Praise for AFRICA'S CHILD

Nhambu and I grew up at the Don Bosco Orphanage and School together. **Africa's Child** is the voice of many Kifungilo children who are unable to put into words their experiences as succinctly and honestly as Nhambu has. What inspires me most about Nhambu is her love and passion for Africa, in spite of her heartbreaking childhood. **Africa's Child** is a gift to all of us.

~ *Imelda S. Browne, CTA, Senior Travel Counselor, AAA Travel*

Africa's Child is a captivating and exhilarating read, alternately heartrending and inspiring. Told through the eyes of a keenly perceptive and precocious child coming of age in colonial East Africa, Nhambu's intensely penetrating insights into complex race, gender, and power relations forge a uniquely personal story that leaves the reader yearning for more.

~ *Natasha C. Vaubel, Scholar of African history, literature and film, Former Associate Professor of Comparative Culture, Aichi University, Japan.*

I've known Maria Nhambu since 1976 when she came to teach at Central High School where I was principal. With my encouragement, she created and taught an African Studies program. Now, reading **Africa's Child**, I understand how much of Africa she brought to her students. Her story is intimately tied to Africa's story, America's story and history. An invaluable book for anyone passionate about Africa and the human condition.

~ *Joyce Taborn Jackson, Ph.D., Licensed Psychologist*

Africa's Child is a story of a soul that triumphed over odds that appeared insurmountable. Maria Nhambu's recounting of her African childhood both charms and horrifies us. Nhambu showed both strength and growth of unconquerable Spirit as she followed God's mysterious plan for her. Yes, Nhambu had a place in the world. Yes, she had something great to share, and yes, there was clearly a force for good at work in her life as she walked the path set before her. **Africa's Child** is a life's adventure that movies are made of and truly a story for our time.

~ *Reverend Nancy Norman, Unity of Delray Beach, Florida*

Nhambu's incredible childhood story is an engrossing and important read for teachers, foster parents, and child-care professionals.

~ *Helene Turnbull, MSW Minneapolis Public Schools;*
Author, Agnes and Diana and Lipskis Of Lodz

Africa's Child is so engaging that I could not put it down. This story of a girl's triumphs and trials as she comes of age in Africa is a historical, cultural, social, religious and educational feast. You will want to read it again because Nhambu will have become your friend and inspiration.

~ *Dr. Dallas L. Browne, Ph.D., Retired Professor of Anthropology,*
Southern Illinois University; Honorary Consul for Tanzania,
St. Louis and Chicago; Author, Culture—The Soul
of Africa and the Coming Gold Rush

Nhambu is an amazing woman with a graceful power that emanates from her. Her story is inspirational and motivational. She grew up with some of the harshest experiences, yet she was able to weave a gold thread of life, love, faith, and freedom through every experience she endured. She held to her own light and truth even though she was often in a sea of darkness.

~ *Kristen Bomas, Speaker, Author, Seminar Leader,*
The Circle: A Kristen Bomas Company

I finished reading **Africa's Child** and the best way I could express my celebration was to dance— just as she taught me. Nhambu has given us and generations yet to be born a treasure.

~ *Diane Gayes R.N., Certified Instructor, Aerobics With Soul®*

Mary Rose Ryan, the abandoned and abused child you will meet in this story, remarkably transformed herself into the accomplished Maria Nhambu, creator of *Aerobics With Soul®*, African art collector, teacher, mother, international traveler, writer and more. Her indomitable spirit and courage as she struggles for survival will cause you to cheer as you weep while you follow this amazing story. I was fortunate enough to be the one who could stand in for her mother and offer her a new life in America where she could fulfill many of her dreams. Our journey together has been among the greatest blessings of my life.

~ Catherine Ann Murray Mamer, Advocate for the Homeless; Former Director of the Peace House Community, Minneapolis, Minnesota

Beautifully detailed and powerfully captivating, Nhambu's story, **Africa's Child**, is a testimony of hope and a blueprint for many who feel orphaned and misplaced. With mindful tenacity, she demonstrates belief in the power of possibility and proves that she is, indeed, Africa's child.

~ Grace Hill Rogers, Retired English secondary teacher and principal; Recipient of Teacher of the Year by Minnesota Alliance of Black Educators and many other awards and recognitions.

Africa's Child takes the reader on a journey of pure perception. Honest, painful, and humorous at times, the story is a testament to the power of human determination to be true to oneself at all costs and to do whatever it takes to survive and thrive.

~ Karl Nhambu Bergh, son, Buddhist teacher. MA, Advanced Buddhist Studies, Maitripa College

Africa's Child is a captivating and intensely private view of a young woman's experience growing up in a German orphanage for mixed race children in Tanzania. From lonely and curious Fat Mary to the bright and beautiful Nhambu, the reader walks into her world and gains a candid and inspirational account of her transformation into physical, psychological and sexual maturity.

~ James M. Gayes, MD

One of the most uplifting and inspirational books I have ever read. Nhambu is the epitome of resilience and perseverance.

This book is alive with piercing yet surprising (and often funny) insights into the nature of people and places in Tanzania. The young Nhambu is a keen observer of the world around her, and she recounts her remarkable story with a disarming directness and a fresh, unique view. The vibrant heart of this book is the author's love for Mama Africa, her source of refuge and the crucible for the alchemy of her life. An homage to what it means to be fully alive and human.

Dancing Soul Trilogy ⚬ Book One

Africa's Child

A Memoir

Maria Nhambu

Delray Beach, Florida

Published by

Dancing Twiga Press
Delray Beach, Florida
www.MariaNhambu.com

ISBN 978-0-9972561-0-9 soft cover
ISBN 978-0-9972561-1-6 mobi
ISBN 978-0-9972561-2-3 epub

Cover and text design by Bookwrights
Front cover photo by Ron Michaelson
Back cover photo of Nhambu by Daphney Antoine
Printed in the United States of America

To my children Katarina and Karl
and to all the children of Kifungilo

Dancing Soul Trilogy

Africa's Child
America's Daughter (to come)
Drum Beats, Heart Beats (to come)

Map of Africa Showing Tanzania

Map of Tanzania Showing
Locations Mentioned in Text

Contents

28   Farewell to Kifungilo   120
29   First Bus Ride   124
30   An African Guardian Angel   131
31   Welcome to Mhonda   139
32   Half-Caste Teacher   142
33   The Bed   149
34   Mary Two   155
35   First Bra   158
36   Delirium   162
37   Missing Anatomy   170
38   Back on the Bus   176
39   Home   179
40   Terror   187
41   Proof Positive   195
42   BBC News   200
43   Territorial Exams   204
44   Flashback   210
45   The Americans   213
46   New Friends   221
47   Sister Martin Corde   228
48   Reel Life   233
49   More Than Friendship   236
50   Little Red Devil   242
51   Awakening   254
52   The Telephone   262
53   Miss Murray   268
54   End of the Road   276
55   Miracle   284
56   First Job   291
57   An American Passport   299
58   Betrayal of Trust   304
59   *Kwaheri Africa!* Goodbye Africa!   306
60   Africa's Gift   308

     Glossary   312
     Acknowledgments   318
     About the Author   322

Foreword

first met Maria Nhambu when she was teaching a dance class at Rancho La Puerta in Mexico. Nhambu, as friends call her, is known for her *Aerobics With Soul* exercise routine, a beautiful series she developed based on tribal dances she learned growing up in East Africa. One year she agreed to come to the Children's Defense Fund (CDF)'s Alex Haley Farm outside Knoxville, Tennessee, to integrate dance classes into the women leaders' spiritual retreat with which we begin each New Year. Her passion and joy in her heritage were infectious, and her sense of being home at Haley farm, bought by the author of *Roots*, led her a number of years later to contribute a large portion of her African art collection to CDF-Haley Farm. It feels as if it always belonged there. Many who watch her joyful dancing would hardly guess that the woman who celebrates her African roots and dances with such grace and love today endured the unbearably difficult childhood she writes about in *Africa's Child*.

Africa's Child is an unforgettable and searingly personal book. Readers will be absorbed in Nhambu's storytelling and come away understanding the most minute details of her life as a ward of the German Precious Blood Sisters Convent's orphanage for half-caste and unwanted children at Kifungilo, high in the Usambara Mountains in postwar Tanganyika (now Tanzania). It is profoundly moving to see this world through the eyes of an exceedingly vulnerable little girl. We hear "Fat Mary" as she prays to find her mother. We share in the refuge of her childhood friendships and the terrors of beatings by the bigger girls. We know her times of loneliness, neglect, confusion, and sadness, and struggle with her in sickness as she comes close to death. And we watch as she faces challenge after challenge that could easily have broken her spirit. Ultimately she suffered racial and religious prejudice and emotional, physical, and sexual abuse, often from the adults who should have protected her.

Africa's Child is compelling not only because of its vivid picture of Nhambu's experience, but because her story is shared by millions of children who are left behind, forgotten, and unwanted today, not just in Africa but in the United States and all around the world. Her story of resilience and faith will bring hope to them. When teachers and caregivers called her a "child of sin" and *"schwarzer Teufel"*— "black devil"—she held to her belief that she was a child of God. When she realized she was smart at school, she furiously latched on to the belief that education was the key to her escape and studied with all her might. In the face of repeated obstacles and injustices, she continued to analyze the world around her with wit and a sharp sense of humor. Above all, as a very young child she decided one day that even if there was no other person in the world who loved and wanted her, she was going to love and care for herself—and that decision changed the course of her life.

How many children are never able to make that wonderful leap? Nhambu instinctively knew that she belonged to God although her life told her she belonged to no one. How many other children never believe in themselves and give in to the outside voices of the world that falsely tell them they are bad, unwanted, not valuable, and not loved? Many adults let Nhambu down, but a few caring teachers and mentors along the way stepped in to give her encouragement and real hope, and those few were enough to make a real difference. How many children never find a single reassuring adult hand or word of encouragement to hold on to? And how do these children's stories end? Anybody in a classroom or working with children in any institution unable to affirm their basic sacredness should please go do something else.

Africa's Child is a powerful reminder that we must *never* give up on any child. Every child must know that she is a child of God. As adults we must be willing to make a difference in our most vulnerable children's lives and refuse to abandon them to neglect, despair, and the hate-filled ideology which becomes an outlet for too many desperate young people around the world who lack positive outlets. I hope this book will compel readers to individual compassion and collective work to reach out to and raise

Africa's child, America's child, and children everywhere. In the words of poet Carl Sandburg: "There is only one child in the world and the child's name is All Children."

Marian Wright Edelman
President and Founder
Children's Defense Fund

A Note from the Author

This is my personal story of my life at the Don Bosco Home in Kifungilo.

Meeting years later with others who had been at the orphanage with me, I had a great revelation. Even though we were at the same place at the same time, our personal memories differed, sometimes markedly.

Of course, anytime two or more of us got together, whether in Tanzania, another African country, or in America or Europe, we would spend hours reminiscing about our childhood at the Don Bosco Home Orphanage. We would laugh until we cried. We could spend days talking and never run out of memories and stories about all the happenings and the naughty things we used to do. We reminded each other of incidents we'd forgotten, and those who were older told us stories about ourselves that we were too young to remember.

It has been my experience that human beings often forget or take for granted the good and happy times of their lives, but they always remember the bad and unhappy times. Yet, when we former Kifungilo children got together, although we all agreed that we'd had a hard life at the orphanage, we only talked about the good times, the funny times, the mischievous times.

I think that was because the individual circumstances that brought us to the orphanage differed. Some of us were true orphans, some had one parent (usually an African mother), some had both parents, some had siblings, while others lived close to the orphanage and spent time regularly with their families.

Visiting with Kifungilo girls and boys over the years has always been one of the true pleasures in my life. When we see each other so many years after leaving Kifungilo, we know beyond a doubt that we are family, and we love each other. My extended Kifungilo family is one of the most precious gifts that the orphanage has given me.

I deliberately wrote in great detail about the social and cultural aspects of my upbringing and education that I know are unfamiliar to the Western reader. Above all, in my memoir I am relating my personal relationship with Africa. I cannot presume to know how others at the orphanage felt about the country of Tanzania or the continent of Africa.

Some names, locations and details have been changed to protect privacy.

Prologue

In the piercing cold and windy afternoon of January 4, 1944, a brown Bedford box-body car crawled and bumped along a rough, dusty road high in the Usambara Mountains of Tanganyika, East Africa. Hesitantly it reached its destination: Kifungilo—"gusts of wind" in Kisambaa, the language of the local African tribe. Kifungilo was the home of the Don Bosco Orphanage and School for mixed race, half-caste, unwanted and orphaned children run by German Catholic Sisters of the Precious Blood Order.

A black-mustached *mzungu*—white person—emerged from the driver's side. He was dressed in khaki bush fatigues, a checkered white and blue shirt, a heavy navy blue windbreaker, and brown hiking boots. A beige pith helmet was strapped under his chin. He walked around the front of the car and opened the passenger door, lifting out a short, heavy woman and carefully placing her on the ground. Her gray silk headscarf fluttered in the wind and across her face as she steadied herself. With one hand the man tried to keep her green and yellow plaid skirt from billowing in the strong wind while supporting her heavy frame with the other. The two walked very slowly. It was an effort for the woman to climb the four short steps to the convent door. In her arms she carried a small bundle, buried like a treasure under several receiving blankets.

Mother Ancilla, the Superior of the convent, greeted the couple with a smile and a hearty handshake. They all went inside. A half an hour later, the man and woman emerged, followed by three nuns who hurriedly bid them farewell with more handshakes and rhythmic nods of their heads.

The wind assisted the man as he lifted the woman to her seat. He then quickly climbed into the driver's side of the car. Everything was quiet for a few minutes; then, abruptly, the engine sputtered, shrieked, rattled, and died. On the fourth try it decided to cooperate, and the car noisily labored to take its passengers beyond the convent and onto the cypress tree-lined road along which they had come.

Before the First World War, Tanganyika was a German Territory and Germans flocked to it as the British had flocked to Kenya in Karen Blixen's day. Under German rule, German laymen and missionaries had the run of the country and established several mission stations, churches, homesteads, coffee farms, and estates all over the mountainous countryside.

In 1932, Mother Ubalda, who came across the valley from Gare, an established Benedictine Mission, purchased a huge estate from a German farmer in order to build a retirement home for the many German Precious Blood Sisters who had lived most of their lives in Africa and wanted to die there, as well as for those who were too old and sickly to make a final trip back home to Germany.

Two years later, moved by the suffering, neglect, and abandonment of half-caste girls and boys, she decided to open an orphanage. With typical German logic and practical organizational ability, Mother Ubalda first built a convent for the nuns who would then build the orphanage with their own hands. Kifungilo was a replica of any small German hamlet nestled into the slopes of the hills along the Rhine, except it was located seven thousand feet high in the Usambara Mountains of eastern Tanganyika, which became Tanzania in 1964.

Half-castes were usually the illegitimate children of African women and European missionaries, explorers, businessmen, government employees, exiles, and tourists. Occasionally the liaisons were legal and the children legitimate. The half-castes were "love children" at best, "mistakes" at worst.

The African community usually rejected its half-caste children, so Mother Ubalda hired people to go into African huts and flush out her first charges, hidden away in villages and towns all over the country. As word of the Kifungilo home spread, boys and girls in all shades of black, brown, and yellow, and ranging in age from a few days to twenty years old, were brought to her. Another nun—Sister Silvestris—came to Kifungilo from Germany in 1934 to become their "mother." Older orphans—the "big girls"—helped her with the everyday grooming and care of up to seventy-five little children.

As for the bundle dropped off on that frigid January day, the Sisters passed it from one to the other as they laughed and chatted and made baby sounds of delight. A loud cry from the days-old baby girl stopped the merriment, and the nuns retreated inside to begin raising yet another unwanted child.

I was that child. The nuns became my guardians. The orphanage became my home.

1

Where Is My Mother?

As a child I prayed often and I prayed hard. Like all children of the orphanage and boarding school at Kifungilo, I was required to say many prayers in Latin when we went to church every day. But I often stayed after services to pray in Swahili for my one great longing—to find my mother.

I liked the prayers I made up best. I felt that Jesus stopped what he was doing and listened to me, and he sometimes talked to me even though I was not praying in Latin. I began my prayer sessions by kneeling in a corner near a Nativity scene. Making the sign of the cross to get Jesus' attention, I'd say, "Baby Jesus, this is Mary." Jesus, who remained a baby for me during all my years at the orphanage, replied, "*I know.*"

I went straight to the point. "I am now five years old. Have you found my mother yet?"

I didn't know my birthday, but my friend Elizabeth was five, and we decided that I was five years old too. I hoped that Jesus would have good news for me and that my mother would come to take me away from the orphanage.

"*You must believe Sister Silvestris, your Kifungilo mother. She told you your prayers will be answered one day,*" he replied.

"How far away is one day?"

He was quiet for a long time. Then he answered, "*You will always have a mother to take care of you.*"

"But I want my real mother. She wouldn't beat me and call me a *schwarzer Teufel.*"

"You're not a 'black devil.' And you will always have a mother," he repeated and closed his eyes. This meant that Baby Jesus was tired, and although he still listened to me, he didn't answer.

I discussed with Jesus the trials of my life in the orphanage—being hungry, having the other orphans call me "Fat Mary" and "Piggy," getting a deserved beating with a cane from Sister Silvestris, and most feared of all—getting undeserved thrashings, along with blows, kicks and punches, from one of the big orphan girls. I promised to be a very good girl and said goodbye to Baby Jesus. After each prayer session, I left the quiet church with the faith and hope I needed to face my life.

For Mass, I wore my one Sunday dress and my one pair of shoes. As I walked down the five steps from the church on a Sunday, admiring my white canvas shoes and wondering when Jesus would find my mother, I heard a small voice: "Mary, why do you stay in church any longer than you have to? What are you doing there?"

"Praying," I said, catching up to Elizabeth, my dearest and best friend. She, unlike me who had been abandoned by my parents, had both a father and a mother. Because in this orphanage not everyone was an orphan, there were painful inequities in how we were treated by the Sisters and the big girls. Children who had both parents received privileged treatment. Also, the orphanage was reputed to have the best school for half-caste children in the country, so interracial couples and single parents who loved, wanted, and cared for their children brought them to Kifungilo to be educated. They visited their children often, brought them gifts of food, toys, and clothing and took them home for the holidays. Most children had at least an African mother and they were treated the next best. Some, like me, were true orphans and didn't have these benefits.

Elizabeth loved me although I wondered why when she listed all the things wrong with me: "Mary, you are fat, and you have a round face. You stretch out my shoes and mess up my doll. You always ask to share my candy, you don't have a mother, and you cry all the time."

I was happy she had waited for me, so I just listened as she recited my faults.

"The only good thing about you, Fat Mary, is your nice hair. And you make me laugh when we play."

"Please, please, Elizabeth, just for today don't call me Fat Mary."

"That's what Sister Silvestris calls you. And you are fat!" With both hands she pinched my cheeks just like Sister Silvestris and mimicked, "Ziz ees mien Fett Mary." We both laughed, and then I grew serious.

"If you don't call me that name today, I promise not to cry all day, no matter what."

Holding hands, we started toward the children's quarters, up a hill beyond the convent. We skipped along the cobblestone path, past the life-sized statue of Saint Joseph, past the big metal prayer bell encased in its ten-foot ivy arch, past the convent building housing over twenty-five German nuns. We sat down on the ground by the fishpond in front of the grotto of Our Lady of Fatima. Below us, to our left, was a wide valley with scattered African villages.

Elizabeth wore a pink shirtwaist dress with blue daisies and a white Peter Pan collar. Her black patent leather shoes had straps that fastened with rhinestone buttons. Her pink socks were trimmed with dark blue lace. Tied around her black, coarse, dense hair was a wide yellow ribbon that ended in a bow on top of her head. I often felt annoyed when she played with my hair as she started doing now, but today I was grateful she had waited for me so I didn't complain. She removed the tiny red ribbons from the ends of my pigtails and undid one long braid and then the other. The comb she used on my hair was missing most of its teeth. I didn't fuss because she was my friend.

She piled my hair on top of my head and, as I held it in place with both hands, she tied her yellow ribbon around my head and made a large bow on top. I let my hair fall down over the ribbon and felt very pretty. Now it was her turn. I planted the comb into her scalp and tried to rake the tangles out of her frizzy, kinky, disobedient hair while she yelped and jumped with each jab. I managed to make two loopy braids almost like the ones she undid from my hair and tied my tiny ribbons at the ends to keep the braids from coming undone. Elizabeth said she felt pretty too.

We continued our ascent to the children's quarters, running along the steep road lined with eucalyptus trees, past Sister Nerea's dentistry, where she provided dental services for patients from near and far, past the brickmaking pit, past the bas relief of Saint Don Bosco after whom our orphanage was named because he was the patron saint of abandoned children. Then we climbed three short stone steps and burst into the dining hall. We were late for breakfast. That meant that we would be punished either by having our food taken away or by being beaten with a stick. The other children were already seated on benches, ten to a side, facing the three-by-eight-foot table.

The best part of Sunday, besides not having chores, was our breakfast of one slice of wheat bread set at each place on the rough wooden table and a tumbler of sweetened peppermint tea. To pay homage to the big girls in charge of bathing us, washing our clothes, and combing our hair, we little girls carried our slices of bread in the palms of our hands to the big girls. They would help themselves to a piece or not take it. My big girl was Zami. She had darker skin, a long face with an irregular dark brown mole on the tip of her nose, coarse black hair, large breasts, a pot belly, and no waistline. As I held my piece of bread up to her, she took one look at my new hairdo.

"You don't like my braiding?" She breathed down on me as I looked up at her terrifying face. "Why are you so late for breakfast?"

"I was playing with Elizabeth. She did my hair."

Zami's huge belly jiggled as she grabbed my upper arms. "Don't mess with my work."

"Please don't beat me. I won't do it again, I promise." She pinched my arms hard and shook me until I almost dropped the bread. When she let go, I set the bread on the table and started to run away from her. She grabbed my skirt with one hand and pulled my hair with the other saying, "Next time get my bread here on time, you stupid pig."

"I will, I promise." As I turned to walk back to my table, she reached under my skirt and grabbed a thick fold of skin on my thigh and pinched me hard.

Another big girl congratulated her. "You have to teach these brats some manners!"

"Not like that." Rosa, who was sitting near Zami, stood up and confronted her. Rosa had been in charge of me from age two to five, before I was given to Zami. "You're cruel to Mary. You're the only one who takes the whole slice of bread. What's she supposed to eat?"

"Shut your mouth!" Zami growled at her.

"You're always beating the poor girl. It isn't right."

"I said shut up, you bloody fool," Zami shouted, slamming her fist on the table.

"I'm not afraid of you!" Rosa, who was about half the size of Zami and had severe asthma, spat at her from her corner of the table.

Zami leapt from the bench, grabbed Rosa by her shoulders, and threw her to the floor. Plates and spoons flew in all directions as the big girls took sides. Most of them cheered Zami on, but the little children rooted for Rosa. Zami pinned Rosa to the ground and sat on her.

"*Mama yangu!* What's going on? Is it Zami again?" Sister Silvestris strode briskly across the dining room using her favorite Swahili expression of surprise and dismay. "Zami, Zami, why are you so violent? Stop right now." Zami continued hitting Rosa on the face and chest and pulling her hair. "Zami, I said stop it!" Sister's face was red and she made the grinding sound with her teeth that always preceded a severe beating. Zami let go of Rosa. Still huffing and puffing, swearing and clenching her fists, Zami cut her way through the now quiet crowd and slid to her place at the table.

"What happened?" Sister asked. No one said a word. Even Rosa, whose right eye was starting to swell and whose nose was bleeding, said nothing. When Sister saw how badly Rosa was hurt, she went for the stick she stored in her cupboard. She then beat Zami with it from head to foot until she ran out of the dining room shouting obscenities at both Sister and Rosa.

"*Hasira, hasira.*" Sister shook her head. "Anger. Such anger. We must pray for Zami and her terrible temper."

I was trembling with fear, but I remembered my earlier promise to Elizabeth that no matter what happened that day, I wouldn't cry. I controlled the forbidden tears in my heaving chest and took my seat. I couldn't look at Rosa. The big girls were comforting her. I reached for my cup and took a big gulp of sweet tea. With each swallow, I hacked away at the lump in my chest. When my cup was empty, the lump was smaller.

Elizabeth sat at a table across from me. I was determined to show her how strong I was. Since I had already swallowed my tears, I knew if I looked at her now, I wouldn't cry. She tilted her head to one side, and smiling, she showed me bits and pieces of bread she had collected from the other children at her table. Sister Silvestris rang the bell to dismiss us and we raced out the door. Outside, I savored the scrunched up morsels of bread that Elizabeth ceremoniously placed in my hand, one by one.

2

The Doll

 On Sunday, with no chores, we played most of the day until it was time for church and afternoon Benediction. Visitors often came from Lushoto, the nearest town thirteen miles south of the orphanage. They were usually *wazungu*—Europeans or any white people—who came to enjoy the afternoon and stroll through the beautiful orphanage grounds.

After three groups of visitors had come and gone, yet another car hummed in the distance as it climbed the hill to the orphanage. Elizabeth and I were sitting in front of the dining room eagerly waiting for lunch, which on Sundays consisted of white rice, cabbage, and sometimes a piece of meat. Our ears were on full alert waiting for the lunch bell when Julitta, another orphan, came running toward us shouting, "Elizabeth! Elizabeth, your mother is here."

"My mother is here! My mother!" Elizabeth jumped up and ran toward the convent where guests were received. I tried to run as fast as she did, but I couldn't keep up.

"Elizabeth, wait for me!"

"Go back, Mary. You can't come. She's not your mother." I stopped dead in my tracks, overwhelmed by the reminder that although Elizabeth was my friend, she was different from me. She had a mother and I did not. "You can have my lunch, and I'll save some *pipi* for you."

Her offer of candy was small comfort. I turned around and slowly started walking back, trying hard not to cry because Julitta was looking at me. "Mary, you should share Elizabeth's lunch with me because I brought the good news." Being reminded of lunch made me feel better. I gladly shared it with Julitta with the hope that she wouldn't beat me up the next time the big girls made us fight for their entertainment.

After lunch I waited for Elizabeth at the top of the hill where I could look down towards the car and the convent. She didn't appear for the longest time. Maybe her mother had come to take her away and she couldn't tell me goodbye. No, she's my friend. She'll come. But the longer I waited, the sadder I got. The differences between us tormented me. She was thin, she had many toys, and she smiled a lot. Even though she had really ugly hair, she had the thing I most wanted—a mother. I was just about to cry when I saw her. If she found me crying, she would pull my hair and tell me that I cried for no reason at all.

When I ran down to meet her, she had a big package. "My mother brought this for you."

"Your mother loves me too?"

"Yes, she does, and I think I know what it is."

We sat right in the middle of the road and I carefully opened the package. "It's a doll just like yours!" Her skin was white and her cheeks pink. Her eyes were blue with lashes the same color as her silky long, straight blond hair. When I tipped her, her eyes closed, and they opened wide again when I held her upright. Her tiny, partly open mouth had very thin bright red lips just like the much-admired European lips. She wore a lacy red dress with puffed sleeves and black lace binding. I lifted the dress. Underneath were pink nylon panties with elastic around the legs and waistline. I pulled her panties down and checked the belly button.

"Look! My doll can talk!" I pushed in the large belly button, and a loud "Maa-maa" came from inside. "I am your mama," I said as I held her very tight. Then I hugged Elizabeth and kissed her on the forehead. "Thank you for being my friend."

"Now that you have your own doll, promise not to touch mine."

Her mother visited often, but once Elizabeth had her presents, she didn't care to spend more time with her, so Elizabeth wasn't happy when I wanted to go and thank her mother. That meant we had to walk up to the little hut on the hill near the children's quarters where African mothers stayed when they visited their children. If her mother were a *mzungu*, she would have used the guesthouse by the convent. We skipped along clutching our dolls and came to the hut for African parents where Elizabeth's mother was standing.

She was wearing a red and white polka dot short-sleeved blouse with some buttons missing. Wrapped around her plump stomach was a green, white, and black *khanga*, the everyday East African women's dress. She had pink rubber thongs on her feet and her toenails were painted red. Her hair was even rougher and kinkier than Elizabeth's.

"Here come the best friends," she said hugging her daughter.

Then she hugged me and I started to cry. "She cries because she doesn't have a mother," Elizabeth said.

"Little Mary," she said, "everyone has a mother."

"No, I don't. Something is wrong with me because mine didn't want me."

Her mother held me, and then I cried so loudly that she put her hand over my mouth. "Please don't cry, little one. Your mother will come someday."

"No she won't. Even Baby Jesus can't find her," I sobbed.

"She must be very busy. If I see her, I'll tell her to come and visit you."

"Why doesn't she want me?" I cried, wiping my nose and eyes on my sleeve. The sobs came fewer and softer. As I stopped crying, I looked up and saw short, old Mother Rufina, the Superior for the Sisters, slowly walking up the hill toward us.

"Now hurry and play with the other children," she said, shooing Elizabeth and me onto the narrow footpath that led back to the children's quarters. As we raced down the hill, she reminded us, "Remember to share your toys with those who have none."

Elizabeth and I played with our dolls in front of the statue of Blessed Martin. I had mastered the art of making dolls from scraps of cloth and string, so keeping in mind what Mother Rufina told us, I gave my handmade doll to Julitta who came to join us by the statue. Her dolls always fell apart.

The three of us sat rocking our dolls in front of Blessed Martin as he watched over us. Martin, a half-caste member of the Dominican Order, lived and worked in a monastery in sixteenth century Lima, Peru, and was the patron of mixed race people. Because all the saints

I'd seen in pictures and statues in church and around the orphanage were *wazungu,* I thought that because he wasn't white, he couldn't be a saint. He was finally declared a saint in 1962. Whenever we needed anything for the orphanage, from clothing to rain, Sister Silvestris sent us to kneel on the grass in front of his statue and pray.

It was time for supper. Elizabeth and I folded our hands in prayer and asked Blessed Martin to send me a mother very soon. Julitta didn't wait for us. I heard her singing noisily to her doll as she disappeared down the steps. She was as happy with my old hand-made cloth doll as Elizabeth and I were with our prized store-bought plastic ones.

3

Village Mothers

 I was sure that my prayers for a mother had been answered one day when four of us children went with Sister Silvestris to bring food and medicine to sick people in the village of Kiuzai, a couple of miles from the orphanage. Sister visited the sick often, and if we were good, we could accompany her. Before handing out the provisions, she would instruct them about the Catholic faith in hopes of sending another soul to heaven. Many visits ended with promises from the "pagans" to come to the mission for religious instruction that Sister hoped would eventually lead to baptism. In return, the potential converts got blankets, clothing, or sugar. As we approached, village children ran to meet us with outstretched hands asking for *pipi* and other treats.

The village of Kiuzai, squeezed into the flat ground between two hills, had three large huts and six smaller ones within a fence enclosure made of thorn tree branches. The hut frames were formed by flexible tree poles interwoven around the four large posts that made up the structure. The walls were soft red clay and mud smoothed on by hand and baked by the sun.

Sister Silvestris, with her aspirin and holy water, stooped to enter a dark, smoky hut while we remained outside. In the middle of the village courtyard, three old women were sitting on the ground by a fire, smoking long pipes stuffed with chunks of homegrown tobacco. The women chatted, nodding and shaking their heads as they fanned the smoke away from their faces. Orange flames hugged a small, black clay pot sitting on three rocks near the women where they cooked their evening meal of *ugali*, a thick porridge made out of water and corn flour. Their bare, parched breasts dangled from their chests and rested on the colorful *khangas* wrapped around their stomachs. They offered us pieces of sweet potato that had been roasted over the charcoals.

"Here, little girls, taste this," the oldest woman said. As usual, in matters concerning food, I gladly accepted, conveniently forgetting all admonitions. I could hear Sister Silvestris' voice in my head telling us that we must never accept or eat anything from the Wasambaa because they are dirty people and their food is contaminated. The other girls didn't accept any food and continued playing.

"*Asante sana*," I thanked her in Swahili, and then I sat with the women and enjoyed my sweet potato while they felt my hair and touched my face with their rough hands.

"Feel this hair." Three sets of rugged hands very gently squeezed my hair against my scalp.

"It's like the silky hair on an ear of maize," said one.

"To me it feels like the cloth that the Arab from the city sells us," replied another.

"No," said the oldest woman, "It's like ostrich feathers."

They then examined the buttons on my dress and checked my knickers. "Why does she wear these things?" asked one.

"The Sisters at the mission use them," answered another.

They passed me from one to the other and fed me more sweet potato. It felt like Christmas. After a while, the oldest woman motioned to the village children who were staring at me, "Come and play with this nice child."

The children rushed up and started touching me from head to toe. "Your skin isn't black like mine."

"Why is your hair so funny?" One asked if she could have some of my hair.

It felt great to be admired. "Sure!" I said undoing my braids for them as they fluffed out my hair. One girl pulled a long strand from the top of my head while another wanted a lighter one from the side, and another took one from the back where my hair was straighter. They carefully wrapped the strands of hair they had pulled out so gently around their middle fingers. I admired their beautiful cornrows and felt the tight plaits close to the scalp. Their hair was the same rough texture as Elizabeth's hair.

I remembered Elizabeth's mother saying that everyone has a mother. In a timid voice I asked the oldest woman, "Do you know if my mother lives in this village? Could one of you be my mother?"

The one with very white hair answered, "Pretty little girl, in this village all the mothers belong to all the children, and all the children belong to all the mothers. If you cannot find your mother, we will all be your mother."

Sister Silvestris came out of a hut and motioned for us to follow her. Although I was very happy to be called pretty and have so many mothers, I sensed that my real mother was not here. All the way back to Kifungilo, I walked with my chin on my chest, thinking about what the village mothers had said. Now I knew for certain that it was not Elizabeth who was different. It was me. I was alone. I had no one. No mother, no father, no brothers, no sisters, no grandmas, no grandpas, no uncles, no aunties, no cousins, and no tribe. I'd seen the children at the orphanage laugh or cry when they received news about a family member. I would never receive such news and no family would laugh or cry for me. That day I understood with sharp clarity that I didn't have a mother who wanted me.

Was there anybody who wanted me? The Sisters cared for me, but did they really want me? I couldn't answer those questions, but then I realized there was someone who wanted me. I wanted me. I wanted to love the one no one else loved—fat me, just as I was. That same day I created another Fat Mary in my mind, who would love me and whom I would love no matter what. I promised her I would take care of her. I would be in charge of her like Zami was in charge of me, but I'd never beat her or take her food.

Fat Mary wasn't like the imaginary friends that other kids had. My Fat Mary and I were more like twins who took care of each other. She was responsible for bearing the emotional and psychological pain of events and issues in my life that I couldn't face and couldn't understand. She also safeguarded the meaningful and happy moments of my childhood and flashed them before me when I needed to be reminded that there was a lot of goodness around me. She provided me with the balance necessary to cope with the tribulations of my existence. More than anything, she was my constant companion who would never abandon me. The only responsibility I had to her was to shower her with unconditional love. I wanted her to live and be happy. I knew that I couldn't give her complete happiness at the orphanage, so I made up my mind someday, somehow, to take her away from Kifungilo. I would be a good mother to my own Fat Mary.

As we approached the children's quarters, the buildings grew larger and our shadows grew longer. The orphanage seemed inviting and serene under the orange glow of the setting sun. Although the air was crisp and piercing, I was flushed with warmth from the satisfaction of knowing that I was wanted and loved by someone. Fat Mary belonged to me and from now on, I would never be alone.

4

Visitors at Kifungilo

 The industrious German nuns who ran the Don Bosco Orphanage at Kifungilo were fully self-sufficient. They grew a large assortment of vegetables from artichokes to zucchini and temperate zone fruits such as pears, plums, apples, peaches, and figs as well as tropical fruits including pineapples, bananas, pawpaws, guavas, jackfruit, and custard apple, each in its season. They ate their produce raw, cooked, or canned in sweet syrups, or preserved by drying in the sun. They planted grains such as wheat, barley and maize, and made their own flour for bread and pastries. They grew white and red grapes for eating and to make wine for Mass. Whenever there was a surplus of fruit that was not eaten fresh or sealed in jars as jam, the children got some.

The nuns kept cows, sheep, and goats for meat, milk and butter, and sold the hides to Indian merchants and shopkeepers in nearby Lushoto. They in turn sold them to the Africans for making drums, bags, and a variety of artifacts. The pigs raised by the nuns were enormous. Some were used for bacon, ham, pork, and sausage, while others were raised for cooking fat, which was also sold to the *wazungu* in town. The nuns raised chickens, ducks, geese, turkeys, and rabbits. Two large artificial ponds, graced by swans and water lilies, provided the Sisters not only with a tranquil spot for meditation, but also with fish to eat on Fridays.

The setting the nuns chose was high in the forested Usambara Mountains. When the Germans ruled Tanganyika, they built beautiful cobblestone roads and stone arch bridges at some of its most impossible climatic and topographical locations. To this day, many of their masterpieces stand in defiance of time and in contrast to the

sorry attempts at road building by the British who took over after
the First World War. The Mombo-Lushoto escarpment road, with
its thirteen-mile snake-like extension to Kifungilo, was famously regarded as the most treacherous road in East Africa. When originally
built, it climbed up steep mountains that were often in the clouds,
descended into deep narrow valleys that never saw the sun, tun-
neled through mountains of solid rock, passed over bridges, rivers
and waterfalls, and swung over swamps and lakes.

The nuns had lined the last mile of the narrow dirt road with
twin columns of tall, elegant cypress trees that gave Kifungilo a
stately and disciplined approach. This was the road that the Germans and Africans had built entirely by hand. This was the road
that I watched with longing for hours on end as my way out of the
orphanage.

As soon as we heard the distant hum of a car motor on visiting
days, we ran up the road to it. "Wait for me, wait for me!" was my
everlasting refrain with any activity involving speed. Although I was
usually ignored, whenever Rosa was going to meet a car, she waited
for me and held my hand. She often had to drag me because I was
so fat that I tired too easily to run the entire mile. We arrived at
the cypress trees in varying states of exhaustion. Surrounding the
slow-moving car, we accompanied it down to the convent, singing
and dancing. All visitors to Kifungilo on a Sunday knew about, expected, and seemed to enjoy this hearty welcome.

"My dear, isn't this wonderfully charming?"

"Look at those enormous cows in the meadow."

"I heard they make the red tiles for their roofs here."

"How lucky for these unfortunate children to have such a place.
If they had parents, they wouldn't be living like this."

"These German nuns are bloody clever. And that's from an
Englishman."

"God will reward them for making a home for these bastard
children."

"You know, one of your bloody relatives could have fathered a
child that's here. What happened to your housemaid's half-breed

son? Rumor has it that your uncle is the father and that he refused to support the girl."

"Are these children going to move so we can get through?"

"They seem perfectly happy to stare at us. They must know that one of their parents is white. Just step on the petrol and they'll scamper away."

We thought that the *wazungu* were very funny people indeed as they made faces and pointed through the open car windows at the picturesque mission station. Why would they come to Kifungilo, a place we all dreamt of leaving some day? The fact that Kifungilo was one of the most beautiful spots in the country was completely lost on us.

The *wazungu* feasted their eyes on the two fishponds that glistened like mirrors at the bottom of the slope. Cows, sheep, and goats grazed lazily among the bees and butterflies on the sloping dandelion-filled meadow. Terraces of vegetables, budding fruit trees, and flowers hugged the hillsides. Several brick and red tile-roofed buildings were scattered in every direction and others peeked above the foliage. Hand-dug irrigation canals lined with blue and white chrysanthemums and calla lilies wound their way up from a river in the valley through the terraces and disappeared into the horizon. Pale gray clouds hovered above the Usambara Mountains and cast shadows over the African villages clustered within fenced compounds amidst the jagged blue-green cultivated terrain.

We followed the car, imitating the gawking visitors and their British accents, until it curved around our school. We waved goodbye and the visitors waved back. The car continued on a quarter of a mile or so to the convent where the road ended. As they got out of the car, visitors inhaled the cool, fresh air, delicately perfumed by the multi-colored rose bushes in front of the convent and subtly blended with the scent of nearby pines.

We were often called to entertain the visitors in the hope that they would donate money and clothing to the orphanage. Standing in a tight group, we listened as a Sister greeted the visitors and told them how lucky we were to be at Kifungilo. She reminded everyone that we were unwanted by our African mothers or by our *wazungu* fathers because we were children of sin.

Sometimes the visitors would ask our names and ages and give us candy or a shilling. We then sang for them. Often we went through this ritual three times in one day. One of our songs was about the wind.

Can you hear—the wind is singing.
Whoo...oooo...oooo....it comes along.
Trees are swinging, trees are swinging
As it sings its merry song.
Birds are flying, can you see them?
Flying high up in the sky.
Would you like to be a birdie,
Stretch your arms and try to fly?
Let us try, let us try.
But no, no, we cannot fly.

Because of the altitude, high hills and low swooping valleys, the wind in Kifungilo was often chilly and constant. The wind was the one natural element that tortured me the most. I often sang these verses over and over to myself, trying to recruit the wind as transportation for my imagination. "Hey Wind!" I'd say. The wind never answered, so I carried on the conversation with Fat Mary's help because she always answered me. "Can we fly over the mountains to look for my mother?"

"You've been a good girl, so I will take you." I closed my eyes and the short trip began. On the other side of the mountain, a woman very much like Rosa, but with darker skin, greeted me with open arms. She kissed me and hugged me. She gave me candy and then ran her fingers through my hair before she caressed it, combed and braided it. She smoothed warm jasmine oil over my face and rubbed it on my ashen arms and legs. *"My dear little Mary, I am sorry that I had to send you to Kifungilo. Please remember that I love you very, very much. One day I shall come to take you home."*

"Are you sure you love me?" I asked my imagined mother.

"So very much."

"Mother, am I a child of sin?"

"Who told you that? You are my child and a child of God. No one is a child of sin."

"Then why do the Sisters say we are unwanted children of sin?" She was silent.

The wind always interrupted the conversations with my imaginary mother and put an end to my reveries. A few minutes after it had carried me over the mountain, it reverted to its natural temperament: mean, ruthless, and unpredictable. It never became my friend. I often watched it blow chilly, thin mountain air across valleys and plains. To wake me up from my daydreams, it sneaked through my clenched teeth, boldly rushed into my nostrils, ran through my ears, and raced down my spine and knocked my knees together. It coiled around me like a dust devil, grabbed me by the ankles and battered me until there was no doubt in my mind that I had never left Kifungilo. In Kifungilo it whistled through the keyholes and squeezed through the crevices of locked doors and windows. At night, it groaned and hissed and shrieked like the eerie voices of mourning Wasambaa from the surrounding villages.

5

The Crying Room

The orphanage had a multipurpose room that squatted between the dining room and the dormitory. Built into the walls and extending from floor to ceiling were one-foot-square open wooden cubicles where we kept our few possessions: a Sunday dress, two weekday dresses, a sweater, a crocheted beret for church, two pairs of knickers that served as panties, one pair of shoes and a pair of socks. The cubicles belonging to children with parents were full to the top. These girls hid their dolls, ribbons, fancy plastic hair clips, candy, biscuits, and many other goodies behind the rows of folded clothes. Guarding their belongings was a full-time job, just as it was also a full-time job for the have-not children to figure out ways and means of stealing whatever they could. *Nyumba ile* or "that room" was a playroom, a nap and changing room—and the place where the big girls tortured the little girls.

Every so often the big girls arranged fights between little girls and bet on which little girl would cry first. There was no prize because this was done only for their entertainment. The little children would be pushed to the middle of the room. All fights began with *kusonya* or steupsing—a sound made by sucking the teeth and used in parts of Africa and the Caribbean to express disgust. The longer and louder the "steups," the greater the disapproval expressed. One child would steups at the other who would then steups back. We alternated between steupsing and yelling "*Bladiful!*" (our version of "bloody fool") at each other until the aggressor started the fight. Then the two would slap, punch, kick, spit and pull each other's hair while the big girls took sides and cheered them on. The one who cried first was the loser. The winner was congratulated while the loser was called names and sent out of *nyumba ile* in shame. I was usually picked to fight when no one was left. I started crying a long time before my turn, so the big girls learned not to bet on me.

From time to time—we never knew which nights—at about 9:30 after Sister Silvestris turned off the lights in her room adjacent to the dormitory, another form of torture began. "Bedwetters, quick, out of your beds," commanded one of the big girls. "Don't make a sound." Several cold and terrified little children left their beds and walked fearfully into *nyumba ile*.

"Take your nightgowns off and line up against the wall," another voice hissed at us in the dark room. Four huge black forms loomed over us.

I started to cry, "Please don't beat me. I'll never wet the bed again."

"Shut up, you fat pig! You're first." Together the big girls reached for me, pulling my braids, grabbing my arms and thighs with their big hands. Over and over they tossed me up in the air while they laughed and chanted "*Kikojozi kakojoa, na nguo kazitia moto,*" accusing the bedwetter of peeing on herself to keep warm. Pulling and pinching me, they taunted: "What a big stomach and fat buttocks! Funny short legs! She smells bad. Except for her long hair, she's just like a pig."

Every cell in my body cried out at their torment, but the big girls never heard a sound from me. If they had, they would have let me fall to the ground. Any child that cried out had her head banged on the floor and a rag dipped in urine tied over her mouth. I learned to hold back my tears and cry only when I was safely back in bed.

The next victim was Christina who was older than the rest of us.

"Look at this skinny thing!"

"Hey, she's getting breasts—just little bumps."

"Her hair down there is thin. Not much to hold on to."

The big girls pulled and pinched Christina's breasts and hung onto her pubic hair as they tossed her in the air. Christina didn't make a sound either as they tortured her. Then they were ready for the next child. It was dark and I never knew how many children were beaten each time, because I was disorientated and drunk with pain. I was usually the last one back to bed.

"What are you waiting for, fat pig?" A big girl kicked me across the chest. I stood up and wobbled towards the door when I remembered that I was naked. Shaking with fear and cold, I felt for my nightdress on the floor, picked it up, and returned to the sleeping room, sliding my way along the walls in the dark until I found my bed. When Sister Silvestris saw our battered bodies the next day and asked us what had happened, we said that we had fallen out of bed or bumped into the walls during the night.

I rarely wet my bed. Knowing their ordeal in *nyumba ile*, I felt sorry for those who frequently did, especially Julitta, who was a true orphan like me. Although Julitta was very strong and beat up most of us in our arranged fights, she couldn't escape her fate in *nyumba ile*. A chronic bedwetter, she was always tortured. One time when she came back to her bed, instead of quietly crying herself to sleep as usual, she sobbed and groaned without stopping. I listened to her and heard her pain. Elizabeth, who shared my bed, slept soundly. I sat up in bed and opened my eyes wide even though I was afraid of the dark. Through the blackness of the night I could see Julitta's tears. They came in large drops that floated in the darkness like a broken string of white beads.

I crawled on all fours feeling my way to Julitta's row and got into her already wet bed. I wiped the warm tears from her cheeks and worked them into her rough hair. She wept and wept until finally she put her arm around my shoulder and, after a while, fell asleep.

The next morning Elizabeth and I had just finished making our bed when we heard Sister Silvestris unlock the heavy metal door and shine her flashlight into our eyes. Her five-foot figure was clad in her Precious Blood Sisters regalia. Her habit consisted of a black, long-sleeved pleated wool robe with a long scapular over it. Only a small square of her face was visible under her headdress made up of a starched square piece of cloth that covered her forehead and touched her black-rimmed spectacles. Her white veil was tucked under a stiffened square at the top of her head and flowed to her shoulders. From underneath the starched white round bib covering her chest hung a large silver crucifix on a red cord. Black woolen socks and heavy-duty, eight-holed black lace-up shoes with thick two-inch heels completed her pre-Vatican II nun's garb.

"Get up, get up, little children," she called to those still in their beds. She moved down the row of beds. "You shouldn't cover your face when you sleep," she said, lifting the heavy homemade wool blanket from Rosemary's face who groaned and slid to the foot of the bed, wrapping herself in a big ball. Sister pulled Rosemary out of bed. "Don't make such a face," Sister told her. "You're a bad girl and you need to go to church."

"I don't want to go to heaven," Rosemary pouted. Sister could never win an argument with Rosemary. I secretly admired Rosemary because she was not afraid of beatings or punishment, and she talked back to Sisters and big girls alike.

Every morning when Sister opened the sleeping room door, she brought with her an icy blade of wind that mercilessly cut into our ribs. After supervising the big girls as they combed our hair and helped us dress, she inspected the floor where she typically found several puddles of urine.

"*Mama yangu.* You naughty, naughty children. Who did this?"

We scattered from her and hung onto the cold walls. The toilets were down the hill from where we slept, and since the Wasambaa often came to the orphanage to scare us and steal whatever was left outside, we used the *debe*, a several-gallon metal container in a corner of the dormitory, for our toilet during the night. Another reason why we would never go outside in the dark was that we were petrified of Bobby and Suzy, the two huge German shepherd watchdogs who were let out after the generator was turned off. They barked angrily all night long, terrorizing man and beast alike, and they bit everyone except their trainer, Sister Fabiana, and the Sambaa night watchmen who patrolled the compound from 9 p.m. to 5 a.m. Their barks echoed eerily throughout the valley and surrounding villages.

Fear of the dogs and the occasional Sambaa villager who subdued the dogs with food and tranquilizers and then peeped into the sleeping room windows to scare us, made us dread getting out of our beds at night for any reason. When we had to go in the middle of the night, we were supposed to walk in the dark to the *debe* which was far from the beds. But some of us had perfected the art of silent peeing and instead walked slowly from our beds to another area of the room tightly holding our legs together and letting the warm urine trickle down our thighs, legs, ankles and onto the floor. It was not hard for Sister to find out who the culprits were because we stunk in the morning. Any punishment from Sister, though, was better than the ordeal of the bedwetters in *nyumba ile*.

"Fat Mary, did you do this?" She pointed to a large pool of urine near her feet.

"I didn't do that one."

"It doesn't make any difference which puddle you made." She wrote down the names of the guilty. We would be punished in the evening.

Evening came. In Sister Silvestris' right hand was a list of names wrapped around a bottle of holy water, and in her left hand she carried four sticks of various weight, color, and length. She liked green twigs from young trees because they were elastic, thin, and light. We preferred the dried sticks, because they were hollow and didn't hurt as much as the flexible green ones. She called out the names of the children who had misbehaved, or wet their beds or the floor during the week. One by one, we got out of bed and huddled in a corner in front of the room.

"Julitta, you wet your bed, got into a fight, and skipped church. Nora, you stole apples from Father Gattang's room. Elise, you took a spoon from the dining room. Rosemary, you made a face and talked back to Sister Theonesta. Antonette, you told a lie. Fat Mary, you peed on the floor and didn't pay attention in church."

Julitta was first. She lay on her stomach on top of a wooden bed with no mattress. Sister raised the stick and struck her across the buttocks. Four sticks for each offence. Julitta didn't cry. Elise, Antonette, Nora, and Rosemary received their punishments. Then it was my turn. Loud sobs came from under Rosa's bed.

"Where is Fat Mary?" Sister was getting angry now. She picked a long stick that was firmer than the others, leaned down, and indiscriminately hit at me. "Rosa, make her come out." Instead, Rosa tried to shield me with her blanket making Sister angrier. "Why do you think you can hide?" She tipped Rosa's bed over and continued hitting me.

"She's supposed to get only eight sticks," Rosa said.

"And she chose to get more by hiding."

It took me a long time to realize that the pain and anxiety of

Sister's random strikes were far worse than the swelling on my buttocks had I lain on the bed without a fuss.

After the beatings, Sister, whose face was red from the effort, sat down on the sacrificial bed, exhausted and maybe a little remorseful. "I never want to beat you. But I am your mother and I have to raise you as good Catholic children. You don't understand now, but it is for your own good."

For a half an hour, she listened to our sobs and sighs and groans. When we had cried ourselves to sleep, she walked around each bed and blessed us with holy water.

"Sleep well, my children, I am always praying for you." She turned off the lights and locked the door from the outside.

6

Monday

I could only enjoy my favorite pastime—daydreaming—when my chores were done each day. Monday was the worst day for chores.

"Get up, you ugly, lazy pig." Zami greeted me at six o'clock Monday morning and any morning when I didn't wake up before she did.

"I said get up!" Zami pulled off the olive wool blanket, grabbed me by the arm and flung me to the floor. I sat on the ice-cold floor trembling. Zami felt the center of the thin sisal mattress with her hand and, tossing it on the floor over me, checked the straw bottom of the bed for wetness. She pulled me up by the back my neck. "You're safe today." Her foul morning breath blew over my head as she banged my face against the bed frame. "Go make my bed, and if I find wrinkles in it again, I'll break your bones." She let go of me and I fell back onto the mattress. Elizabeth helped me up, and we ran to the other side of the room, stepping over and into scattered pee puddles, where she helped me make Zami's huge bed. I said a prayer of thanksgiving. My bed was dry. I was spared the torture in *nyumba ile*.

The bell for Mass rang. Barefoot, we headed down the road in the dark and formed two lines in front of the church as we waited for the nuns inside to finish morning prayers. They chanted endlessly in Latin while we shivered outside hearing the rustle of their habits as they bowed and genuflected. Finally the short, bent-over figure of Mother Rufina, the Mother Superior, opened the door.

"Fold your hands together," she instructed us. We pressed our trembling, freezing hands together. "Dip your third finger in the Holy water bowl to make the sign of the cross, cross, cross." Mother Rufina often repeated what she said as least three times. "Mary, show the children the right way to make the sign of the cross." Beaming with pride, I went to the front of the line, dipped my third finger in the holy water, touched my forehead, chest, left shoulder, right shoulder, and folded my hands together. "Very good, my child, very good, very good. Now you can enter."

The big girls nicknamed Mother Rufina *Ntendezeze* in reference to the back and forth motion of playing the *zeze*, an African stringed instrument. Besides repeating her words, she usually took one step back for every two steps forward when she walked.

Two by two, boys on the right, girls on the left, we filed into the church and marched to the front. There were a few boys at the orphanage, but they lived in a separate house. For all activities, we were grouped according to gender: boys first, girls second; boys to the right, girls to the left; boys in front, girls in the back. After genuflecting, we each knelt in our assigned places, ten to a pew.

Dear Father Gattang always seemed to say Mass in slow motion. We couldn't kneel without fidgeting for the whole hour, but we didn't dare move because ever-vigilant Sister Silvestris counted all the empty places on the benches and noted which children had dirty berets or ripped dresses. She remembered who prayed and sang, who dozed off, and who talked or laughed. Any infractions would be added to the offenses we accumulated during the day, and we would be punished with the usual beatings.

One morning, Zami forced me to miss Mass. She squeezed me behind the toilet door as soon as I was up and said, "I want some sugar, apples, and cooking oil."

The big girls knew we'd be beaten for skipping church, yet they hid us under beds, behind doors and bushes, or up trees, and gave us lists of items to pilfer during the hour that Sister Silvestris was in church. I was almost always caught when I stole for Zami. We took plums, pears, peaches, and passion fruit from the orchard. We dug up carrots, sweet potatoes, rutabagas, and radishes from the garden. Stealthily we filled small bags and tin cans with sugar, rice, simsim cooking oil, and flour from the storeroom, and emptied whole containers of chocolates, candy, biscuits, sunlight soap, coconut hair oil, and toothpaste from Sister's room. When we were caught, the big girl who sent us to steal beat us in private for being caught, and Sister Silvestris beat us in public for our moral lapse.

After Mass, we ran uphill to the dining room and ate *uji*, a slippery porridge made out of corn flour, water, and salt. Sometimes we had a spoonful or two of milk.

"Delphina, can I please have some of your sugar for my porridge?"

Delphina and her three siblings weren't orphans, and they got whatever they wanted from their Greek father and African mother. Delphina's parents were the only mixed couple who visited their children together. "I can't give you any. It already melted."

"Then can I have some of the porridge that's under the melted sugar?"

"No, today I can't share with you," she replied, as she vigorously stirred her porridge with a large metal spoon. So I watched her and timed the swallowing of my *uji* with hers, imagining that my porridge was sweetened too.

The bell rang and we jumped from our benches. Outside, Delphina took my hand and said, "I'll save some sugar for you tomorrow, Mary. I won't tell Zami. I don't want her to beat you." Zami was in charge of us both, as well as of Delphina's two sisters and her brother. "I told my mama that Zami beats you. She said that if Zami ever beats me, she'd cut off her hands."

"Really?"

"Yes, my mother can do anything." She continued holding my hand and said that she would tell me something that she had never told anyone. We sat very close together on the grass behind the bushes near *nyumba ile* and she began, "Everybody in our village is petrified of Mama because they think she's a *mchawi*." The word meant witch doctor. "Even my father is afraid of her."

"Your mama is a real *mchawi*?" I pulled away and stared at her in disbelief.

"Don't be afraid of me! I'm not a *mchawi*."

I was trying to absorb the fact that *wachawi* actually existed and have children in Kifungilo, when suddenly I had an idea. "Could she really cut off Zami's hands?"

"She can do anything. Now listen, if you ever say anything about Mama, I'll have her cut off your head." Delphina then told me a story in great detail about an encounter her mother had in the village market with a man who wanted to take her to his house. When she rebuffed him, he insulted her and her "white as a ghost" Greek husband. She returned his insults. He was furious that a woman would talk back to him and began threatening her. Delphina pleaded with her mother not to fight. "You lay a finger on me, and your entire family will die," she told the man, but he hit her across the face anyway. She knocked him to the ground. A woman in the crowd yelled for him to stop, saying that he was tangling with a *mchawi*. He ran away as fast as he could.

Delphina recounted how her mother went home, killed and cooked a black rooster all the while singing a strange song. That night she dressed up in her best *khanga* and went to the man's village, carrying the food in a basket. Delphina secretly followed her. Her mother knocked on the door of a hut and one of the man's wives answered. She told the woman that she had a present from their husband and left the basket with them. The next day, according to Delphina, the three wives and several of the man's children were dead.

I had heard several other stories about *wachawi* and they petrified me. "Is your mother really so powerful? Aren't you scared of her?"

"Yes, even though she says she'd never hurt her own family."

"If your Mama cut off Zami's hands, she could never beat me again. She could cut off Zami's feet too so she couldn't kick me anymore." But Delphina told me that her mother only protects herself and her family.

We had almost forgotten that it was Monday, laundry day. Grabbing our aluminum pails and basins from the storage shed, we went to fetch water. If there was no water from the tap in the children's quarters, we had to make several trips to the river a half mile away in order to fill earthenware barrel-like containers sitting over a log fire that heated the wash water.

Some big girls went down to the Sisters' quarters to wash the huge piles of nuns' habits, sheets, towels, blankets, and sweaters, while others did the children's laundry. Not only did Zami make me wash all the dirty clothes that she was supposed to wash, but also once a month she had me wash her homemade bloody "period" rags. My imagination went wild when I tried to figure out what part of her produced such a vile substance. The menstruation rags were made out of two one-foot-square pieces of cotton sewn together, with one-inch loops on two opposite ends. The corners without hoops were folded toward the center so that the rags were narrow rectangles. The big girls put two or three of these rectangular rags between their legs. They ran a cord through the front loops at the base of the stomach and the back loops over the tailbone and tied the cord at the waist. They used up to a dozen rags a day.

I fetched water and rubbed Zami's menstruation clothes with a strong, light blue-and-white soap bar, scrubbing until my hands were raw. I laid them out on the hibiscus bushes near the toilets and watched them until they dried. If they still looked stained after drying in the sun, I had to wash them again in order to avoid a beating.

Every Monday, I washed a mountain of Zami's large dresses, slips, bras, and panties as well as clothing belonging to the little rich girls under her care, and I spread the clothes on the grass in front of the statue of Blessed Martin to dry. I wondered what he thought of this array of female clothing laid out for his inspection. I stood guard to keep the wind from blowing them away and re-soiling them. By early afternoon, I had folded the dry ones, rewashed the items I didn't get clean the first time, and taken them all to Zami for inspection.

"Why is my towel gray?" she asked, slapping me across the face.

"The color ran when you told me to wash everything in hot water."

"You idiot! You boiled the towel!" She hit me on my right cheek. Smack! She slapped me on the left cheek. "Show me my dresses."

I got hit in response to most of the items I showed her. Her big fat hands came flying at me at regular intervals. When I lost my balance and fell down, I quickly stood up to connect with her hands, otherwise the slaps turned into blows and kicks that landed on my stomach.

"Get out of here, you good for nothing fat pig!"

As soon as I was dismissed, I ran behind Zahabu the woodcutter's shack as fast as my short fat legs could carry me to meet with the other orphans who had also been beaten for imperfectly done laundry. We compared our swellings and bruises, and since we were out of our big girls' earshot, we sobbed and moaned to our hearts' content.

7

The Rest of the Week

 Unless there were special chores like brickmaking, or washing the feet and removing jiggers from the cracked toes of Fupi and other old men of the village who had no one to help them, or gathering firewood to heat water for next week's laundry, we were free until it was time to return to church to say the Rosary. It was dark by the time we sat down for supper, so the generator was turned on and we had light.

A steady clang-clang filled the dining room—the sound of our spoons hitting the rims of our metal plates as we scooped out the dead *wadudu* floating in our kidney bean soup. "Give your bugs to Mary," yelled Serafina. "She eats anything!" We laughed as we gulped down the soup with huge metal spoons that cut the corners of our mouths. Some children couldn't swallow the beans with the bugs, so there was plenty for me. To get the last morsel, I raised the plate to my mouth with both hands and slurped every drop of soup, leaving a wet mask on my face and hair.

Ever since the Germans lost the First and then the Second World War, the Sisters of Kifungilo lived in constant fear of the British who ruled Tanganyika, a former German territory. During the war, German nationals and all non-British citizens had been regarded as enemy aliens and their activities were restricted. The nuns were concerned that the British would impose strict tariffs on goods coming into Tanganyika from Germany and confiscate donations to the orphanage from abroad. They kept a low profile for several years after the war. At times this caused hardships for Kifungilo. Instead of the Sisters going to town when they needed to buy maize, beans, rice, or flour for the children, they asked trusted Germans and other expatriates who lived in town to do them the favor. The *wazungu* expatriates were not always honest, and they often bought low grade, half-full, and spoiled bags of staples, claiming there was nothing better, and pocketed the difference in price.

Other problems with our food supply occurred when the rains didn't come, or when it rained too long and too hard and the road to Lushoto was washed out, or when we had a plague of locusts that stripped the entire orphanage of all foliage and destroyed the crops in a matter of hours. At those times Sister Silvestris had to strictly ration the staples. Often the bags of beans and grains were stored in the dark, insect- and rat-infested *magazine* for so long that by the time we ate them, they were full of bugs. To kill them, Sister Silvestris poured paraffin oil into the storage sacks. Although most of us diligently pushed the dead *wadudu* to the rims of our metal plates as we ate, our breath smelled like paraffin.

After supper, we all had to go to the toilet shed, which consisted of six three-by-four feet chambers of cement, each with a square hole in the ground at one end, and on one side, a wooden door that never stayed shut. Around the shed were hibiscus bushes whose leaves we used for toilet paper. Because of the frantic little hands tugging at them, these plants never bloomed despite their proximity to human compost. A trench that ran the length of the shed collected the deposits, and with the aid of water pumped up from the river, dumped the waste into a huge cesspool a few yards from the shed. Little girls used the two toilets at the end. Because it was dark by six o'clock and we couldn't see where we aimed, the floor of our toilets was always full of diarrhea, feces, and urine. Cleaning the toilets was our most hated chore.

After the toilet rituals, we fetched water from the tap or from the river and poured it into a tin basin in the bathing room adjacent to the toilet shed. We washed up without the aid of soap or towels. The rich girls brushed their teeth with toothbrushes and toothpaste. The rest of us used twigs from the hibiscus bushes to clean our teeth. One by one, we went to the sleeping room, got into our night dresses made of *merikani*—a cheap, shiny cotton textile imported from America—and crawled under the covers.

Each weekday had its own chores. On Tuesdays we ironed. We put pieces of charcoal in heavy metal irons, poured some paraffin over them, lit them with a glowing piece of charcoal from the cooking stove, blew until the coals were red and the iron was hot. The big girls did the ironing, but we had to take the irons outside when they cooled to get them hot again and then carry them back until the day's ironing was done.

Wednesdays, we dispersed over the entire mission grounds picking up leaves and whatever litter the wind had scattered. "The child who collects the most rubbish will get *zawadi*—a nice present," announced Sister Silvestris. "Put your piles of rubbish down by the dump pit and I will inspect them." Sister came with a big bag of *sukari guru* (crystalized brown sugar) and gave the child with the biggest pile the largest piece. It was never me. By nightfall when we crawled into bed, our backs and limbs hurt so much we groaned with every move.

Thursdays we went to the forest to collect firewood for cooking and heating water for bathing and laundry. "Tell me, Fat Mary," Sister Silvestris asked, "why are you so happy on Thursdays when you go to the forest?"

"I find delicious berries, like gooseberries. I chase butterflies, and sometimes I pretend I'm a bird. I can pick pretty wild flowers and weeds and play with the stray goats."

"What do you do when you catch a butterfly?"

"I usually find only dead ones. I spread their wings and imagine how and where they fly."

"That's why your load of wood is so small, Fat Mary. You spend all your time playing. You mustn't eat the wild berries. Some of them are poisonous."

"I know all the bad ones. See, I haven't died yet."

Sister laughed and gently pinched my cheek.

Many times I forgot to collect firewood. Then I'd ask Stefana to share her wood with me, because she always collected the most, and

I shared my gooseberries and pretty dead butterflies with her. We tied strips of flexible green bark around the wood, helped each other load it on our heads, scampered down the hills, showed it to Sister Silvestris, and finally delivered it to Zahabu's wood shack.

On Fridays, while the Sisters and big girls went to Confession, we searched for lice in each other's hair. We separated the hair into narrow rows, ran our fingers along the scalp, and killed the fat lice by pressing them between our thumbnails. The children whose hair was infested with lice eggs were drenched with paraffin oil, the orphanage's all-purpose bug killer. Whenever we could, we removed lice from each other because if Sister found them crawling on our clothing, she scolded the big girl in charge of us, who would then beat us.

On Saturdays, right after breakfast, we ran to the fern tree forest to collect branches for making brooms. We arranged ten two-foot-long branches cut from the trees on the ground and then tied the ends together with strips of bark. We spent the whole morning stooped over, sweeping the entire mission, including the long road that brought visitors to the orphanage. The big girls cleaned the priest's house, as well as the convent and our living quarters. They washed the glass windows with vinegar and newspaper; swept and mopped the cement floors with soap and water; scrubbed, waxed, and polished the wooden floors and stairs with bees wax; changed sheets; fluffed pillows, and aired out the heavy woolen blankets by hanging them over wire clotheslines.

On Saturday afternoons we bathed. A bucket of water was shared by three or four children. If there was no water in the tap by our quarters, we fetched it from the river and heated it for the big girls and the rich girls. Zami, who was in charge of Delphina, had me bathe Delphina along with her two younger sisters, although she was much older and taller than I was. I bathed her as best I could and washed her hair, and then she helped me with her younger siblings. I dried her body, rubbed jasmine oil all over her skin, and put lavender brilliantine on her rough hair before I braided it. Delphina always thanked me and put a dab of her hair dressing aside for me.

After bathing the girls, I heated more water for Zami to bathe in.

When she was done, three or more big girls used the same water, and then, with only two inches of dirty water left in the tin tub, I bathed using Delphina's soap. After I dried myself with her wet towel and put the sweet smelling dab of brilliantine in my hair, she helped me untangle and braid it. When we were all clean, I took them all to Zami for inspection.

8

Adoption

 One Saturday, after sweeping what felt like miles and miles of road, Elizabeth and I fell asleep behind the statue of Blessed Martin. "Piggy! Piggy! Where is that fat pig?" Zami's harsh voice woke me. I opened my eyes to see Zami's beady black ones looking down on me. "Why can't you stay clean?" She slapped me on the thigh and sent me rolling down the hillside toward the river. "Wash your filthy fat body and come right up. Don't be chasing butterflies and picking your stupid weeds. Be back here in two minutes or else!"

At the river I wet the palm of my hand with the freezing water and cleaned my arms and legs. I waved to the ducks sunning nearby. On my way up the hill I found a dead grasshopper. Its wings fell off in my hand. I admired them and envied their ability to fly. I crumpled the wings and blew them back towards the sky. With my foot I made a small hole under a coffee bush and buried the rest of it.

Zami was waiting for me with a comb in her hand. "And how many *wadudu* and birds did you talk to this time, you stupid girl? Go to *nyumba ile* and put on your Sunday dress and shoes and come back here so I can fix your messy hair."

I ripped off my dirty clothes, pulled on my dress, stuffed my feet into my shoes and ran as fast as I could back to Zami. "All that time at the river and you didn't even wash your face!" With her fist under my chin, she jerked my face up. I looked up at her angry face with its tightly puckered lips and protruding mouth. *Thoop, thoop, thoop!* Zami discharged several mouthfuls of warm spit on my forehead, cheeks, and nose. "Now clean your face, you dirty pig."

I spread the sticky spit on my face and rubbed it in, then wiped my hands on the inside of my dress. As Zami combed my hair, I saw Sister Silvestris coming toward us smiling. I ran to her and put my hand in hers. I liked Sister Silvestris so much when she smiled. "My little Fat Mary, we have a guest who would like to see you. You must show her your best manners and don't talk to her too much about Kifungilo."

She didn't need to worry. We were very afraid of the *wazungu,* and the most we'd ever say to them was "yes" or "no."

"Is it another *mzungu* lady who is looking for a child to adopt?"

"Yes, my Fat Mary. Would you like to be adopted?"

"Oh, yes. I pray to Blessed Martin that soon the right *mzungu* lady will pick me, but I also pray to Baby Jesus that he will find my real mother."

"Anything you ask from Baby Jesus, he will give you when the time is right."

"Why do only *wazungu* ladies come to look for children?"

"Because most Africans have enough children of their own, and sometimes they can't take care of them all."

"Did my mother have so many children that she couldn't take care of me?"

"You mustn't ask so many questions, my Fat Mary. Even if you're adopted someday, you must remember that I was your first mother."

We climbed the five rounded red epoxy steps to the open wooden door of the convent and walked to the parlor where *wazungu* guests were received. Sister let go of my hand and left the room, shutting the door behind her.

I spotted the plate of biscuits on a small round table covered with a pink lace doily. Among them were the rectangular, sugary Nice brand biscuits that Elizabeth sometimes shared with me. When I looked up, I saw a *mzungu* lady sitting on the high-backed chair opposite the table. Her face was round and she wore large horn-rimmed glasses. She had on a lavender dress with little white flowers and a narrow white belt with a silver buckle that peeked out of the folds of her large waistline. I couldn't see her feet, but she was tapping a soft, uneven beat on the floor.

I waited for her to grab me and put me on her lap and start kissing and hugging me like the other children told me the *wazu-*

ngu ladies did, but she didn't move. Taking a light blue porcelain teapot from under a tea cozy, she poured tea into a matching cup on a saucer. She put two teaspoons of sugar and a drop of cream in the cup. Preparing another cup of tea exactly the same way, she handed it to me. I put the saucer on the table, held the cup in both hands and drank the tea straight down. I stuck my forefinger in the bottom of the tea cup several times to scoop up the un-melted sugar and spread it over my tongue. I put the cup on the table, wiped my mouth across my sleeve, held my skirt out at the sides, curtseyed, and said, "Thank you, lady."

The lady didn't seem very happy. She didn't smile or ask me any questions. She gave me some biscuits and poured me more tea. I drank four cups of tea and finished all the biscuits on the plate before I noticed that she hadn't touched her cup of tea. She gave that to me too. She pointed to the chair next to me and indicated that I was to sit down. I sat on the floor because I didn't know how to sit in the big cushioned chair. She pointed to the chair again. I looked at her, and I looked at the chair several times before I decided to put one knee on the seat to pull myself up onto it with both hands. I tucked my feet under my dress Buddha-like and stared at the short, round lady.

Who is this woman, I wondered, and why is she looking at me so much without smiling? At least I knew that she didn't like me, so I wasn't going to count the days until I was adopted. She was looking at me so hard that, if she weren't a *mzungu*, I would have asked her if she were my mother and why she didn't want me. When I heard Sister Silvestris' footsteps, I jumped to the floor and stood at attention. She nodded at the lady and told me to go back to the children's quarters.

Elizabeth was waiting for me. "Tell me what happened?" I told her that the *mzungu* lady gave me biscuits and tea.

"Is that all? What did she say?"

"Nothing."

"Why did it take so long? What did she want?"

"Nothing. I think she is the same *mzungu* lady who has looked at me before. She didn't even give me candy or tell me how adorable I am."

"The *wazungu* don't mean what they say. How could anyone call you adorable?"

"A *mzungu* lady visiting Kifungilo once said that I was pretty and adorable and have beautiful black eyes."

"She was lying. But I think you took so long because you're going to be adopted!"

The idea of having a mother or someone who loved me enough to adopt me—even this serious *mzungu* lady—made me giddy.

"I'm going to be adopted! No one will call me 'fat pig' or stupid or beat me anymore."

We held hands and jumped up and down, round and round, until we were dizzy.

The *mzungu* never adopted me. But every so often, I went through this ritual with the same serious lady. I learned how to sit on a high stuffed chair with my legs over the edge, rather than tucked under, how to hold a saucer in one hand and drink from the cup in the other, how to use a tiny spoon to stir sugar, and how to sip my tea slowly without burping or smacking my lips.

I don't remember anyone being adopted and taken away. There must have been some, but we never knew for sure. We would just notice that someone was gone. We didn't ask questions.

But I feared I'd never be adopted because I was so fat, ugly, and stupid. Thinking about this one day, I began feeling bad and was crying loudly when Sister Silvestris passed by.

"Fat Mary, why are you crying now?"

"Because no one wants to adopt me."

"Come, my Fat Mary, here's a toffee." She pulled my head on to her stomach and I cried into her apron.

"Don't cry. You're a good girl. You have a nice home in Kifungilo."

When Sister Silvestris left me, my inner Fat Mary suddenly spoke up. *You are not ugly and stupid, you know.*

"Sister Silvestris often tells me that I'm clever."

You must believe her, Fat Mary insisted. *Sometimes you don't love yourself, and you forget all about me.*

"I do? I'm sorry." Fat Mary was right. As long as I remember to love myself, everything would be OK. I took a deep breath and went to join the other children for supper.

9

Boxes from Germany

The one time of the year when I almost forgot all about my longing for a mother and a family was Christmastime.

After supper on the four Sundays before Christmas, all the little children gathered under the Advent wreath in the recreation hall. Sister Silvestris sat in our midst and told us stories from Germany and stories she made up about miracles that the Christ child performed for Christmas. We knew that she made them up because our names appeared in the stories.

"Please read Hansel and Gretel again," I asked Sister. She read the stories in German, then translated them into the distinctive Kifungilo blend of broken Swahili and limited English.

As Sister tired of recounting stories in a language that only Kifungilo children could understand, the thickness of her German accent made them harsh lullabies. When most of the children were dozing off, Sister's voice faded to a whisper. She closed her storybook and reached for the bag at her side.

The crackling sound of candy wrappers and the ruffling of roasted peanuts in the gunnysack woke the sleeping children like an alarm bell. Little arms reached over heads and in between shoulders to have Sister drop a piece of hard candy and a handful of peanuts into cupped hands. "I didn't get any," we lied, so some of us received more than our share.

"Elizabeth, I got a piece of cherry-flavored candy." I had already popped it in my mouth because I knew she would ask me for it. We used the candy to color our lips red like the *wazungu*. "Stick out your lips." I took the candy out of my mouth and rubbed it across Elizabeth's lips then colored mine.

"Save your peanuts," she reminded me.

I had every intention of saving them in an old sock so I could eat them one by one during the week like the other children, but mine never made it through the night. What I didn't eat in the recreation room, I quietly chewed and savored under my covers in the bed that I shared with Elizabeth. We slept at each end with our feet touching the other's head. No matter how quietly I ate my peanuts, she heard me and every so often, she threw a flurry of little kicks that made me lose a peanut which I then had to search for in the bed and sometimes on the floor. Savoring the peanuts was worth the scratches from her toenails on my face and arms.

On the evening of the last Sunday of Advent, after receiving our peanuts and candy, Sister reminded us of the sacrifices we had to make before Christmas in order to welcome Baby Jesus to the orphanage. "For every sacrifice you make, you can collect grasses and gather moss from the rocks by the waterfalls for the nativity scene. Baby Jesus wants a soft bed, so make many sacrifices."

Babu volunteered to clean old Fupi's hut, and Elizabeth said she'd fetch water from the river to water his maize. Stefana offered to clean the jiggers from his toes. She could dig into Fupi's toes using a thorn without hurting him.

"I'll say extra prayers to Blessed Martin," I added.

"Praying doesn't count," Rosemary objected. "You have to do something hard."

"Fat Mary, you can pray if you want. Baby Jesus always listens to your prayers," said Sister Silvestris.

During the entire week before Christmas, we kept busy cleaning huts for old and sick Wasambaa, watering their plots, giving our candy to the children in the village (a sacrifice I never made), staying in church longer and saying extra prayers for the conversion of pagans, helping each other with our chores, collecting litter and taking it to the dump, returning the cups, plates, and spoons that we had stolen from the dining hall, and not talking after Sister had turned off the lights at night.

Sister Theonesta, who was in charge of teaching the younger children, taught us Christmas carols, plays, and poems that we memorized to perform for the Sisters on Christmas Eve.

We received our yearly allotment of clothes and sometimes a pair of shoes at Christmas time. Two days before Christmas, the children were taken to the dormitory attic to pick a Christmas dress that would be our Sunday dress for the year. We shrieked with excitement as we saw the boxes from Germany full of clothes and shoes. Sister Silvestris told us that the Sisters in Germany collected these clothes for us.

"What will those children wear if they give us their clothes and shoes?" I asked because I couldn't imagine giving my clothes away.

"They are not rich, but they do have more clothes than you. Like them, you must always share your things with those who have less. Now go ahead and choose your Christmas dresses." We began going through the boxes of used clothing, shoes, purses, jewelry and other items.

"What's this?" I asked, holding up an enormous, stiff contraption that had rusted metal hooks hanging from bias tape. I put it over my head and tied the tapes together at my shoulders.

"It must be a stiff sleeveless blouse," I said.

Sister Silvestris looked at me. "Fat Mary, that's not for children. It's a girdle. Look only for dresses with sleeves. Only bad girls wear sleeveless dresses and trousers." I held up a huge satin bra with sharp rods and hooks. "Put that down!" Sister's voice was stern. I dropped the bra, imagining the size of the breasts that would fit in it. "Where are the big girls? Hanna, go call Lizzy and Rosa to come and help me. The children are mixing everything up."

We each tried on several dresses and picked the one we liked the best. Often we quarreled over a particularly pretty dress and Sister would have to intervene. We also chose a pair of shoes. If no donated shoes fit, we had to wait until the following year.

"Children, line up and show me what you found. Lizzy, make sure they have picked something nice, and Rosa, pin their names on the clothes and put them in that empty box for Christmas Eve."

Sister sat on one of the unopened boxes and used her fountain pen with the short wide nib to write our names. I loved to watch Sister write. Whenever I saw her writing, I would run to her and watch her handwriting that flowed so easily and seemed full of meaning.

"Can I please try writing?" I asked Sister.

"Not today, Fat Mary."

I was the last in line because I was so small. As I waited for my turn, I recalled the time when she let me "write" on the back of a used sheet of paper. I gave her my paper full of scribbles when I was done.

"What did you write about?" she asked.

"It's the story of Hansel and Gretel."

"Do you know any other story?"

"Yes, but I don't know how to write the other stories."

"One day when you learn the alphabet, you will be able to write down all the stories in your head. When you grow up, maybe you will be a writer."

"No. I want to be a dancer."

"A dancer! Where did you get that idea?" Sister asked with surprise.

"From the Wasambaa. When we go to the village, I see them dancing and singing."

"I've never seen them."

"They always stop when you come."

"I hope so. From what I've heard, their dancing is sinful. They are almost naked. Many are drunk, and they make terrible noises that come straight from the devil. They fall on each other and lie on the ground for days, forgetting to work. They skip work so often just because they were at a *ngoma*, a tribal dance celebration."

"They seem so happy."

"They dance to forget their miserable lives and escape responsibility. You must never dance like them."

"But I want to dance."

"You don't need to dance. I've never danced. But if you like, I'll ask Sister Theonesta to teach you proper dancing. The German waltz is a very beautiful dance."

I couldn't forget this conversation with Sister Silvestris. I was glad that she never caught me dancing with the Wasambaa. The old women would twirl me around, teach me to shake my hips and chest, and show me a few steps. I'd squeal with delight. I promised myself that when I grew up, I would dance just like them.

It was finally my turn to have my Christmas dress examined.

"Mary, you picked a fine dress," Lizzy said. "Put it on to see how it fits."

"You look very pretty in your new dress," Rosa said with a kind smile. "Come, I'll pin your name on it so nobody else gets it."

"Can I please look at my name?"

Rosa gave me the piece of paper. "This is how to spell your name. F-A-T M-A-R-Y."

"Is F-A-T part of my name too?" I asked as I studied the letters.

"There are other Marys in Kifungilo, so when we say 'Fat Mary,' we know it's you," she said, pinning the paper to my new dress.

"I want to learn to write my name."

"When you do, write only M-A-R-Y."

From then on, I longed for the day when everyone would simply call me "Mary."

10

Trim the Tree

 In preparation for the Christmas celebration, the big girls baked *mtu wa mandazi*—gingerbread men—and Christmas cookies. A pig was slaughtered. We went to the pine forest for a Christmas tree that Zahabu, our woodcutter, chopped down. Singing and dancing, we carried the tree into the recreation room. After that, we were forbidden to enter the recreation room until Christmas Eve. Although Sister Silvestris was very busy and secretive at this time, she was in a good mood. "What does my Fat Mary want for Christmas?"

"I only want lots of food and my mother."

"You can't get everything you want, you know. Some things even Father Christmas can't find. And you mustn't ask for your mother. Remember, I am your mother."

At night we dreamed of our desired presents, and in the morning we'd share our dreams. The first time I said that what I wanted most was my mother, the other children laughed at me, and Serafina said, "Don't you understand that you don't have a family? Ask for something else because your parents probably died in a horrible car accident."

"I don't believe you!" I cried and ran off. I quickly learned not to tell the truth about what I wanted. My other wish was mainly for the kind of treats that the rich girls received from their families—enough biscuits, chocolates, candy, golden syrup, and canned mangos to last me until the following Christmas.

At six o'clock on Christmas Eve, the big girls, already dressed up, came to get us ready. Their hair was arranged in pretty designs and held in place with colorful clips and ribbons. Their lips and cheeks were colored with cherry-flavored candy saved for the occasion. They wore sparkling, multicolored costume jewelry from the boxes of donated items. Their shoes were secondhand high heels they had practiced walking in for weeks. They carried big, beat up, empty *wazungu* purses. We little ones thought the big girls were gorgeous.

With joyful laughter and song, we walked down to the convent to bring the Sisters to our festivities in the recreation hall. I could hardly contain my excitement as we neared the hall. Sister Silvestris ceremoniously opened the door for the Sisters to enter and then shut it. After an eternity of ten minutes, she swung the doors open. Two by two we marched in, forming lines facing the seated Sisters.

The room smelled like a pine forest. Red, blue, green, yellow, and orange tinsel, and large paper bells, trees, and balls hung from the ceiling. Angels made out of bright colored paper with gold and silver wings floated above us. The advent wreath, its last candle still tall, hung from wide purple ribbons in the center of the room. Along the four walls were tables covered with evenly spaced little bundles.

In the front left corner of the room, with candles burning around it, was a cave and a large nativity scene. The moss we had collected covered its floor and walls. At the center was the Holy Family. Baby Jesus had white skin and blond curly hair that caressed his smiling face. Tiny plump hands reached up from under the many layers of clothes that pressed him down onto his bed of the soft grass we had collected. Mary was dressed in a pink tunic and her ocean blue veil was sprinkled with yellow stars. She knelt to the right of her son, with her hands folded on her chest. To the left stood Joseph in a brown tunic with a maroon cape over his shoulders, leaning with both hands on a curved staff.

The Holy Family was surrounded by shepherds with their sheep. The dark-skinned herdsmen wore the same brown tunic as Joseph, but with different color sashes at their waists. They were spread across the scene, their faces set in various expressions of adoration. A black ox, with long curving horns, and an attentive ass stood over the Christ child resting in the manger. A bright silver star dangled from the top of the cave almost touching Jesus' head. To date, I have not seen any other crèche that has measured up to the wonder and promise of this Nativity scene.

Christmas made me think of my missing family, because everyone who had a family went home. As soon as we entered the recreation hall, totally oblivious to the other children's sneers and the stares of the Sisters, I marched straight to the crèche. Kneeling on the cold cement in front of the Holy Family, I gazed at the motionless Baby Jesus as though he would come alive for me. Speaking out loud, I prayed, "Please, please, beautiful baby, send me a mother, or please help my mother find me. I have been praying for a long time. When will you answer my prayers?"

"As soon as I can," he replied.

"Promise me that it will be very soon." I waited for an answer, but Jesus was asleep. I continued praying silently, because I didn't want to wake him up and also because the room became very quiet. Undaunted, I continued praying. Hadn't Sister Silvestris told us that whatever we asked from Baby Jesus at Christmas time would be granted? I believed her. Then, with a strong sense of satisfaction and anticipation, I joined the others who were just about to start entertaining the Sisters without me.

We tried our best to focus on the Sisters, who were beaming and chatting in German, and to keep our eyes off the pile of presents waiting for us on the tables. We sang Christmas carols and performed the Christmas story. I was the Virgin Mary. I knelt with my hands folded across my chest most of the time, but sometimes I stroked the short, nappy hair of little Babu who was playing Baby Jesus, and remembered to give a "heavenly" smile for the nuns just like Sister Theonesta had told me to do. Gemsi played Joseph and knelt next to me clutching his staff. Even though Gemsi was from a large mixed family who lived nearby and whose father, Heini, was the building contractor for the orphanage, the children took part in the Christmas celebration. Reza, Stefana, Imelda, Elise, another Ellen, and Antonette were angels. Wearing beautiful paper wings, they swooshed down from a table on the side and knelt in front of Baby Jesus.

After the Christmas story, we recited poems we had memorized and performed the German waltz with partners—boys with boys, girls with girls. We held each other by both shoulders and moved like stick figures in an orderly fashion. *"Einz, zwei, drei, opp*—one, two, three, up," Sister Theonesta prompted us. This was so different from dancing with the Wasambaa in the village and it never made me smile or scream with delight. The waltz, a new addition this year, pleased the Sisters. They stood up, clapped thunderously, and to our chagrin, wanted several encores. Our faces got longer with each encore. Finally we started singing "Trim the Tree," the last number of our performance.

Who'll come and help to trim the Christmas tree?
Fa-la-la-la-la-la-la!
Make all the branches pretty as can be.
Fa-la-la-la-la-la-la!

Pretending to be candles, angels, crystal balls, and snowflakes, we made a Christmas tree as, one by one, we lay down on the floor. When we finished singing and acting out "Trim the Tree," we went to search for our presents on the table.

For the next hour, the recreation hall buzzed with sounds of joy as we got our gifts. A ten-inch gingerbread man, with raisins for eyes, nose, and mouth, smiled at me. Four little buttons made of white icing ran down his chest. I removed the eyes and buttons, broke off the right arm and ate it right away. As I was chewing, I examined the rest of my presents: a tumbler of roasted peanuts, a little paper bag full of hard candy, a pair of socks, a pair of white patent leather shoes with buckles instead of laces, a cotton slip, a flannel nightgown, two homemade drawstring knickers (our panties), five marbles, a cloth doll that the retired Sisters had made, and the beautiful red dress with light blue trim on the hem that I had picked out from the boxes from Germany.

I was so happy that I put my new dress on top of the one I had on, pulled on my new socks and shoes, and went looking for Sister Silvestris. When she saw me coming, she reached out and put her arms around me, saying, "How pretty you are, my Fat Mary!"

"Thank you very much for my presents, Sister."

She put her finger across my lips. "Hush. You mustn't thank me. Thank Baby Jesus, Father Christmas, and the kind people in Germany."

On Christmas Eve we stayed up and played until nine o'clock. Then at eleven thirty we got up for midnight Mass. I was dreaming of the beautiful hymns we would sing for Mass when the light in the sleeping room went on.

"Wake up, wake up, everyone," Sister Silvestris called. I jumped out of bed when she pulled back my covers. "Get ready quickly. We have to be in church before the nonbelievers and pagans who come just to listen to the organ and don't know anything about Christmas."

I loved midnight Mass. Lizzy pumped the organ and played Shubert's "Ave Maria," "Stille Nacht," and many other Christmas hymns so sweetly that I imagined it was the angels in heaven who sat inside the organ and sang. My favorite Christmas carol was a Swahili one, "Kimya" ("Hush!").

Silence over continents and oceans.
Silence over heaven and earth.
Your Lord and Creator,
Baby Jesus, is falling asleep.
Hush! Hush! He is falling asleep,
Our beloved Baby Jesus.
Hush! Hush! He is falling asleep,
Our beloved Baby Jesus.

After Mass we ran back up to our beds, and when Sister reached the wall to turn off the lights, we all yelled, "Happy Christmas, Sister!"

"Happy, Happy Christmas! My dear children, I pray that you will always remember Christmas in Kifungilo."

My friend Elizabeth always went home with her mother for the holidays. Every year, as I watched her pack her shiny leather suitcase, I dreamt of the day when my mother would come and I would go home. Before I could start my trademark farewell sobs, Elizabeth said with excitement, "Mary, when I return in January, we'll be seven and old enough to start school."

The mere mention of the word school made my heart beat fast. School was the only thing I had to look forward to, and the only thing that might one day get me out of Kifungilo. Elizabeth and I raced toward the green Austin that brought her mother, chanting, "We are seven, seven years old."

I followed the green car with my eyes as it slowly drove past the statue of Blessed Martin, past the hut for African mothers, the gooseberry field and the two-humped cows grazing on the sloping meadow. Then I saw Elizabeth's yellow handkerchief waving from the window. I pulled the ribbons from my pigtails and waved good-bye with both hands. She left me so happy with the thought of school that I forgot to cry.

Oh, how I wept those first few years of my life. My tears came like tropical storms. Every pore in my body wept. I heaved and shuddered and sighed. Everything around me seemed dark and terrifying. But whenever I felt like that, I would have a chat with my own Fat Mary. She was like the sweet fresh air after a rain. She brought me newness, clarity, and relief.

She managed to get in touch with and resurrect the free spirit deep inside me. Being one with this spirit allowed me to soar above my everyday reality. I marveled at the beauty of all life and savored the power and possibilities of my imagination. In these rare moments, I prayed, I danced, and I analyzed. I saw that life was good and bad, beautiful and ugly. I understood that I had to dwell on the good and beautiful in order to keep my imagination, sensitivity, and gratitude intact. I knew it would not be easy to maintain this perspective. I knew I would often twist and turn, bend and crack a little, but I also knew that with Fat Mary, I would never completely break.

11

School

From Christmas to New Year's, I sat by Blessed Martin every day watching for Elizabeth's car. Before she left, she told me, "If you are old enough to start school, you are old enough to stop crying."

"It's easy for you to say."

"You always find reasons to cry, and you carry on whenever the other kids say anything bad about you, but you have to stop. Try not to cry no matter what I say to you: You're fat and you have a round face." I cringed. "You don't wear panties." I pulled my dress down. "You smell." I sniffed my underarms. In an increasingly loud voice she hurled insults at me. "You *Dummkopf!* You're stupid and ugly! Cry baby! Little black gypsy—*schwarzer Ziguener!* Black devil—*schwarzer Teufel!* Your mother doesn't want you!" She stopped to study my reaction. I was contorted in pain, hunched over, fingers plugging my ears, my lips pressed together, and my eyes scrunched shut.

She started laughing at me.

"See, I didn't cry."

"Your eyes didn't cry, but your body did. If you don't do things that get you beaten, then you won't have a reason to cry, and if you don't cry all the time, you'll have more friends."

Out loud, I promised to cry less, but deep down I wondered: Who wants friends who won't let you cry when you're hurting?

Sister Theonesta was the main reason why I was fat because she fed me all the time. She was one of the three nuns who received me when I was brought to the orphanage. It must have been "love at first sight," because she volunteered to raise me until I was old enough for a big girl to take over. I slept in her bed, then on a pillow in a cardboard box. She also made all my clothes, sewing tiny nightgowns and baby clothes out of her old aprons, and crocheting small wool blankets, sweaters, and booties for me. She kept me at her side day and night, singing to me and playing with me. She carried a bottle of milk in her pocket for me and fed me with convent food that she chewed first, and then with children's food that she mashed and mixed with water and sugar.

Rosa told me many stories of my infancy, recounting how Sister Theonesta tucked me in her blue and white pin-striped apron and carried me with her wherever she went, showing me to anybody she could. Sometimes she'd even lift me over her head to present me to the sun and would pray loudly. Raising her arms over her head, Rosa imitated Sister Theonesta. "'Lord, watch over this beautiful baby. May she grow strong and healthy. Give her the strength to live a life worthy of you.' We stopped whatever we were doing and prayed with her." Rosa continued, "You never cried when she held you up and sometimes you even waved your arms as we prayed. Sister really loved you."

"Tell me more."

"She carried you in her apron when she made the outdoor Stations of the Cross. Starting at the first station and making her way up the hill, she'd genuflect at each station. By the time she reached the last station near the cemetery at the top of the hill, you were crying loudly. The other nuns heard you and marveled. They declared that you were a miracle baby who wept out of sympathy for Christ's suffering and death. But eventually someone noticed that you were bruised from hitting the ground every time Sister genuflected."

We attended Sister Theonesta's class three hours a day, five days a week. That schedule alone removed me from the scene of many of my crimes, spared me several beatings, and helped me keep my promise.

Sister's classroom was a rectangular room with four long desks that sat ten children each. In back was a large wooden cupboard for supplies, and on each side wall were two large glass windows. Wide sheets of painted black plywood covered the front wall and served as our blackboard. Facing us in front of the room was a six-foot square table and high back chair that served as Sister's desk.

When short, plump and round Sister Theonesta walked, she shuffled and swayed. The white starched bib of her habit touched her stomach when she sat down. As she taught, she played with her crucifix on the table. Her face had the soft wrinkles of someone who smiled and laughed a lot. Alert and slightly protruding brown eyes made her look like a contented chameleon.

Sister Theonesta taught all the subjects and would be our teacher for four years. Every morning when she entered the room we stood up, and she greeted us singing, "Good morning to you! Good morning to you! You're all in your places with bright smiling faces For this is the way to start a new day."

With our Swahili accents, we hollered back an unrecognizable version of her song ending with "Goody morninghee, Seestah."

"Good morning, children. You may sit down. You must take good care of your slates," she said as she handed them out to us. "You will use them for the next four years." I held my slate with both hands and pressed it to my heart.

"We shall start by learning to sing and write the alphabet."

"I already know the alphabet," I said. I often sat behind the school building memorizing as much as I could of what I heard. I stood and sang the entire alphabet. Sister clapped. The other children hissed.

Throughout the year I excelled in all the subjects. When Sister was not looking, I usually helped Elizabeth and Julitta and any other child who was having trouble and had the wits to sit within a four-foot radius of me. School was my place to shine. In return for helping my classmates, I made them promise not to tease me or call me "Piggy." Julitta was a poor student, so I told her that I would help her only if she didn't hit me too hard when we fought in *nyumba ile*. Children started to like me and play with me more.

As for Sister Theonesta, she still favored me. She called on me to read in front of the class and had me collect all the slates at the end of the day and put them on the table for her to correct. Every now and again I would wipe out half the slate of a classmate who had been mean to me, so she would be punished for not finishing her work.

12

True Confessions

 By my third year, Sister Theonesta had me teach when she left the classroom for a while, but we spent most of the time imitating her voice and her walk. We laughed uncontrollably. I put one child in charge of watching for her return, although if we had been doing what we were supposed to, we would have been able to hear her shuffling feet and hoarse voice. She often sang or talked to herself. She loved to sing and act. She taught us English songs to sing for the *wazungu*, German songs to sing for the Sisters, and Latin songs to sing to God.

She also prepared us for our First Holy Communion by instructing us on Catholic doctrine and morality and for Confession when we didn't live up to those teachings. We spent several months memorizing the catechism and quizzing each other. I made my First Communion with five other girls and one boy.

We looked forward to our first Holy Communion even though, as with much of our religious instruction, we never grasped how the Body and Blood of Christ became a wafer that tasted like paper. We wore lacy white dresses from Germany. Our white chiffon veils were crowned with circles of fresh daisies, and we wore white canvas shoes with white wool socks. The Sisters gave us holy cards of the Virgin Mary and other saints, and Father Gattang gave us each a rosary that would come in handy for saying our penances after we confessed to him.

We rarely understood what we confessed. We simply memorized the sins in the sample confession written in German and translated by Sister Theonesta into our peculiar mix of Swahili and English or "Swang." The confession sample was based on the Ten Commandments:

1. *I am the Lord thy God. Thou shalt not have strange gods before me.*

   At least we knew we didn't commit that sin, like the heathen Wasambaa who worshiped their gods, and the nuns said, the devil.
2. *Thou shalt not take the name of the Lord thy God in vain.*

   We were very guilty of this one because we swore a lot.
3. *Remember to keep holy the Sabbath.*

   No chance of missing church on Sunday.
4. *Honor thy father and mother.*

   No problem for me.
5. *Thou shalt not kill.*

   We had to kill the many snakes, spiders, and *wadudu*—bugs—that crossed our paths and sometimes bit us.
6. *Thou shalt not commit adultery.*

   We never fully understood this commandment. We heard that it had something to do with why we were called "children of sin," so we figured that we must be guilty of it. After confessing it several times when we practiced for confession, Sister Theonesta told us to leave it out.
7. *Thou shalt not steal.*

   We could take an hour to recite the things we stole in one week.
8. *Thou shalt not bear false witness against thy neighbor.*

   This was a big one. We lied and made up stories when we were caught doing something we shouldn't.
9. *Thou shalt not covet thy neighbor's wife.*

   I wondered if the mothers who came to visit their children were wives. If so, I was very guilty of coveting them.
10. *Thou shalt not covet thy neighbor's goods.*

    As long as those goods were food or warm clothing, we coveted them.

Every Friday afternoon, we went to confession in church. The confessional cubicle was made out of polished teak with velvet curtains inside and a cushioned seat for the priest and a kneeler underneath the window on the outside for the sinner. Father Gattang was going deaf, so we could hear others' confessions as we stood in line waiting our turn. Sister Silvestris couldn't understand why every Friday evening she had to break up fights, and why confession made us so noisy and violent. The fights stopped only when we repossessed our stolen items and got even with those who had lied about us.

As I knelt at the confessional, Father Gattang blessed me with the Sign of the Cross, whispered some words in Latin and told me to proceed.

"Bless me father for I have sinned. My last confession was one week ago. Since then, I have taken the Lord's name in vain sixteen times; I have killed forty-seven times; I have stolen many guavas, passion fruit, sweet potatoes, and biscuits from Sister Silvestris' room. I also stole Serafina's sweater and Babu's ball. I wiped off Hanna's slate in school. I have coveted Elizabeth's dolls and shoes and Delphina's butter and golden syrup."

Father coughed several times, then asked, "Are you sorry for your sins?"

"Yes, very sorry, Father."

"Say three rosaries for your penance. Go in peace, my child."

I hurried to my place ignoring the threatening gestures from Hanna and Serafina. To say three rosaries would take an hour, so instead of reciting the complete Hail Mary fifty-three times for each rosary, I skimmed my fingers over the beads and simply said, "Hail Mary, Hail Mary, Hail Mary" one hundred and fifty-nine times. I grouped all the Our Father and Glory Be prayers together and also recited only the first two words of those prayers. I felt guilty and ashamed and thought that maybe my sins wouldn't be forgiven, so I said one long version of the Lord's Prayer and finished with the entire "Glory be to the Father, to the Son and to the Holy Ghost, as it was in the beginning, is now, and ever shall be, world without end. Amen." I then ran out of church and tried to hide from Hanna and Serafina.

"Thief!" shouted Hanna.

"You can't hide from us," yelled Serafina. They found me behind the toilet door and grabbed me.

"We'll teach you a lesson, Piggy. And we'll tell Sister Silvestris that you're a thief."

"Say you're sorry!" Hanna pulled one of my braids and held me down on the toilet floor while they punched and kicked me.

"Let me go!" I begged. Only God knows what they would have done to me if they hadn't heard Sister Silvestris' footsteps. By Monday morning, I started a new list of sins as I found ways to get even with them in the classroom.

Shortly after this incident, Sister Theonesta had me be the teacher again.

"Hanna!" I ordered, mimicking Sister's tone of voice, "Sit here between Philip and Gemsi."

"Please, Mary, they'll pinch me and tease me."

"Serafina, sit between George and Daudi," I commanded. Serafina pouted, but dutifully went to the assigned spot.

We were so indoctrinated to always obey priests, Sisters, teachers, or any grownup that it didn't occur to the children to disobey even if the teacher was little Fat Mary.

Sister Silvestris told us to stay away from the boys because they were naughty. She treated boys as though they were a different species and was very upset when she found out we played together when she wasn't around. The boys wasted no time fulfilling expectations. They tortured Hanna and Serafina by pulling their hair, hiding under their skirts, and poking them.

13

Anatomy Lesson

The biggest problem we had with boys was that we couldn't figure out their anatomy. Because at the orphanage boys and girls were mostly separated, we never saw them naked. How did their pee soar up in the air? Esta and Serafina had answers. They lived with their families in Gare and Kwemashai, villages near Kifungilo. Esta seldom combed her tightly curled brownish-blond hair; her limbs were short and strong, and she was fearless. Esta and Serafina promised to tell us about little boys in exchange for all our Sunday candy and we agreed.

"Well," began Esta, "boys have a finger that grows right here between their legs."

"A finger like this?" I asked, holding up my pinky.

"Yes." Serafina took over. "And when the finger is full, it becomes big and hard, and then boys can pee."

"How big does their finger get?" asked Elizabeth.

"As big as a banana," Esta said.

"To get babies, they put their full fingers in the place we pee from," explained Serafina.

"And that's how babies are made." Esta's tone of voice made it clear the lesson was over. We were incredulous, disgusted, frightened, and now very curious. Soon after that, Elizabeth, Delphina, Stefana, Hanna, Antoinette, and I gathered our Sunday candy and gave it to Esta and Serafina for another lesson. We then moved from the theoretical to the practical.

Esta led us to the only accessible man in our lives, Zahabu, the old woodcutter. We followed her behind the hibiscus bushes near the toilets, past the pigsty to the wooden shed where Zahabu was sleeping. "Wait outside," she whispered and crept into the shed carrying a long stick.

When she gave the signal, we crawled in one by one and sat on the floor around Zahabu. He slept in a sitting position with his jigger-bored feet on the floor and his bent knees touching his chest. On his ancient head, he wore an old black velvet bishop's hat with the red tassel dangling over his hairy left ear. Around his neck he had three rusty padlock keys on a sisal cord. He was snoring loudly.

With the long stick, Esta slowly lifted his worn and dirty brown robe—his *kanzu*—from around his feet and dropped it over his knees. We leaned closer. "I can't see anything," I whispered.

"See this?" With the tip of her stick, Esta moved from side to side something that looked like a three-inch-long, shriveled, rotten banana embedded in clumps of short coarse, grayish-white hair.

We stared in disbelief, and I asked, "Is that it? How can that ugly, lifeless finger make babies?"

Esta defended herself. "I've seen my brother's finger get full, and it gets very big."

We took turns using the stick to move the lifeless thing from side to side and up and down. We were sure that Esta had fooled us in order to get our candy. "This was no big finger," we grumbled to Esta.

Suddenly Zahabu woke up. We flew out of the shed and started running. I was never known for my speed, so Zahabu caught me and took me to Sister Silvestris. Sister loved Zahabu as much as she loved the children and was very protective of him. While he explained what we had done, I shook with fear because the punishment for messing around with Zahabu was to be put with the children's pig in the pigsty near his shed.

14

The Pig

The pigsty was a rectangular structure made out of stone, about eight feet long. The trough where the big girls put the pig's food and water was on the same side as its heavy wooden gate. When Sister opened the door to put me in, the pig thought that I was his food, so he started sniffing me. Sister Silvestris disappeared in a flash, because she couldn't stand to listen to the ensuing duet of screaming and shrieking between the pig and me. Although I had already received this dreaded punishment several times, my fear of the pig never subsided.

A thick, slippery, smelly substance like green mud covered the floor of the pigsty. After about half an hour of trying to climb over the gate and slipping and falling in it, we made our peace. Piggy and Pig were cohabiting, distantly at first but then closely. Because I hadn't named the other naughty children, they came to visit me in the pigsty, trying hard not to laugh.

At nightfall, I squatted by the gate and my namesake put his snout on my thigh, grunting off and on. Then all was quiet. Sister Silvestris appeared and told me I should clean up and go to the sleeping room. Although the other children held their noses when I arrived, my friend Elizabeth pulled back my blankets and welcomed me to bed. She warmed my frozen, smelly feet in her hands until I stopped shaking and weeping.

We were all very afraid of the pig. Little did we know that he was even more afraid of us. The children, especially the boys, poked and hit him with sticks or threw little stones at him when it was their turn to take him out to wash. This made the naturally even-tempered animal aggressive at times, and he would run after us. We eluded him, leaving him free to wander wherever he pleased. He knew the sty that sheltered him, though, and returned every evening for us to feed him. Eventually, we got attached to him and he became our pet. But then came the day when he outgrew his pen and would have to be replaced by another little piglet.

About six months after my stay with the pig, Sister Theonesta announced to the class, "Today we are going to kill the pig. You are excused...." Before she could finish, the floor shook as thirty shouting children ran pell-mell toward the door. Excitement and anticipation about catching the pig won out over our newly cordial relationship with the animal. Esta led the race to the pigsty and I brought up the rear. By the time I got there, the pig was already out and running every which way in total bewilderment.

Laughing and shouting, the children chased it with sticks up the path, running around the hibiscus bushes, screaming as they passed the dining room and crossed the lawn in front of Blessed Martin. The frenzied kids raced all over the grounds, huffing and puffing down the road of the Stations of the Cross, and trampling plants on the graves in the cemetery, They lowered their voices only as they passed by the convent. Then they resumed the chase with more vigor, cutting through the grapevines just beyond the cow shed, the kohlrabi patch, and the thorn bushes. They crossed the log bridge over the river, ran behind the hydroelectric generator plant and up into the broom forest. Ultimately, they tumbled into the river just a few steps behind the pig. Soaking wet and covered with mud, the children and the doomed pig finally arrived at the slaughterhouse, which was right next to a large pigsty where the enormous pigs that the Sisters kept were audibly commiserating with their brother.

Sister Fabiana, who was in charge of the pig-raising process from birth to bacon, and several other Sisters got so involved in the pig-catching spectacle that every time it occurred, at least one of them fainted from having laughed herself into a stupor.

Because I couldn't keep up with the pig or the other children, I went straight to the slaughterhouse and waited behind the building for the pig's arrival. After all was calm, I heard the exhausted pig's last cry as Sister Fabiana killed it. I covered my ears, but my heart raced and my temples pounded. I thought about the night when this same pig grunted contentedly as he rested his snout on my lap. Now he was no more. He was dead. Would that be my fate too? Lately Zami had started calling me Piggy Knife. Was she going to slaughter me with a knife like Sister Fabiana just did to the pig?

The turmoil and confusion I felt led me to my Fat Mary. She and I discussed my fears, and we came up with a solution to help me. From this incident, I developed my tactic of "swallowing." Whenever I was faced with an unbearable pain or hurt, I collected saliva in my mouth and deliberately swallowed the emotion. I would give it to Fat Mary to keep for future reflection so that I could continue with whatever was at hand. I seldom had the luxury to work through the confusion I felt during a painful episode, but Fat Mary guarded these emotions and thoughts for me until I had the time and maturity to analyze and learn from them.

The next day the children got another tiny pig to feed until it was fat enough to provide bacon, sausage, ham, and cooking fat for the Sisters and children. Because we got to pick at the leftover cooked meat on the bones at slaughter time, we all enjoyed eating our pig. I always chewed the bones to a pulp, trying to swallow all my sorrows about the pig.

To this day, however, no matter how my pork is prepared, it is bittersweet.

15

Bricks

 There were other occasions when we were permitted to yell and scream and get disgustingly filthy. Kifungilo was gradually expanding to accommodate boarders who were drawn by the school's reputation. At the end of my second year in school, when I was nine years old, the largest building I had ever seen was completed near the school. It had three stories and several large rooms.

The bottom floor had a dining room on one side and a recreation room on the other. The recreation room took the place of *nyumba ile* as an all-purpose room, but luckily Sister locked all doors at night, so the big girls couldn't sneak out to beat the bedwetters. Between the two sections of the large house was a winding wooden staircase that we had to wax and polish every Saturday. The staircase took us to two dormitories on the second floor: one for the big girls and one for the little ones. The boys slept in a house on the other side of the school. We had a hard time pronouncing the word "dormitory," so we continued to call it the sleeping room, but show-offs like me called it the "domtree." Between the dorm rooms were cubicles with Asian toilets. The squat toilets were porcelain bowls embedded in the floor which we flushed by pulling a chain attached to a water tank mounted high on the back wall. Most important of all, there were locks on the half-sized wooden doors of the cubicles so they stayed shut when we were inside.

Along the wall near the toilets in each dorm were six porcelain sinks with cold running water. Sister Silvestris' room was tucked in the west corner of the little girls' dorm. Our new metal beds had spring coils that made sharp, squeaky noises every time we moved.

The third floor was the attic where we dried our clothes when it was raining. There the big girls had wooden boxes with locks for keeping their valued possessions such as items they stole or pretty clothes they had accumulated from Christmases past. Sister had a large room on the south side of the attic where the boxes of donations from Germany were stored.

Facing the cypress-lined road outside the new house was a verandah with a cement railing and narrow boxes of red and white geraniums sitting on a ledge. This imposing brick building with its silver corrugated iron roof was now the first structure seen from any approach to Kifungilo. It truly had everything we could imagine a house would have—running water, indoor toilets and sinks, wooden floors, metal beds with springs, and more than one electric bulb hanging from the ceiling of each room. We felt we were living like *wazungu*!

We were very proud of the new house because we took part in its construction. Saturday afternoons, after the entire mission had been cleaned and swept, Heini, the foreman in charge of building projects, tutored us in brickmaking in the large pit next to Sister Nerea's dentistry. Big girls scraped and dug the red soil from the sides of the pit with a hoe, and we carried it on our heads in aluminum basins called *karai* and dumped it into the water that we'd already hauled from the river to the pit. Singing exuberantly, laughing and splashing each other, we frolicked as we mixed the mud and water, kneading the mixture with our feet and squeezing it between our toes. Still sitting in the mud, we formed globs of the heavy goo into rough balls and packed them into yard-long wooden frames with rectangular partitions. We patted the mixture into place and then used a smooth, narrow board to remove the excess mud. Next we helped each other carry our frames to a corner of the pit and set them in neat rows to dry in the sun.

After we each had made twenty bricks, we slipped and slid up the walls of the pit and went looking for Sister Silvestris. We found her in the sewing room. Her penguin-coiffed head nodded as she pumped the old Pfaff sewing machine. She put aside the one-size-fits-all khaki shorts that she was making and came to the door with a big smile.

"Who am I? Who am I?" we chanted. We were so caked with mud that we were unrecognizable. Sister Silvestris' eyes were the smallest eyes I'd ever seen, but she had no trouble identifying us from our silhouettes. Yet she played along with us.

We figured she recognized our voices, so we didn't laugh or make a sound, no matter how far off she faked guessing our identities. "Zis mast bee Julitta, nein? . . . und zis ees Hanna . . . und zis ze Fett Merry."

"Nein! Nein! Nein! Nein!" we sang in unison at each wrong guess. We enjoyed this charade, especially because she couldn't resist touching us for clues and then resting her hand on her cheek to think. In the end, the child that she couldn't recognize got a handful of peanuts from Sister whose bib, veil, and face were now also covered with mud.

Our enthusiasm for making bricks didn't always produce a usable product. A few days later when the bricks were dry, we removed them from the frame and carried our masterpieces from the pit to the kiln a little distance away where they would be fired. Heini was waiting to inspect them and refused any imperfect ones. "Put your bricks here," Heini instructed me. "This one is perfect, and this one is very good, and this one is also perfect. Your bricks are very well made, Mary *Mdogo*. You are done." Heini always called me Mary *Mdogo*, Little Mary, because I was small and short.

To my dismay, I always made acceptable bricks, so I didn't get to frolic in the mud a second time. We helped him pile the sun-dried bricks in narrow six-foot-high hollow pyramids that had openings on one side. He arranged branches inside the pyramids, and after dowsing them with kerosene, he lit the fire. We watched the flames leap and crackle into the bricks above. When the branches were reduced to smoldering coals, we again loaded the kiln with firewood and built a door of brick. This process was repeated until the bricks were sufficiently fired; then the fire was allowed to burn down, and the bricks left to bake for several days during which we'd huddle close to the pyramids to soak up the heat.

When the fired bricks cooled, we carried them from the kiln to the building site by forming a long line and tossing the bricks from one to another down the line. Occasionally we got carried away and dropped the bricks or chipped them and got into trouble with Heini.

16

Castor Oil

 Because the nearest hospital was in Lushoto thirteen miles away, Sister Silvestris was also our doctor, nurse, and bedside companion when we got ill. She almost always knew what was wrong with us and devised some very creative treatments. When we had whooping cough, we were isolated in the infirmary and given aspirin. When we had measles and smallpox, she rubbed us with a thick, yellow sulfur ointment and gave us aspirin. When we had mumps she wrapped hot bacon in a scarf, tied it around our cheeks, and gave us aspirin. When we had chicken pox, she sprinkled homemade cornstarch on our rashes and gave us aspirin. At times, up to ten children would be in the infirmary suffering from various childhood diseases, all recuperating with the aid of aspirin.

We regularly invented reasons to get permission to visit the children in the infirmary. Because they usually didn't feel like eating and seldom finished the special food they got from the Sisters' kitchen, we would help them clean their plates. One day, with my mouth watering, I was making the rounds of the infirmary when I discovered that someone had beaten me to it. Disappointed, I sat by Imelda's bedside and watched her puffy, red face lying still on the pillow. Her straight, black hair was covered by a pink bandage that went around her face and ended in a double knot under her chin.

"Mary, I'm so g-glad you're h-here." She tried to speak even though her lips hardly moved. Without shame, I asked, "Who took your leftover food?" Imelda was younger than me, so I spoke with some authority.

"I was asleep and didn't see anyone. Would you undo my bandage and retie the knot so it's on top my head?"

She grimaced with pain while I slowly unwrapped the bandage. I found thick strips of bacon stuck to her swollen cheeks. Sister Silvestris used warm bacon to reduce the swelling of mumps, reheating it every few hours.

"You can have the bacon, Mary."

I gently peeled the bacon from her cheeks and tucked it in the elastic waistband of my panties. "Thank you very much, Imelda." I retied the bandage around her head as she wanted and waddled out of the room with the bulge of bacon strips over my stomach.

Elizabeth met me behind the statue of Blessed Martin. "What did you get?" she asked.

"Our favorite!" She reached under my skirt and pulled the bacon from my panties. We laid it on the grass and carefully separated the fat from the meat. She gave me all the fat while she ate the meat. We savored every morsel, ignoring its greenish hue and then licked our fingers, one by one. With a final long stroke of the tongue, we cleaned our palms.

"Will Sister Silvestris notice that Imelda's bacon is gone?" Elizabeth asked.

"I made Imelda promise not to tell."

"But if she does, I'll swear to Sister that it was you who went into the infirmary."

"If you do, I'll tell her that you lent me your panties with the strong elastic to hide the bacon."

"Then she'll beat both of us!"

"And we'll cry together."

"When I get the mumps, Mary, I'll give you my bacon."

"When I get the mumps, I'll eat my own bacon!" Neither of us got the mumps.

"Doctor" Silvestris also practiced preventive medicine. Once every three months, she put us through a detested castor oil ritual to flush out parasites that we acquired by scavenging for food and eating whatever we found. The night before the dreaded day, our supper consisted of one metal tumbler of sweet tea made from young eucalyptus leaves and a chenopodium pill that killed the worms that bloated our stomachs. The pill made us belch often and we felt nauseated. We went to bed at six instead of eight, our stomachs grumbling all night long. The following day, eucalyptus tea would be our only nourishment. In the morning after church, we lined up on the school verandah. Sister Silvestris stood facing us at the head of the line with a large spoon in one hand and her bottle of castor oil in the other. On either side of her she had a big girl to help in case any of us tried to run away.

"Open wide . . . one spoon . . . two spoons . . . good!" Sister praised each child who did as told. I had started my facial distortions as soon as I got in line. By the time it was my turn Sister had to laugh. "And who is this miserable child?"

"It's Piggy Knife, the fat pig," Zami replied.

"You mustn't call her a pig." Sister straightened her rubber apron and brandished her spoon. "Come, Fat Mary, take your medicine."

I stood bravely in front of her until the spoon forced open my tightly shut mouth. When the cold, thick oil reached my tongue, I gagged, sputtered, and spat onto Sister's rubber apron. "*Mama yangu!*" Sister exclaimed as I tried to flee. The other big girl sat me on the floor and Zami anchored me to the verandah with her great weight. She pried open my jaws while Sister repeatedly poured castor oil down my throat. "You must not be so stubborn, Fat Mary. For this you will be punished in the evening."

We didn't eat all day. The castor oil stripped our stomachs and forced us to spend most of our time near the toilets. All our senses were assaulted. Groaning, sputtering, and farting noises shook the shed as children emptied their bowels. The floor was swarming with live ringworms, round worms, and tapeworms that were purged from our stomachs. We held our nostrils to avoid the stench. Several children fainted from weakness and the smell. At the end of the day, with every ounce of energy spent, we walked to the sleeping room like zombies, hoping that when we woke up, we would feel human again.

In school the next day, Sister Theonesta knew the sorry physical state we were in. She let us rest our heads on our arms and sleep at our desks. We didn't even go out to point at the sky and follow the tiny silver object when we heard a plane.

17

When Molly Was a Baby

 After four years with Sister Theonesta, those who qualified went on to Sister Clotilda's classroom. We had to be able to recite the alphabet; copy words from the board in a straight line on our slates; write and recite the multiplication tables from one to twelve; do two-figure additions, subtractions, and multiplications; and sing songs in Latin, German, and "Swanglish." We had to have read the Catechism, made our First Holy Communion and mastered the art of Confession. Understanding what we read and sang was not a priority. To teach us songs, Sister Theonesta would write the words on the board—words we could barely read and didn't understand—and we memorized them by repeating them after her. Only when we could recite the words, German accent and all, did we learn the melody.

Sister Theonesta also had two requirements before we could leave her. First, we had to sing and act out her favorite song, "When Molly Was a Baby." Each week we lined up in front of the room and took turns acting out the stages in Molly's life. Sister stood in front of us, and with a ruler for a director's baton in one hand and a baby's milk bottle in the other, she counted, "*Einz, zwei, drei!* Hanna!" Hanna stepped out of the line, took the milk bottle from Sister, stuck the nipple into an imaginary baby's mouth, and pretending to rock the baby in her arms, sang:

When Molly was a baby, a baby, a baby,
When Molly was a baby, a baby was she.
She went this way, and that way,
And this way and that way.
When Molly was a baby, a baby was she!

Hanna stepped back into the line and Sister held up a slate and piece of chalk and called on Stefana. She stepped out, and pretending to write, sang lyrics about Molly as a school girl. Molly's biography continued with verses about being a grown up and more props from Sister. Serafina, who knew a thing or two about the facts of life because she lived at home, made us laugh when she pretended to put on rouge and lipstick, puckered her lips, and winked at Delphina's brother Phillip. With great enthusiasm we sang and acted out verses about Molly the nurse, the nun, the teacher, the wife, and Molly the grandmother, and finally a corpse. For the finale, Sister Theonesta gestured herself into a frenzy directing the ear-splitting encore of all the stages in Molly's life sung and acted out at the same time. Often we got really carried away, and Sister would laugh so hard that she couldn't stop. Then she'd tell us to go outside to look for an airplane.

We performed this song on feast days, and we sang it for the *wazungu* who came to visit. We sang it when life was bleak, like when the rains didn't come and we had very little food left in the storeroom. Sister Theonesta had us sing it after funerals, too. She said that we should imitate the Wasambaa and not only mourn the passing of our loved ones, but also celebrate the reunion of their souls with God.

Because I was such a show off, I never had a problem with performing. I did have a problem, though, with Sister's other requirement. At year's end she measured each of us on the back of the classroom door. If our shoulders didn't reach the yellow mark cut into the wood, we were too short to graduate to Sister Clotilda's class.

Fortunately and unfortunately for me, I remained with Sister Theonesta in the fourth grade for three years. It was fortunate because she favored me, and even though she was no longer in charge of me, she didn't stop feeding me. When I stayed behind to collect the slates, she'd give me a butter and sausage sandwich or a slice of yellow pound cake from the Sisters' dining room. It was unfortunate because I was losing valuable time in my plan to become educated enough to leave Kifungilo, and I was getting fatter by the day.

On feast days, when the weather was good, Heini packed the little children in the back of his lorry and drove us for a picnic to Rangwe or Sakarani, two Benedictine Mission Stations not far from Kifungilo, or to the waterfalls, about five miles away. Our picnics at the waterfalls were the most special occasions for us next to Christmas. Most of us had never been in a car or any motor vehicle, so when the lorry started moving, we fell on top of each other. We eventually figured out how to sit securely on the truck's flatbed or stand up holding onto the wooden railings. We screamed as the trees and villages raced by and the not so gentle breeze chilled our faces and raised havoc with our hair. "Faster, faster," we begged Heini.

Sister Silvestris and the big girls had started walking to the falls early in the morning. We met them there with the food and picnic supplies. We could swim in the icy water in our underwear, but I seldom swam because I usually lost the heavy woolen knickers, held up by a thick string at my waist, that Sister made. When they got wet, they came down to my knees. Elizabeth and the other children with parents swam in nylon panties that had elastic at the legs and waist.

We played hide and seek around the boulders and in the dense forest behind the waterfalls, and we collected moss and many kinds of ferns and wildflowers. Our lunch was jam sandwiches and sugared water, and Sister gave us guavas and one piece of hard candy each. We thanked God for the many saints in heaven whose feast days gave us picnics at the waterfalls! About four o'clock, we piled into the lorry and sang all the way back to Kifungilo.

18

A Funeral

By the end of my third year in the fourth grade, Sister Theonesta was transferred to Pemba, a speck of an island in the Indian Ocean, just off the coast of Zanzibar, where the Precious Blood Sisters ran a hospital. Her leaving was bittersweet because, with no height requirement, I could continue my education. But life in Kifungilo without her was almost unbearable. She didn't say goodbye. Sister Silvestris simply told us that there would be no more school for the rest of the year because Sister Theonesta had left Kifungilo.

One Sunday, when Elizabeth and I were fixing each other's hair, we heard the huge iron bell in the ivy tower ring. It was not the ring of the Angelus, nor was it the ring that called the nuns to church for midday prayers. It was a slow, forlorn ring that went on and on. We stopped playing when we realized that it was the ring for the death of a nun. Most of the Sisters seemed ancient to us, so it could have been any of the Sisters who we figured were hundreds of years old. We had to wait until the evening when Sister Silvestris came to bless us with holy water to find out. She usually prayed with us and congratulated us when we behaved. This night she didn't speak for a long time.

She turned off the lights and in a trembling whisper said, "My children, today we have lost our dear Mother Ancilla, who has gone to prepare a place for you in heaven. She loved you all very much. She built Don Bosco Home for you. She made the beautiful statues you see in Kifungilo. Next time you pray to Blessed Martin, remember her. She made that statue especially for you. Tomorrow morning, wear your Sunday clothes for the funeral. Good night, children."

In the morning, on our way to church, we collected flowers and made colorful bouquets to take with us. When we entered the church, the Sisters, dressed in official black, were mourning and whispering prayers in Latin and German. A wooden casket, made by Heini, was in the center of the aisle.

We filed past the casket and saw Mother Ancilla in full habit, lying with her head resting on a small pillow and her purple hands holding a black rosary. I felt no emotion as I looked at her. She was so peaceful and seemed to smile. I could hear her tell me, "Good little girl, you must always pray hard, work hard, and play hard."

Father Gattang said Mass then blessed Mother Ancilla with holy water and incense, while we sang several verses of *Dies irae, dies illa,* a sorrowful Latin chant. The procession left the church and slowly climbed to the cemetery. It was headed by Heini and three Wasambaa, including Zahabu, carrying the casket over their heads, followed by the children with flowers, the Sisters and the priest.

The ceremony by the freshly dug grave near the black wooden crucifix that dominated the cemetery was as long as everything Father Gattang presided over. At the end of the rituals, the children made a circle around the pit where Heini and Zahabu had lowered Mother Ancilla's casket, and one by one, with a quiet prayer, we tossed our flowers into the grave.

My prayer was "Thank you, Mother Ancilla, for building a home for us. I do not mean to be ungrateful, but now that you are living with God in heaven, please find another place for me. Please take me away from Kifungilo. Amen."

The Sisters stayed in the cemetery when the funeral was over, while the children walked down the road of the Stations of the Cross and did our best to remain sad for the rest of the day. If Sister Theonesta had still been in Kifungilo, she would have had us sing "When Molly Was a Baby" to cheer us up.

19

Blood and Sticks

 The years spent in Sister Theonesta's class were not equivalent to conventional grade school. We had no set curriculum, and Sister taught the same subjects in the same way each year. At age eleven, I started school with the big girls in Sister Clotilda's classroom in what used to be the sewing room. It was three times larger than Sister Theonesta's classroom. Blackboards along the four walls were separated by storage cupboards with heavy wooden doors and big padlocks. Two bare light bulbs hung from the ceiling on either end of the room.

German and English textbooks and Bibles, piles of paper, bottles of ink, and erasers along with skeins of wool, knitting and crochet needles covered the tables in front. Our desks had an inkwell on the right side and storage space underneath. New students received one pencil, a ruler, and an eraser. Older students had a pen holder and several nibs that they dipped into the inkwells. The first thing we did every morning was to carefully draw parallel lines on the paper we were given. I treasured my school supplies and was proud to write on paper instead of a slate.

Sister Clotilda taught us skills we would need if we left Kifungilo—sewing, mending, ironing, knitting, crocheting, and cooking. We had already mastered the very important tasks of cleaning, scrubbing, washing and bathing. To survive if we ever left Kifungilo, we had to speak English, so instruction was always in Sister's heavily accented German-English.

We had no textbooks. Sister Clotilda wrote everything on the board and we copied it. Her back to us, she held a huge book in her left hand, and writing as fast as she could, filled the blackboards around the room. As she ran out of blackboard space, one of the girls erased the first blackboard and all subsequent ones, so she could continue her writing orgy without interruption. On and on she wrote, all morning, all day, every day.

By the end of the year with Sister Clotilda, we had written our own textbooks that we sewed together with strands of red wool. We wrote about plants and animals, the history and geography of Germany, and the history and doctrine of the Roman Catholic Church. From the Bible we copied the passages that admonished us to avoid sin. We memorized the contents of our thick handwritten books and analyzed them to learn English grammar.

She hated the scraping of our desks against the floor as we shifted to read the boards around us, so we became veritable contortionists trying to see the writing on the back wall without moving. The only sounds we heard during our writing marathons were the scribbling of her chalk, the rustling of her habit, our sniffles and coughs, the constant rubbing of our erasers, and the distant thumping of Zahabu chopping wood outside his shed.

It was very hard to keep up with her because some of us were just learning to use paper and pencil, and we had to write straight and stay on the lines in order to avoid Sister's stick. I had never seen English like this and had no idea what the words meant and could hardly pronounce them. We were leaning about human anatomy by studying the digestive, respiratory, and circulatory systems. Consistent with our convent education, the reproductive system did not exist. I started copying from the first board.

The Circulatory System.

The circulatory system, in which the blood is propelled throughout the body, consists of four types of hollow chambers: 1) the heart, or the central pump; 2) the arteries, or efferent vessels, delivering the blood to the tissues; 3) the capillaries representing a fine network of very small vessels contained within the body tissues; and 4) the veins, larger vessels, returning the blood back to the heart....

Next, with no help on pronunciation or meaning, we had to memorize the information and present it to the class. Sister Clotilda called us up one by one. I was sure that when she prayed, she petitioned God for opportunities to beat us. To me, she was proof of the devil's existence. She beat someone every day. In spite of the fear I felt, I actually liked school, and I memorized hard until I could recite the whole fifteen minutes of the "The Circulatory System" without hesitation. Elizabeth and I studied together, and the other children were envious of the fluency with which we poured out our gibberish.

I watched the other girls tremble when their turn came to recite in front of the class then go back to their desks in tears. Very few were able to remember past the fifth paragraph, so most everyone got a beating. I was confident I'd do well. At last, my opportunity to shine came. But as I approached the front of the room, the sight of Sister's stern face and the stick poised to strike caused my brain to sizzle and burn, erasing the Circulatory System.

"De surk letry seestm een weech de blud ees p . . . lll . . . ahh . . .uhh... De surk letry seestm een de blud. . . ahh... de surk letry. . . ah . . . de surk . . . ah, ah . . ."

"Two sticks!" Sister Clotilda yelled. She was standing by the window across from the door, her white habit powdered with yellow chalk. In her left hand, she held the red cord of her crucifix; in her right was a long, thick stick.

Head down and arms at my sides, I stiffly walked over to her and stretched out my right palm for her to hit, and then my left palm. She raised her arm high above her head and came down with full force on each hand. She struck me so hard the second time that she almost lost her balance.

"Continue," she ordered.

Sobbing and sniffling, I started again: "De surk letry . . . ah ahh . . . de surk . . . ah . . ." I blanked out. Nothing was clear to me except the writing on the wall—I knew that she would beat me until I recited the whole chapter without a mistake. Sure enough she yelled "four sticks" and I went to receive them. Each time I was stuck, she doubled the number of sticks and started counting from the beginning. By the time she was at thirty-two on her way to sixty-four strikes, my whole body writhed with pain.

I was so numbed by the pain that I didn't notice or feel that the stick had cut my left hand, and it was bleeding profusely. She continued: "thirty-three, thirty-four, thirty-five, thirty-six . . ." I saw the stick turn dark. "Thirty-eight, thirty-nine, forty, forty-one, forty-two, forty-three . . ." The floor was getting sticky, and Sister Clotilda's face came in and out of focus. The front of her white habit was speckled with my blood.

The next thing I knew, I was in the dentistry with Lizzy.

"Ssshhh, Mary. I'll put *dawa*—medicine—on your hand."

"Th-thank you, Lizzy," I managed to say between sobs.

Lizzy was the one big girl who always protected and defended the little children. Apparently, while I was being beaten, someone from class went to get her. She came into the classroom and without saying a word to Sister took me out and down to the dentistry. She cleaned my swollen, bleeding hand with warm water and iodine, then gently spread sulphur ointment on it, wrapped it in a bandage, and put my arm in a sling.

"I'll take you to Sister Silvestris." She held my good hand and took me to Sister in the sewing room.

"Now, now, my Fat Mary." She put her knitting down and held my head across her chest. "What happened to you?" I couldn't speak through my sobs. Lizzy told her the whole story.

"*Mama yangu, mama yangu,*" Sister whispered, shaking her head.

Sister Silvestris put me in the infirmary, gave me aspirin, and brought me chamomile tea with sugar, and a plate full of jam-filled cookies. I finished all the cookies and tea, and crawled under the covers. I don't know how long she sat with me because she didn't say a word, and when I awoke, she was gone.

It was no secret that Sister Clotilda regarded Sister Silvestris as an uneducated nun whose only contribution to Kifungilo was babysitting the *schwarze Teufel*. She frequently belittled Sister Silvestris in front of us.

On one "castor oil" Monday afternoon, we were copying from the blackboard while Sister Clotilda walked around the classroom. One of the girls was nauseated and weak and hadn't done any work. Sister Clotilda pulled her from the desk to the front of the room where she collapsed on the floor. Calling her *schwarzer Teufel*, the nun picked up a stick and started beating her mercilessly. Then she kicked and stepped on her, making the poor girl soil herself, the floor, and Sister's robes. We were horrified. I ran to the dentistry to get Lizzy who intervened again.

I had a long talk with my dear Fat Mary that night, because I had many questions. Could someone actually be beaten to death by such a nun? Did Mother Rufina, the new Superior, know that Sister Clotilda was so cruel? Who let her work with children? Could nuns go to hell?

Fat Mary told me she didn't know the answers to my questions, but she reminded me that it was her role to take my worries and burdens and keep them for me until a time when I could understand them.

20

Lady Twining

 Sister Clotilda was the "intellectual" at the mission. She spoke English very well, so she usually accompanied visitors who came to offer help for the orphanage. They were mostly high-ranking *wazungu* who sometimes felt that they had to support missionary work in order to remain in good standing among their compatriots. Lady Twining came twice a month to teach us about Girl Guides and Brownies. She was the wife of Sir Edward Twining, the British governor of Tanganyika. They were part of the famous Twining tea merchant family and lived at the Governor's Lodge on a nearby estate in Magamba.

Girl Guides wore dark blue uniforms made out of smooth cotton fabric with two buttoned lapels and light blue neckties with silver shamrock badges that had a big "G" on them. They wore their Sunday shoes with their uniforms. Brownies, the littler girls, wore the same style uniform as the Girl Guides except in dark brown, with yellow neckties and brass badges with a "B." I had prayed to be picked to become a Brownie because I would finally have official permission to dance. Apart from being instructed in First Aid and outdoor survival skills and activities, we were taught country dancing by Lady Twining and other *wazungu* volunteers. Ironically I received my first, and only, formal dancing lessons from a member of the English aristocracy.

Now that I was thirteen, Sister Silvestris put me in charge of the ancient RCA Victor's "His Master's Voice" gramophone that a kind benefactor had donated to the orphanage. For years I had persistently begged her to let me "make the music."

"See, Sister, I can dance just like the *wazungu*," I would say before I performed a few of the country dance steps that I'd watched the Girl Guides learn. I made a veritable spectacle of myself by mouthing the words of "English Country Garden" and dancing with all my might and skill.

"All right, Fat Mary," she finally gave in one day. "You can be in charge of the gramophone. When you become a Girl Guide, you won't have to dance like the Wasambaa anymore."

"Thank you, Sister. I promise I will dance only like Lady Twining."

If she only knew how often I hid in the toilet and danced just like the Wasambaa, she would have taken my gramophone privilege away. I could hear their drums—energetic and lively if for a celebration, or heavy and sad for mourning rituals—whenever nearby villagers danced. My frequent walks to the village with Sister Silvestris emboldened me to set out on my own. The first time, I crept along the path, then went from bush to bush until I could see the dancers. I loved the free and natural way the dancers moved. Their bodies glistened. It seemed as if they had no cares in the world. I memorized the movements, imitating them from my post behind the bushes, and practiced dancing on the path back to the orphanage.

Whenever I skipped Mass or evening Benediction, which was often because that was the only time I could steal food for Zami, I hid behind the door in the toilets until Sister and the children had gone down the hill to church. When my stealing chores were done, I'd go back to the toilets to dance like the Wasambaa. I shook my hips and shoulders and expressed my joy of dancing to the toilets as though they would clap for me. I danced up and down the narrow aisle along the row of stalls, and in and out of each of the toilets. I made sure that "Fat Mary" was watching, because she approved of me even when I slipped and fell on the filthy floor, or bumped into the walls of the tiny stalls as I hitched up my skirt and twirled with delight.

Every Wednesday, I fetched the gramophone from Sister's room where it was under lock and key. It was only brought out for very special occasions, such as the dance lessons or when Sister Theonesta taught us the German waltz to perform on Christmas Eve. I carefully wiped the 78 rpm-speed vinyl record with my hand, put it on the red felt base of the turntable, wound the power handle until it wouldn't move, picked up the arm with the needle at its circular head, cautiously placed it on the record, and sang "Que Sera Sera" along with Doris Day:

> *Kay sad eye sad eye*
> *woteva wheelde, wheelde*
> *de fewchas nat usya see*
> *Kay sad eye sad eye*

I sang all the verses of all the songs, though I understood little. I butchered Gene Autry's "He'll be Coming Round the Mountain" and Roy Roger's "Home on the Range." I relished imitating the slow, sweet voice of Patti Page singing "The Tennessee Waltz." I improvised the lyrics, but sang with so much gusto that one day when Lady Twining and a group of *wazungu* came to Kifungilo for Girl Guides, Sister Silvestris told me to sing for them.

I sang my three songs, carefully imitating each singer's voice, and I added a mixture of Lady Twining's country dance steps. Sister Silvestris and the *wazungu* laughed uproariously. The more they laughed, the louder I sang and the harder I danced. When I had finished, I curtseyed. They all clapped and Lady Twining gave me a shilling and said, "When you grow up, you will be an actress and a dancer. You must never stop dancing, little one." When the *wazungu* left, I gave my shilling to Sister Silvestris.

The satisfaction I got from being the focal point of Lady Twining's entertainment, I carefully stored up against future bad times. I showed off my singing to the other children, who were very impressed that I knew the words to the songs even though none of us understood them.

21

Rosa's Wedding

Apart from her duty of beating children to a pulp, Sister Clotilda also taught the biggest girls, ages sixteen and up, about marriage and how to be good wives. She taught them to sew dresses, shirts, trousers, and panties; to knit and crochet sweaters, socks and blankets, and to embroider pillowcases and tablecloths. They were never taught anything about sex or babies except that they should baptize their children and do what their husbands wanted.

Up until now these girls had been told that most men were evil and would lead them into temptation and sin. What's more, they had no personal knowledge of boys their own age. When boys at the orphanage turned nine and ten, most were sent to Ndanda, an all-boys mission school in the southern part of the country, run by Holy Ghost Fathers and Precious Blood Sisters.

Although some big girls worked as nurses in hospitals, cooks in small hotels, and caregivers to retired *wazungu*, and a few became nuns, for most of them marriage was their way to leave Kifungilo. Kifungilo girls were very desirable to African and half-caste men. They had the reputation of being hard workers, clean, obedient, and faithful. Men came from all over the country to woo them. Even some of the boys who had been sent to Ndanda eventually came back to find wives. The men came on Sundays, and the girls dressed up in anticipation of their freedom and a man's touch or loving look.

The big girls seemed to know a thing or two about touching and kissing. There were several big girl "couples" that were inseparable. They washed each other's clothes, shared each other's food, and often disappeared behind the bend in the river when we went swimming. They did each other's chores, walked hand in hand, and after Sister Silvestris turned off the lights at night, they slept in each other's beds.

For two weeks every September or October, Rosminian priests and brothers from the surrounding missions came to Kifungilo for their annual retreat. Even as a little girl, I looked forward to their coming. We helped the Sisters clean the many rooms of the guest house down by Father Gattang's quarters, launder sheets and towels, peel potatoes, cut and pit peaches for drying in the sun and for canning. Best of all, we licked piles of dishes that had wonderful morsels of exquisite food before we washed them.

Up to twenty-five priests came to enjoy the cool air and to be pampered by the German nuns. It was an escape from their dreary, solitary, impoverished, and often alcoholic lives in the bush. They wandered over the mission grounds in their white robes, smoking pipes as they said their prayers and meditated. Some of them meditated on the big girls and Wasambaa women working in the fields. The big girls fixed themselves up extra nice and would just happen to find themselves in the orchards, down by the river, and at the outskirts of the mission grounds where the priests strolled.

One priest in particular was especially active during his retreat. Elizabeth and I secretly followed the big girls and hid behind bushes each time we saw them descend into the orchards. We felt a mix of delight and disgust watching him seduce the Kifungilo girls or the African women, and thought we might finally witness the repulsive act Esta told us about when we peeked at Zahabu's penis. But because the nuns had successfully instilled in Kifungilo girls a fear of the male organ, the girls accepted fondling and kissing, then pulled away from the priest and ran off.

The big girls looked forward to the coming of potential husbands. Whenever a male suitor arrived, Sister Clotilda picked several girls and sent them down to the convent one at a time to meet the suitor.

One day Rosa was sent down, and Elizabeth and I watched nearby. She was beautiful! Her smooth dark hair flowed over her shoulders, and she wore a red dress with white flowers, a white patent leather belt, dangling red rhinestone earrings with matching necklace and bracelet that she got from the German Christmas boxes, and two-inch heels. She carried a white purse over her arm.

Sister Clotilda and Sister Silvestris greeted a young man named George, a half-caste who had a sister in Kifungilo. George had probably heard about Rosa from his sister and was coming to ask for her hand.

"Rosa is hardworking, can cook very well, sews beautiful flowers on her tablecloths, and is very kind to the little children," we heard Sister Silvestris announce.

"I'm sure he'll choose her," Elizabeth whispered.

I hoped not, so I said he wouldn't take her because her skin wasn't fair.

"Well, my skin is lighter than yours, but you have nicer hair. I think you're too fat, but men like fat women. This morning Sister Silvestris told Tina that no one would marry her because she was so thin."

"Sister only worries about big girls who are thin because they could get sick and not be able to work. When I'm a big girl, I'll be thin, no matter what Sister says."

"You will never be thin."

After meeting with George, Rosa saw us and came over, smiling. She looked so happy that for a moment I forgot to be sad. Elizabeth poked me. "See? I told you Rosa will get married and leave Kifungilo. Now who's going to protect you from Zami and the other big girls?"

I lowered my head and was about to cry when Rosa asked, "What's the matter, my little Mary?"

"Are you going away?"

"Yes. This is the happiest day of my life. I will be leaving Kifungilo for good."

"Will you take me with you?"

"I'd like to, Mary, but I can't." Stroking my braids, she said, "But you can be one of the flower girls at my wedding."

I jumped up and down with joy. "Thank you, Rosa." My sadness flew away with those words. She also chose Mary Jameson and the two of us were inseparable for the few months until the wedding and were the happiest, most envied girls in Kifungilo.

For the wedding we wore our First Communion dresses and lace veils with daisies in our hair. After the big girls dressed us, Sister Fabiana drove us and Rosa to Gare in the Sisters' blue Volkswagen van where we waited at the church for Sisters Silvestris and Clotilda, the big girls in their Girl Guide uniforms, and the children who walked the eight miles to Gare.

The church was decorated with white flowers, ribbons and paper bells that caught the colors of the stained glass windows. Rosa entered, dressed in white. To me she looked like the angel in the picture on the wall. She carried a bouquet of white and pink roses mixed with delicate smoke ferns, and wore a string of chipped fake pearls and white plastic heels. She smiled a lot, but wheezed from her asthma.

Lizzy started playing the organ as only she could. Everyone sang several verses of a Latin song while we walked down the aisle to the altar. Rosa and George exchanged vows before Communion. At the end of Mass, George and Rosa led the procession out of the church followed by Mary Jameson and me. We sat on benches behind the church and ate sausage sandwiches on white bread and fluffy white wedding cake. The others began walking back but Mary Jameson and I would return by car with the Sisters.

"Will Rosa leave Kifungilo today?" I asked Sister Silvestris.

"Yes, Rosa and George will move to a large city on the coast." Sister anticipated what I was about to do and scolded, "This is a big day for Rosa, Fat Mary. You mustn't let her see you cry."

"Goodbye, my sweet, sweet Mary," Rosa wheezed, holding my hands. "I promise to visit you."

I looked up into her face, and with the biggest smile I could manage, said, "I shall wait for you. Goodbye, Rosa."

That night in my bed, I thought about Rosa and Sister Theonesta. I asked Fat Mary if she knew why the two people who loved me had been taken from my life. I remembered the kind words Rosa said to me. Her soft voice echoed in my head and made me smile with love for her. Fat Mary smiled with me and I gradually became overwhelmed by a feeling of joy and peace in my heart. I fell asleep hugging my pillow, knowing that somewhere far away from Kifungilo lived a person who loved me and would come to visit me.

A year and a half later, Rosa came to show us her first child, Marianne, named after me and Anne, another girl she had taken care of. She brought biscuits for all the children and a doll and leather shoes for me. I deeply wished I were Marianne and had Rosa as my mother. She visited twice a year for three years. The third year she came, I accompanied her and Sister Silvestris to see one of the big girls, Florida, in the infirmary. For three months she had been feeling weak and was throwing up in the morning. Sister Silvestris tried everything, but nothing helped. We prayed to Blessed Martin and Saint Don Bosco every evening for her.

Rosa sat on Florida's bed and talked to her for a long time, asking her many questions and touching her stomach. "She's not sick," she told Sister. "She's at least five months pregnant."

Sister's tiny eyes grew large. "What do you mean? How can this happen in Kifungilo?"

"It must have happened during the month she was assigned to work with Mweta tending the livestock for Sister Fabiana."

"Is this true?" Sister asked Florida, who nodded yes.

Florida had told us that she liked to work with Mweta—a man so trusted by Sister Fabiana that she left him in charge of the farm whenever she chauffeured the Sisters to Lushoto and around the country. Florida said he treated her very well, and she often shared with us the gifts of food and homemade perfume that he brought her from his village.

"Do you know that you have committed a mortal sin?"

"Yes," Florida replied.

"You must go to Confession on Friday. We shall all pray for your forgiveness."

"What's wrong with her? What mortal sin did she commit? Is God punishing her?" I asked Sister.

"Questions, questions. Fat Mary, you mustn't tell anyone what Rosa said."

I only told Elizabeth that Florida was sick because she committed a mortal sin.

Later in the week, Sister Silvestris told us that Blessed Martin had answered our prayers and Florida would be going away for treatment. We didn't see Florida or Mweta anymore, and Rosa never visited Kifungilo again.

22

The European Hospital

Castor oil and chenopodium tea kept the children surprisingly healthy considering how we weren't concerned with sanitation pertaining to what we ate. But there were always outbreaks of infectious diseases in the surrounding African villages. Sister took some children with her to bring medicine to ailing Wasambaa. Sometimes we walked five miles along narrow paths, through forests, hills, and valleys.

One day, I accompanied her to visit the sick in Mkuzi, a village a few miles away from Kifungilo. Sister was concerned about a particular family because out of six children, four were *zeruzeru*—albino. It was the first time I saw "white" people living like Africans in poor villages, wearing tattered clothes. Three girls and one boy had very white, almost transparent, freckled skin and blond kinky hair. Their white-lashed eyelids, noses, lips, and ears were covered with open wounds and blisters. I was full of questions.

"Why are they living here, so poor and dirty when their skin is white?"

"Because they are not really Europeans. They are Africans."

"White Africans!" I exclaimed.

"They are Wasambaa except that their skin has no color."

"Are they poor because they're not white Europeans?"

"We have poor white people in Germany also."

I couldn't imagine white people who were poor. When we returned to Kifungilo that night, I told my friend Elizabeth that there were poor white people in Germany. She didn't believe me.

A few days after my experience with the albinos, a typhoid fever epidemic struck the orphanage due to dead rats in the water tank.

Eight children, including me, came down with severe headaches, high fever, and vomiting. Two of us were so ill that we were taken to the hospital in Lushoto. Lizzy helped Sister Silvestris carry us to the van, and both accompanied Sister Fabiana to the hospital. There they helped us walk up the steps of the hospital and down the hall to the examining room for African patients. Under the British, both health care and education were segregated with separate schools and hospitals for Africans, Europeans, and Aga Khans (members of the Ismaili sect of Shiite Muslims).

The benches lining both sides of the corridor to the examination room in the African Hospital were filled with patients of all ages and their relatives. Many of the sick recognized Sister Silvestris because she had been to their villages delivering food, clothing, medicine, and the word of God. They bowed their heads and greeted her with "*Tumsifu Yesu Kristu*" (Praise the Lord Jesus).

"*Milele na milele. Amina*" (Now and forever. Amen), Sister replied.

They motioned for us to go ahead of them. Sister took the two of us inside where the African doctor greeted her the same way. She told him our symptoms. Without examining us, he said we had typhoid and must be admitted.

All forty beds in the foul-smelling ward were occupied with groaning, crying children and adults. Patients' relatives sat and slept on the floor beside each narrow metal bed. They also cooked for their sick on the hospital grounds. The nurse set up two wood and canvas cots while Sister unpacked the sheets and blankets she had brought. Lizzy put two large bottles of orange juice, sandwiches, and a box of Marie biscuits by each of our cots then helped us into bed. Before leaving, Sister Silvestris prayed over us and sprinkled us with holy water.

The otherwise noisy ward fell silent as everyone watched us settle in. But as soon as Sister Silvestris and Lizzy left, the able-bodied got into fights, some of them falling over us as they grabbed our food. We were too sick to defend ourselves. A nurse came in to break up the fighting and stuck a thermometer in my mouth. I couldn't keep it between my lips because I was shaking from chills and fever.

At night I was awakened by the wailing of the mother of a boy three beds away from me. When the doctor came in, he announced in a deep low voice, "*Kwisha. Pole sana mama.*" (It's over. My deepest sympathy, Mama.) The relatives of the other patients in the ward tried to console the distraught woman.

I pulled my covers over my face trying to hide from death and listened to the throbbing in my head. I was shivering so violently that my cot moved two feet to the right touching the bed of the groaning old man next to me. A knot in my stomach was getting tighter and tighter, and I could barely breathe the foul air in the ward. I knew death was making its way to my bed.

Sister Silvestris brought us food daily. We told her what happened the first time, so she stayed with us until we had eaten. After three days, the other girl was well enough to go back to Kifungilo, but I remained. For the first time in my life, the sight of food made me sick. Sister Silvestris broke the sandwich she brought into pieces and tried to feed me. I couldn't open my mouth wide enough, so she gave me orange juice with a spoon that she took from her pocket. She kept touching my forehead and my body and shaking me and talking to me, but I couldn't hear her words and slowly drifted into unconsciousness.

When I came to, I was sure that I had died and was in heaven. I was lying in a large mahogany bed with a white mosquito net suspended from a knot in the center above it. My sheets were starched, and on top of them, three soft pink blankets hugged the contours of my body. I could smell lilac talcum powder and hear the babbling of a stream. Although the room was dimly lit, I could see that it was small and that mine was the only bed. I didn't feel any pain. I looked around for one of the old dead nuns from Kifungilo to take my hand and present me to God.

Instead of a nun, I saw a short *mzungu* lady, very much like the one who taught me how to drink tea from a porcelain cup and saucer, sitting in a wooden chair on the other side of the mosquito net with her arms folded across her stomach. We looked at each other. After a while, she stood up, rearranged and tucked in the net over my mattress. She looked at me a while longer, blew out the candle, and left. "Please God," I prayed, "don't let anyone take me from here."

The lady returned. She slowly pulled the net from under the

mattress, sat by my feet and said, "You will stay here until you are well."

"Oh thank you, thank you, lady," I answered. She stood up, tucked the net back in, looked at me for a while longer, and left. I knew then that I wouldn't die because I had my own room and my own *mzungu* nurse.

I sank into my cloud bed and fell asleep. When I woke up, Elizabeth was playing with my hair. "Elizabeth? Is it you?"

She jumped up and ran out of the room yelling, "She's talking! Sister Silvestris, Mary is talking."

I heard Sister Silvestris say, "Shh . . . shh. We're in the hospital." She rushed to my bedside. Sister felt my forehead and smiled. As she gave me a handful of soft toffees, she told me that the children in Kifungilo prayed every day to Blessed Martin for me.

Sister left and Elizabeth came back in. "Mary, we thought you were going to die. You weren't moving and you didn't answer Sister. You wouldn't eat. Your eyes were closed all the time. Two weeks ago you were moved to the European Hospital with the European doctors. Sister Silvestris came to see you every day."

I was so happy to see, hear, smell, and feel my friend Elizabeth that I gave her all the toffees.

Every evening after dark, when she thought I was asleep, the *mzungu* lady came to sit on the chair in my room. I heard her sigh and yawn. I watched her tuck my mosquito net under the mattress. I saw her when she stood up and rearranged her dress. She continued looking at me for a long time and then left. She never spoke to me.

I remained in the hospital for two more weeks and recuperated in bed in Kifungilo for another three weeks before going back to Sister Clotilda's classroom.

23

Thin Mary

While I was recuperating at Kifungilo, I thought a lot about my life and about life and death, heaven and hell, good and evil, thin and fat, wealth and poverty. I wondered why I didn't die and if it meant that God wanted me on earth. Though it was barely a month since I got sick, I felt like it had been a year. Sister Silvestris was especially good to me and visited me often. She instructed me to rest in the afternoons and excused me from all chores. I had to go to church only on Sundays.

One morning while I was lying in bed listening to the cold silence in the big dormitory after everyone had gone to daily Mass, I found myself wondering if anything in Kifungilo would be different had I died. I thought about those who died in the African hospital, and I envied them a little. I could still hear the anguished cries of their relatives. I felt sad for them and began whimpering and sniffling and wiping away my tears when I was startled by Sister Silvestris' voice. "Fat Mary, why are you crying? Are you getting sick again? What's the matter?" I reached for her outstretched hands.

"I was thinking of the Africans who died in the hospital. Why did they die and not me?"

"You almost died, but you're alive now, and we are very happy."

"Why didn't I die?"

"Your time hasn't come yet. You mustn't think about death. When you think too much about dying, you forget to live."

"Sometimes I feel very alone, like there's no one else in the world with me. I want to go to heaven where I'll find many good people."

"But you aren't alone, Fat Mary, the orphanage is full of people. I left church early because I want to tell you something."

"What?"

"You are no longer my Fat Mary. You've become so thin and weak that you won't get well unless I fatten you up. You shall have special food from the Sisters' kitchen every day until you're stronger, but you must eat everything like you did when you were little."

She patted my cheek, then told me a story. "I remember when you were just learning to walk, and Sister Theonesta and I made a bet on who could walk faster, you or Julitta. Both of you were the same age, but you were so fat that we couldn't see your neck or knees. Julitta was much shorter and thinner. Of course, Sister Theonesta bet on you. We stood at one end of the long table in the sewing room and held out our hands urging you both to walk to us. You were not interested in walking at all. At every step you sat or fell down, but Julitta walked without stopping to the end of the table and I won the bet. You were a very happy baby, Fat Mary. You laughed all the time, you went to anyone, and you ate everything and anything."

Sister paused for a while, and then the smile on her face turned to a concerned frown. "Even before you got typhoid, I noticed that you were often sad. Is there a reason?"

"I wish I had a mother who loved me, and brothers and sisters, and a real home where I could go for my holidays, and that the children at Kifungilo wouldn't tease me so much, and that Zami would go away. But most of all I wish you would stop calling me Fat Mary."

"I have no choice now, because you're no longer fat," she said as she pinched my sunken cheeks.

"But I don't feel any different than I did before. I thought thin people were always happy, and that there was a 'thin' feeling, just like there's a 'fat' feeling. Please Sister, don't make me fat again."

"I like all my children fat. If you weren't fat, you might not have survived typhoid. You must eat all your food every day. I won't give you permission to go back to school until you're fatter. Mary, I didn't make you fat. God made you fat."

"And he took my mother away! I'm tired of having no village and no tribe. I'm tired of being poor, tired of wondering what will happen to me when I grow up, tired of being beaten, tired of begging to be loved. And I'm very tired of praying. I'm tired of my life. I wish I had died in the hospital!" I don't know what came over me to make me talk like that to Sister, and I don't know why she tolerated it.

"I believe there's a reason why you didn't die. God must have special plans for you," she said. "And who beats you all the time?"

"Sister Clotilda and Zami and some of the other big girls."

"Sister Clotilda is your teacher and she must have good reasons to beat you. But you must tell me when Zami or anyone else beats you."

"I can't understand God. Why is he good to some children and not to others? Why doesn't Baby Jesus ever answer my prayers?"

"I promise you, Mary, all your prayers will be answered someday. You must believe that, and you must never stop praying. You think and think, and you ask questions that no one can answer. I know that you're a good girl and God loves you."

"I just wish somebody here on earth loved me too. Sister Theonesta loved me and she was transferred to Pemba, and Rosa got married and went away. I hope Elizabeth will never leave me."

"Do you think I love you?"

"Sometimes."

"It's hard to love so many children equally, but when you grow up, I hope you will understand that I really do love you and all my Kifungilo children."

I didn't fully believe her. Noises from running children grew nearer, and Sister left to chaperone them. "Eat all your food every day and you will be fat again," Sister whispered as she closed the door.

When I could no longer hear her footsteps, I got out of bed and unsteadily walked over to the open window near the verandah to look at my reflection in the glass. I almost didn't recognize myself. The only part of my face that hadn't changed was my eyes, but even they seemed bigger and blacker. I liked what I saw. I was thin. I slowly turned around to see all of me in the reflection. Yes, I liked this person in the window. Imagine, me—thin! I was thinner than Elizabeth. I heard footsteps come up the stairway so I made my way back to bed. It was Anne with my breakfast tray. I was glad it was Anne because I liked her and she was always smiling.

"I'm not going to eat all that. Sister Silvestris wants me to eat and get fat. I'll never be fat again."

Anne set the tray in front of me. "Mary, you'll die if you don't eat. Why do you think Sister takes food to the Wasambaa? She says they're sick because they don't have enough to eat."

"If food makes me fat, how come Lucinda is so thin even though she eats a lot?"

"Because she's tall. Look, you've got fresh baked bread with butter and jam."

"And you. Why are you thin?" She ignored me as she uncovered a plate of eggs sitting on strips of my beloved bacon.

"Sister told me to stay with you until you finish all your food." She poured syrup on a thick German pancake.

"Why do I get fat from eating? Anne, you can have my food. I'm going to be thin the rest of my life."

"Well, if you eat a little, I'll help you eat the rest."

That morning I learned that I mustn't stop praying and that Sister Silvestris tried to love all the children in Kifungilo equally. Most of all I learned that although food didn't make everyone fat, it made me fat, and no matter what Sister Silvestris wanted, I knew that I wasn't happy when I was fat. From that day forward, I picked at my food, and after each meal I looked at my image in the window glass. That first image of Thin Mary is permanently etched in my memory.

24

The Informer

When I returned to school about six weeks later, no one, not even Sister Silvestris, called me Fat Mary anymore. Although my physical image had changed, I felt no different inside. I still felt unloved, and my longing for my mother and resolve to leave Kifungilo obsessed me. Sister Clotilda continued to harass and beat me. Zami worked me even harder and continued calling me "Piggy Knife." When I searched for my own Fat Mary, I was happy to find her alive and healthy—and still fat.

One day after school, Zami saw me napping on the grass in front of Blessed Martin. She yanked me up by the arm and growled into my face, "You have a lot of work to make up. You're taller now and since you're not such a fat pig anymore, you should work longer and harder."

For the first time in my life, I yanked my arm away from her and talked back. "Zami, I almost died in the hospital. I wish I had died, then I wouldn't have to be your slave."

"Are you talking back to me? I'm going to teach you a lesson once and for all."

I didn't wait for the lesson. I started running as fast as I could. For the first time, she didn't catch me. I ran straight into the sewing room yelling, "Sister Silvestris, Zami wants to beat me! I'm afraid she's going to kill me!"

"Ssshhhh!" Sister put the child's dress she was mending on the table. "Where's Zami? What did you do? Don't be afraid. She cannot kill you." Zami stood at the door gesturing up a storm as she ranted and raved about what she would do to me.

"Why are you always so angry? Why do you want to beat Mary?"

"Beat her? I'm going to kill her! She talked back to me! No one messes with me. She's so cheeky since she's been sick. If typhoid couldn't kill her, I will."

"You cannot kill anybody, but I know you beat her a lot before she was sick. She has suffered enough. You must help me make her strong and healthy. Now go away and leave her alone." Sister went back to her sewing. Before Zami left, she stood by the door, blocking the light with her enormous frame. Her big stomach shook each time she sprayed a mouthful of saliva in my direction. Sister let her vent her rage, while I crawled under the long table that Julitta and I had competed on when we were toddlers. When she left, it looked like it had rained in the sewing room.

"Come out from under the table, Mary. No one will beat you. What did you do to make Zami so furious?"

"I reminded her that I almost died and told her she shouldn't make me do all her work for her anymore."

"What work?"

"I washed and folded all her clothes—even her *vikatasi* that are filled with blood every month. When there was no water in the tap, she sent me to the river to get a thousand pails of water and fetch firewood to heat the water for bathing Delphina and her sisters, plus all the other children you put in her care. She had me steal fruit from the garden and food from your bedroom and storeroom, and she took my slice of bread every Sunday morning. I have to hide from her because when she sees me, she pinches me, pulls my hair, or spits in my face for no reason at all."

"Are you telling the truth?"

"Yes, I am."

"*Mama yangu!*"

"Other big girls also beat their children. One day Suzana beat Antonette with an iron rod because she tore her blouse when she was washing it."

"This is the truth? *Mama yangu!*" Sister shook her head.

"And sometimes, when we were still in the old sleeping room, after you turned off the lights in the dormitory, the big girls took the bedwetters to *nyumba ile* and tortured them." I also told her how the big girls made us fight each other until one child cried. I said I never got too beaten up because I cried long before I had to start fighting. Sister began to laugh but caught herself. Maybe she remembered that I did the same before my beatings from her.

"Why didn't I know about this?"

"Because it happened when you were at church or the convent for meals. One of us would watch and give a warning when you were coming up the hill, then everything would go back to normal. Besides, if we told you anything that the big girls did behind your back, we'd be beaten even more."

"*Mama yangu!*"

"They also call you *Kuru* because they say you look like a crow."

"This I know, but I'm very surprised to hear about the big girls. Mary, you're older now, so you mustn't be afraid to tell me everything. What names did they give the other Sisters?"

"Well, Mother Rufina is called *Ntendezeze* because of how she moves. Sister Theonesta was called *Uvundo* (stinky) and Sister Agathana was *Mastiff* (stiff). Elizabeth and I had a nickname for Sister Clotilda. We called her 'Heetla.'"

"What do you know about Hitler?" Sister seemed surprised.

"When the Sisters speak German among themselves, they use the word Heetla often and always lower their voices. We decided there was something about Heetla they didn't like. The big girls and some little children understand when you speak German. And we know when you talk about us."

"*Mama yangu!*" Sister just smiled. "So can you speak German, my clever Mary?"

"I can't speak it, but I can understand everything the Sisters say."

Sister's smile abruptly disappeared and she was quiet for a long time. "You mustn't call Sister Clotilda 'Hitler' because it's a man's name. Do the big girls have names for the children too?"

"I think 'Piggy Knife' is the worst, but the big girls called Lucinda *Chura* because she has bulging eyes, thin lips, and a wide mouth like a frog. Margaret they call Moonface because her face is perfectly round."

"Such naughty, naughty children. What shall I do with you? What else do the big girls do that I don't know about?"

"They steal cooking oil and spices from the Sisters' kitchen, and rice, flour, sugar, and salt from the storeroom, and they cook their own meals on open fires behind Zahabu's shed when you're in church. Also, they know that you're afraid of rats, so whenever they want you to stop scolding us or leave the room, they bring in one of the big rats from the field and let it loose near you. They like seeing you run every which way and climb on tables and chairs."

"*Mama yangu!* Mary, you mustn't be afraid of the big girls. It's not good to be afraid of people."

"But Sister, we're all afraid of you!"

"I know that. You must understand that I have to discipline you, and some of you are very bad. It's my duty to beat you when you're naughty or when you sin. I always feel bad after beating the children."

"At least we know that when you beat us, it's because we've done something wrong. The big girls often beat us and we don't always know why."

"You do understand that I have to discipline you. Go now, and remember not to be afraid again."

I repeated "I'll never be afraid again" several times to myself as I stood up and tiptoed out the door of the sewing room. My body felt light and my mind clear. It was the good feeling I had after crying when I was younger. As I passed the statue of Blessed Martin, I recalled how often I hid behind his cloak when I cried so Elizabeth wouldn't scold me. I was proud of what I had told Sister, and now I wanted to find my friend and tell her, but she was nowhere in sight. I knew the children would be happy that Sister knew everything, especially if it meant that they were not going to be beaten anymore. I would no longer be a scared child. Repercussions from Zami and the other big girls never entered my mind.

25

Eyes of Stone

 That evening when Sister came to the little girls' dormitory to bless us goodnight, she sat on an empty bed in the center of the room, gave a heavy sigh, and said, "Today, Mary told me many things about the big girls that I didn't know. She told me that they beat you and take your food and candy and give you their work to do. If she's telling the truth, raise your hands."

Not a single hand went up. "Is she telling the truth?" Sister asked again. Dead silence. I raised my hand. Then Elizabeth raised hers. I relaxed a little. Sister asked one more time, "Is it true that the big girls beat you?"

One by one whispers of "Yes" came from several beds, but no more hands went up.

"*Mama yangu!*" was all that Sister said. Then, after a few moments, "From now on, you must tell me when the big girls hurt you or take your food. You mustn't be afraid. Come, my little ones. Let's pray for our big girls." We got out of bed, knelt by her feet, and repeated The Lord's Prayer phrase by phrase, repeating *Forgive us our trespasses as we forgive those who trespass against us* several times.

"Sleep well," Sister said as she sprinkled us with holy water and locked us in.

The Lord's Prayer rang in my ears, in my heart, and in my soul. I said it over and over. The longer I prayed, the better I felt. I was almost grateful that I hadn't died from typhoid. I remember how well Sister cared for me when I was ill. I said the whole Lord's Prayer one more time just for Sister Silvestris.

The next day we trembled as we watched our big girls collect sticks, pins, matches, ropes, and wire. We knew what they were for.

At night when Sister had turned off the lights, I heard Zami's unmistakable footsteps tramp through the hallway past the toilets and into the children's quiet dormitory. She marched to the far wall and in a semi-whisper announced, "Tomorrow when Sister goes down for lunch, everyone who told on the big girls go behind Zahabu's shed. You'd better all be there. We know who you are."

I was neither surprised nor frightened. I wondered whether I should alert Sister Silvestris, but before I knew it, Zami reached under the blankets, dragged me down toward the metal frame at the foot of the bed, and landed a thundering blow to my stomach. "You will die tomorrow!"

I must have passed out, because the next thing I knew it was morning and I was coughing up clumps of blood.

After morning class, before lunch, a few of us children gathered behind Zahabu's wood shack. Along the rough splintered walls of the shed were small piles of homemade torture instruments. Each of us instinctively knew which pile belonged to our big girl and waited by it. The torturers appeared en masse and grabbed their victims. I heard someone say, "See this match? I'm going to burn your eyelashes."

Zami grabbed my arms and tied them with a rope to one of the loose planks that stuck out from the wall of the dilapidated shack. From her pile on the ground, she took a stick from a thorn tree with the thorns intact and beat me with it. "By the time I'm finished with you, you won't be able to open your big mouth for a long time." She hit me across the face several times and then twisted my lips with her fingers. She proceeded to alternately kick me in the stomach and beat me on the head with the thorny stick. I watched her as if curious to see what torture tactic she'd use next. Amidst the crying and whimpering around me, I heard our tired voices from the night before saying the Lord's Prayer. I didn't flinch and I didn't cry. She continued hitting and kicking me, and pinching and twisting my flesh with her fingers as though I were a blob of dough. She was the last one to stop. From the beginning to the end of this ordeal, I stared at her with eyes of stone.

This time, after the thrashing, I felt as though I had just witnessed someone else's abuse. I realized that I was no longer afraid of

Zami. I touched my swelling face with my cold hands. I touched my arms, chest, buttocks and legs, and the pain subsided. My body was red with tiny bleeding cuts from the thorns. I took hesitant steps to the nearby tap and cleaned up.

Throughout class that afternoon I half stood, half sat, and fidgeted on my seat as if the thorns from Zami's stick were still pricking me. Sister Clotilda asked nothing and we said nothing. She often collaborated with the big girls or didn't stop them when she knew their plans. To Sister Silvestris we continued to give the same made up reasons why we were black and blue and swollen or couldn't walk that we gave before. She knew the real reason now, but did not punish the big girls. Could it be that she too was afraid of them?

At night, when I lay down to sleep, a familiar voice spoke to me. *You're growing big and strong. You must always love yourself. I will never leave you.* It was my Fat Mary. We hadn't talked for a long time, and I was amazed at how young and childlike her voice was.

"Why aren't you thin like me?" I asked her, "Don't you know that I've been sick and that I no longer cry?"

You're growing up fast. No matter how big you get, I will remain your little Fat Mary. I am very proud of you.

"Fat Mary, you will live in me forever."

When I woke up in the morning, I was very stiff and it hurt to sit down. Although the beaten children were in misery, to my surprise they talked to me and consoled me as though I wasn't the cause of this most recent assault. I had turned a new leaf. They had turned a new leaf. Everything was somehow bearable. I even looked forward to showing Sister Clotilda that I wasn't afraid of her. As a result of my telling on the big girls, the beatings subsided because the children now weren't as afraid of them. As soon as they knew that blows were coming, they took off screaming, "I'm going to tell Sister Silvestris!"

Most big girls stopped dead in their tracks but not Zami. Although I could run faster than before, Zami often caught me and continued to beat me. She did however notice the change in me and was frustrated that I didn't cry no matter what she did to me.

It was also good know that Fat Mary approved of my metamorphosis. The more I changed, the more she remained the same.

26

Kwisha! It's Over!

 My friend Elizabeth was happy that I was thin like her and that I no longer cried, but one day she said to me, "Mary, you've changed too much. When you stopped crying, you stopped laughing too."

"You always told me tears didn't help. You were wrong. After a good cry, I'd feel better and then I could laugh again. Now that I don't cry anymore, I can't laugh as easily. And now I worry more about what will happen when school is finished. I don't want to become a nun or stay in Kifungilo forever. What will you do?"

"My mother will take me home. She can't take you, but you'll always be my first and best friend." Somehow, the thought of one day parting from Elizabeth forever didn't upset me as much. I had other things on my mind.

"I want to run away from Kifungilo," I told her.

"Are you crazy? Where will you go?"

"Someplace where I can go to middle school and then to secondary school."

"You'll be finishing fourth grade soon."

"Sixth grade," I corrected her.

"But the years of school with Sister Theonesta don't count. If you go to a government school, you might have to repeat the first grades."

"You mean nothing we learned in Kifungilo counts in government schools?"

"Nothing," said Elizabeth. "The nuns taught us only what they knew. They aren't real teachers."

"I overheard Mother Rufina and Sister Silvestris talk about sending some girls to an African School in Kongei that accepts half-castes."

"If you do go to a government school, then what?"

"I don't know, but continuing with school is the only thing important to me now."

One day, two weeks after I overheard their conversation, Sister Silvestris, Sister Clotilda, and Mother Rufina stood waiting for us in the classroom when we entered. What had we done? We sat quietly, our faces reflecting their somber mood. Mother Rufina stepped forward, cleared her throat several times, and smiled at us. Sighs of relief filled the classroom.

"My dear children," she began, "we have decided to send some of you away, away, away for proper schooling." My heart started racing. I had to concentrate to hear her words. "In Kifungilo we give you a basic education, but we are not affiliated with the government, so even though you are much better educated, educated, educated than the Wasambaa who attend government schools, we cannot give you a Primary School Certificate. We have therefore chosen a few of you to go to Kongei where our Precious Blood Sisters run the Middle School for the government. You will be tested when you get there, so you won't have to repeat, repeat, repeat any grades."

Sister Clotilda couldn't wait to add, "I'm sure you'll be the best pupils in Kongei because of the quality education you've had with me."

"And with Sister Theonesta," added Sister Silvestris.

As far as I was concerned, Sister Clotilda was the worst teacher. I couldn't recall much of what I'd learned from her, although the scar in my hand guaranteed that I would remember bits and pieces about the circulatory system for the rest of my life.

"Who wants to go to Kongei?" Mother Rufina asked. All hands went up.

"We have to pay your school fees, so we've picked five of you for now, and if we have the money, we shall send more girls next year." My racing heart stopped and my stomach tightened. I knew I was left out. She took a piece of paper from her pocket, unfolded it, and called the names of the chosen: "Antonette, Elise, Nora, Imelda, and Julitta."

The first four jumped from their desks, clapped loudly, and shouted, "Thank you, thank you!" Sister Clotilda ordered them to sit down and be still.

Julitta ignored her and cried out, "No! I don't want to go to school. I won't go!"

"*Mama yangu*, Julitta!" exclaimed Sister Silvestris.

"Please, please, can I go instead?" I pleaded.

"No, Mary," Mother Rufina said sternly. "You will not go to Kongei. Julitta will go." Then she added, "Kongei is an African school. You will be the only half-castes there. Conditions are primitive, primitive, primitive. Africans don't know the European way of living. You are spoiled. Here in Kifungilo we have given you much more, much more, much more than the Africans have."

I couldn't believe that I wasn't chosen to go to Kongei. Had this happened to me before my reform, I would have begged, carried on, and cried my heart out. Instead, I looked at the three nuns in front of me with disgust and disbelief. Sister Clotilda sneered at me. "You aren't smart enough, Mary."

"Don't be so sad," countered Sister Silvestris. "One day you'll also go away to school."

"You mustn't be angry, Little Mary," said Mother Rufina. "Your time will come." I made such a terrible face they had to laugh. The chosen few congratulated one another as the rest of us watched them with profound envy. That day I left the classroom with a heart heavier than my body.

Why did I continue to believe that one day, through education, I would leave Kifungilo? Was Sister Silvestris lying to me when she said I was clever? Maybe Sister Clotilda was right. Must I erase the images in my head of sitting in a classroom with proper teachers and proper exams to finally obtain the coveted Standard Eight School Certificate? Was it my destiny to remain in Kifungilo and become one of the big girls? That possibility seldom entered my mind because as a child I was so sure that some *mzungu* would adopt me.

When I was constantly rejected, it became clear to me that the only way I could leave Kifungilo was to get educated enough to find a job with a *mzungu* or become a good wife to a husband who would treat me well because with a Standard Eight School Certificate, I would be more valuable to him.

I left the three Sisters and the chosen girls and walked alone to the statue of Blessed Martin. I gazed at his cement face. I couldn't pray. I felt like my intestines were tying themselves in knots. The cramps were similar to the awful pains and nausea of castor oil day. No matter what position I took—sitting, kneeling, or standing in front of Blessed Martin—the pain wouldn't go away. I tried to distract myself by thinking of my friend Elizabeth or Christmastime in Kifungilo, but it became obvious that the true cause of my pain was once again showing its face. That very familiar feeling of being unwanted, unchosen, rejected, and abandoned was gnawing at my insides. I wanted the pain in my stomach to stop. I wanted the ache in my heart to stop. I wanted the loneliness of being an orphan to stop. I didn't want to carry the heavy, indescribable misery of my life anymore. I wanted it all to stop.

Then I remembered something. I had accompanied Sister Silvestris to the village of Kiuzai when the father of a very sick child came to Kifungilo begging her to save his daughter's life. Sister dropped everything and grabbed a large bottle of holy water from the infirmary, put it in the deep pocket of her habit, and picked up her first-aid basket and handed it to me. We followed the father, praying out loud as we hurried to the village several miles away. Approaching the village, we heard wailing coming from the sick child's hut. It stopped when Sister entered. I heard her comforting each member of the family gathered around the sick child. Then she prayed out loud, blessed the child, and sprinkled holy water inside, then outside the house. The wailing that had stopped when Sister arrived began again when she left the hut. The little girl had died.

Sister shook her head sadly repeating, "*Kwisha, kwisha.*"

I asked her why the girl died. She said the little girl had drunk a whole bottle of Dettol, a strong antiseptic that most households kept on hand. "Even if she had gotten to the hospital," Sister said in a quiet voice, "she wouldn't have lived. I have lost another little one." We walked home in silence.

Sitting on the grass in front of the statue of Blessed Martin, I knew what I would do. What's the use of living if I couldn't go to school? It was very clear to me that I was doomed to live my entire life as an unwanted child in Kifungilo. That burden would never go away. Yes, I would do it. I was satisfied with my decision. My stomach cramps slowly disappeared as I got up and went to the infirmary where I was sure I could find a bottle of Dettol.

No Sisters were at the infirmary when I walked in. I saw Sister's first-aid basket on the table but there was no Dettol in it. I looked around. Two younger children were in the beds. One was groaning softly in her sleep and the other was moving restlessly. I tiptoed over to a cabinet, opened it, and found what I was looking for. There were several bottles of Dettol. I grabbed the first one and hid it under my sweater. The sick child who was awake called out for Sister and for water, but I slipped out the door and quietly closed it.

I thought for a moment about where to go. Someone might see me if I went to the lavatories in the new dormitory. I could go by the river or behind Zahabu's woodshed, or to our pig's sty. I rejected each idea. Then I decided to go to the cemetery. I had often reached a point of despair before and had thought of drowning myself in the pond near the cemetery, but it was too shallow. I had heard of children being killed by cars, but drivers coming up the narrow, winding Kifungilo road usually drove cautiously.

No one was at the cemetery. I saw the grave of Mother Ancilla, who started the orphanage for us. Across from her there was one big grave for the babies and little children who had died at the orphanage. On it there was a solitary wooden cross and a large, rough gravestone with no names. I sat on the children's gravestone, opened the bottle, and started swallowing. It tasted awful and burned my mouth and throat, but I drank it all and threw the bottle as far away as I could. Almost immediately, my stomach churned, I felt flushed, my head began to throb, and my vision got blurry. I put my head down on the cool gravestone. "*Kwisha*," I whispered. "*Kwisha*."

I heard a voice talking to me. I could barely open my eyes. A young nun was hovering over me. I didn't recognize her and I thought I must have died, but I felt so sick that I knew I hadn't. The nun spoke only German and I understood her to say she had just arrived from Germany and what could she do to help me. I threw up then struggled to my feet. I indicated I wanted to go to the dorm, and she helped me walk the distance there, half carrying me. I collapsed on my bed.

For several days, I was miserable. I suffered from severe stomach aches, fever, diarrhea, and dizziness. No one ever found out what made me so sick, but I found out why I didn't die. Sister Silvestris always diluted her Dettol to make it last longer.

27

Furaha! Joy!

 Instead of attending classes, the lucky girls began preparing for their departure to Kongei while the rest of us kept on memorizing blackboards full of information. I continued to be despondent and was disappointed I hadn't succeeded with the Dettol.

Finally the big day for the girls' departure to Kongei arrived. Everyone turned out to wish Imelda, Julitta, Antonette, Elise, and Nora goodbye. Sister Silvestris led the way as the fortunate girls, with their sweaters tied around their waists and their new suitcases on their heads, started down the eight-mile path that would take them to their African boarding school. Elizabeth and I waved and watched the long line of bright colors wind down the slope and climb up and down the hills and valleys of the fertile countryside.

"I never thought I would feel this way," I said, "but I am sad to see them leave Kifungilo. Sister Silvestris says we're lucky to have so many brothers and sisters. Maybe she's right. I feel like a part of my life is leaving me."

Elizabeth knew that I was trying to make the best of things. "Maybe Mother Rufina wants to find a European school for you."

"Can you picture me in a European school? I wouldn't know how to talk with the *wazungu*. I'd rather go to an African School where my English would be better understood and I could learn their dances. They use their whole bodies for dancing, not just feet and arms like the *wazungu*. They laugh and sing and clap and touch each other, and even cry when they dance. Maybe I'm not a hundred percent African, but when I dance, I know I'm one of them."

"Oh no! I prefer being a *mzungu* because *wazungu* are clean and rich and pretty," said my friend.

112

"So that's why you try to talk like Lady Twining?" I couldn't re-sist commenting on her accent when she spoke English.

"She's British, so her English is the best. The nuns speak terri-ble English. Even the *wazungu* don't understand them. Imagine how our English—taught to us by German nuns—sounds to the British. They laugh at us when we speak."

Easter came and the scholars from Kongei returned home to Kifungilo for the two-week holiday. As soon as we saw the line of suitcases snaking up the hill on the students' heads, we ran to meet them. I reached Nora, who held on to the suitcase on her head with one hand, and fell into step with her. "What was real school like? What did you learn? How were your teachers? Were you the only half-castes in Kongei?"

"Mary, you're so lucky you weren't chosen to go. Life in Kongei was very, very hard. We had to get up early in the morning to hoe the fields just like the Wasambaa even though we didn't know how to hoe. The Africans made fun of us all the time and called us *cho-tara, kilokote* (bastards, gutter children)."

"What did they teach you?"

"Little that we didn't already know. We learned a lot from Sister Theonesta, and compared to the Africans, we're excellent in English. And all we ate was *ugali* and *kunde* every day. Always the same stiff corn porridge and beans with hardly ever any cassava or greens, And just like the Wasambaa, we sat on the ground and cooked in large petrol barrels over open fires."

Nora slid the suitcase from her head and set it on the path. "Lis-ten, Mary, let me tell you something. As poor as those of us who have no parents think we are, Africans are even poorer. They don't have Sunday shoes, they don't wear panties, they've never seen a petticoat, and they had no sweaters. Even though Kongei isn't as cold as Kifungilo, most of the Africans were freezing. Besides their school uniforms, the only thing they had to wear were their *khan-gas*. Many times parents came to school to take their children home because they couldn't pay the fees or they needed help in the fields. We're rich compared to most of the African students in Kongei, even though they have parents."

"Did the sisters and teachers beat you?"

"No one was ever beaten, but when we did something wrong, we had to hoe in the field all day or carry water from the river. And we couldn't join the fun on feast days. You would have loved learning songs in Kisambaa and Kiswahili, and dancing like the Wasambaa, though we didn't want to."

I had to go to Kongei. Imagine having permission to dance like the Wasambaa! "Do you think Mother Rufina would let me go with you after the holidays?" Nora stood up, put her *n'gata*—a balancing circle made out of dried banana leaves—on her head, and swung her warped suitcase on top of it.

"Mary, you don't know what hard life is. I'm not going back."

I heard Sister Silvestris say she was happy to have all her children back and that we would have a *sikukuu*, a feast day. She barely hid her pleasure at hearing how the girls now appreciated Kifungilo. They complained about working in the hot fields, the bad food, and being called names.

"I'm not going back to Kongei," Julitta announced and the others joined her.

"*Mama yangu!* You have to go back," insisted Sister Silvestris. "Your school fees are paid for the whole year. Now put your suitcases in the attic and go bathe in the river. I'm sure you missed the cold water," Sister teased.

It was time for the girls to leave again for Kongei. All of them were going back except Julitta. As it turned out, she was allowed to stay because she still wet her bed and that was an embarrassment to the Sisters of Kifungilo. We accompanied our four classmates down the road, but this time the mood was somber and the pace was slow as they reluctantly disappeared back into their hard lives.

They didn't return until the long holidays that began in late December. Their stories were the same: the hard life, terrible food, humiliation, and loneliness. But just as Mother Rufina predicted, they were now appreciative of the opportunity they'd been given, and they were determined to persevere until they graduated from Standard Eight. At the end of their four years of study in Kongei, they would sit for the Territorial Exams, and if they passed, they would be deemed highly educated. Again at Christmas I had my special time with Baby Jesus. I no longer asked him for my mother. Instead, I asked him to send me away to school. By now I was accustomed to not getting an answer, but I still liked talking to him. Maybe asking him to find my mother was asking too much. Now I told him that all I wanted was an eighth grade education.

In the festively decorated recreation room, the little children performed "Trim the Tree" for the appreciative old nuns. I didn't participate because I was almost a big girl. Afterward, hoping she'd have news for me, I searched for Mother Rufina. She greeted me with a smile.

"Mary, I have very good news, good news, good news for you. When school starts in February, you shall go far away from Kifungilo to a school called Mhonda. We have found school fees to send five girls."

All I heard was "Far away from Kifungilo to a school..." The phrase danced in my head. I will go far away from the orphanage, I will get an education, I will travel, I will see another place in Tanganyika, and most importantly, I will start forgetting my childhood. All I felt was *furaha,* joy!

Mhonda was the other school that the Precious Blood Sisters operated for the government besides Kongei. The school was a whole day's travel by bus, Sister told me. "Mary, I know you have had only the equivalent of a fourth grade education here, and middle school in Mhonda begins with Standard Seven, but I'm confident you'll be one of the best, the best, the best students from Kifungilo. Unlike some of our girls, you know the value of education."

"You won't regret sending me to school and paying my fees. I will work very hard so that one day I'll be able to pay you back."

"You know you have to pay back the school fees?"

"No, but I want to show how grateful I am to the nuns for raising me when my parents didn't want me. I'll always be grateful, Mother Rufina."

"There are many things a young girl cannot understand," she mumbled to herself. Her small frame seemed weighed down by the complex contents of her mind.

"Mother, imagine me, Fat Mary, Mary *Mdogo*, Piggy Knife getting to the eighth grade!"

"One day, Mary, you will make us very proud."

I went back to Baby Jesus in the Nativity scene. I wondered if he had answered my prayers, or if it was inevitable that I go on to school. "Thank you, Baby Jesus," I said anyway.

I went to my assigned spot toward the end of the long row of tables and found my Christmas presents. These gifts that had meant so much in the past now seemed insignificant in light of what Mother Rufina had just told me. I wondered if Sister Silvestris would let me pick an additional dress out of the boxes from Germany, or if the long-sleeved, red taffeta one I chose for this Christmas would be the only Sunday dress I would take to Mhonda. I couldn't think of anything else except leaving Kifungilo. I tried to imagine sitting in a bus for the first time and what life would be like far away from Kifungilo. Would the teachers beat me and the Africans call me *chotara* and *kilokote*? Would I have a friend like Elizabeth?

I thought of my friend who had gone home to her family for Christmas. I longed to tell her the good news. I knew she would say, "I told you so. See, I prayed so much for you and now you're finally leaving." Will I ever see her again, I wondered. Was school worth losing everything for—even a best, forever friend?

Breaking my reverie, Sister Silvestris came over to me with her arms wide open. "So, now you're happy, my Fat Mary. You will finally go away to school. Kate, Lucinda, Stefana, and Mary Jameson are also going. Mhonda is two hundred miles from here, so you will only come home to Kifungilo once a year. You'll be the youngest, so the bigger girls will watch out for you." Sister went to talk to the other girls.

I doubted the others would watch out for me, but I did wonder how we'd all fare at Mhonda. Kate was older and had lighter skin than mine. Although her hair was shoulder length, it was rough and kinky. Would she have a harder time at the African school because she was so fair, or would the Africans prefer lighter skin? Stefana and Mary Jameson, both darker than me, were sweet and gentle. Stefana was very disciplined, clean and hardworking, and she took great pride in her personal grooming. Her clothes were always spotless. I, on the other hand, was considered lazy because I was fat as a child. Sometimes that criticism was justified because personal grooming and cleanliness were a bother to me, and I did my chores hastily to leave time for daydreaming and studying.

Lucinda changed her mood like a chameleon changes colors. She took great pains to win a friendship, but once anyone became her friend, she could turn into a bully. I was an on-again-off-again friend of hers. While becoming friends, she'd spoil me with attention and share everything. But when she decided to befriend another girl, I'd be ignored. Then I'd do whatever she wanted in order to be in her good graces again. She was the only one I wished wasn't going to Mhonda with us.

I counted the days until the first of February. At night I dreamed of Mhonda, wondering if it would be as bad as Kongei. I imagined the subjects I'd learn and how smart I'd be when I returned to Kifungilo. I spent more time with Elizabeth, but we didn't talk much. I think we were preparing ourselves for my departure. She was the only person I would miss. I longed to be away from Sister Silvestris because lately I never knew what mood she'd be in. I had to be on my guard and that was stressful. When I was little, she was sweeter and more accommodating, and I could ask her anything. Now she seemed harassed and impatient, and she often yelled at us as she prepared us to go to school far away from her.

The day before we left, she called us to the sewing room to give us our supplies and rules to live by. "Sit on the bench and be quiet," she ordered. She showed us the suitcases Zahabu made for us. The wood was conditioned with palm oil to keep it from cracking and warping. Lucinda grabbed the largest one. Kate took the next largest, and Stefana, Mary Jameson, and I got the smallest ones. I handled my homemade wooden *sanduku* as if it were made of soft leather like the one Elizabeth had. I felt the rough insides, and I admired the big silver nails embedded into the four corners joining the rectangular pinewood panels. The other girls put their suitcases on the floor and listened to Sister Silvestris, but I held mine on my lap and mentally packed it. First, I put in my many dreams and hopes for my future. On top of them I folded and arranged all my worldly possessions. The last thing to go in was my determination to create a new life from the rubble of my childhood. I would not fail! I lowered the lid. I squeezed a padlock through the tiny metal hoop, locked it, and hid the key in my heart.

"For the ten months you'll be gone," Sister was saying, "you'll need two Sunday dresses, two *suruwali* (Sister Silvestris' homemade boxer-like cotton panties), one petticoat, your one pair of shoes and two pairs of socks, one bar of yellow Sunlight soap for bathing, and two bars of blue detergent soap for washing your clothes. I bought these special combs for you. The one with big teeth is to remove your tangles, and the one with tiny teeth is for combing the lice out of your hair."

"I haven't had lice for a long time," I said.

"You never know what you'll bring back to Kifungilo from the Africans. Africans are dirty people," she said waving the lice combs at us. "See what our girls looked like when they returned from Kongei! *Mama yangu!* They bring back lice and bugs and have open sores on their legs. Such *uchafu,* such filth. I'm ashamed of them. You must obey the same rules of cleanliness we practice in Kifungilo. Tell me what they are."

"Wash your face and comb your hair every morning and evening, take a bath once a week and change your *suruwali.* Wash your clothes each week and iron your Sunday dress," we recited.

"If you do this all year, I shall be very proud of you. Now, pack your supplies in your *sanduku.* Sister Florestina, the headmistress at Mhonda, will give you each two school uniforms that Mother Rufina has paid for."

We meticulously folded and packed every item into our suitcases. I couldn't believe that the day I had dreamed of and prayed for so often and for so long was just a night away. I lifted my suitcase to my head, but I couldn't balance it there like the Africans and some Kifungilo girls. I grabbed it as it slid off my slippery hair. My future lay in that box.

"Early tomorrow," Sister continued instructing us, "meet at the garage. Sister Fabiana will drive you to Lushoto and then to Mombo. I will come along to make sure you get safely on the bus for Turiani.

Now, go to the convent and say goodbye to the Sisters and to Father Gattang."

From the moment I learned I was going away to school, my attachment to my life in Kifungilo all but ceased to exist. I knew I could leave without a shred of sadness or nostalgia. I could see that Stefana and Kate were apprehensive. They hadn't smiled or uttered a word since we were called to the sewing room. Because Mary Jameson and I were flower girls in Rosa's wedding, I felt a little closer to her than to the others. As we walked to the convent, I told her I was glad she'd be in Mhonda with me.

"Mary, you seem happy to be leaving Kifungilo."

"I'm happy because it means I'm finally getting an education."

"The idea of going to an African School and working in the fields in the hot sun makes me wish I could stay in Kifungilo forever. I don't really want an education."

"Is that true, Mary Jameson? When I get educated, I'll know what to do with my life. I don't want to stay in Kifungilo. If I reach the eighth grade, I'll have more choices and the nuns will let me leave Kifungilo."

"I haven't thought about my future. Maybe I don't care about it that much."

"You have a mother and a brother who care about you. If I don't care about myself, no one will. It's up to me to do what I can to be happy and have a good life. I don't even think that much about my mother or a family anymore. I just know I'm responsible for me, and going to school will help me take care of myself."

At the convent, the door opened and a few sisters led by Mother Rufina came out. "Here are the lucky girls, lucky girls, lucky girls who will leave us for school in Mhonda," Mother Rufina said as she and the other nuns shook our hands goodbye. I took her small hand in mine. "Thank you for letting me go, Mother."

She held my hand tightly. "You are happy now, Mary. You must work hard, hard, hard and give Kifungilo a good name. We want our girls to do better than the African girls."

28

Farewell to Kifungilo

Only after students started going to Kongei and Mhonda, did I hear the Sisters refer to us as something other than Africans and *schwarze Kinder*. They had made it perfectly clear to us that we were not Europeans, but never clarified our status relative to Africans. Even though we were half European, the nuns had always treated us like Africans, but when they compared us to Africans, they told us that we were better than them, but still worse than Europeans.

The farewell queue of nuns filed in front of us. Some of the Sisters gave us holy cards with pictures of the Virgin Mary, the Sacred Heart of Jesus, Saint Joseph, and Saint Don Bosco.

"I want to give you each twenty shillings," Mother Rufina announced. Twenty whole shillings was the most money I ever had in my life. I started planning all the things I would buy with it. I would get shoes, a satin dress, lacy nylon panties, and maybe a pair of socks—all brand new. I was sure twenty shillings would buy everything I wanted. I examined the crisp, clean bill. From its center, the familiar face of Queen Elizabeth II gazed solemnly at me. It was the same portrait of our beloved Sovereign in full regalia that hung in several buildings throughout the orphanage. We practically adored Queen Elizabeth. She was our ideal of beauty, grace, wealth, and power. I folded my twenty shilling note and carefully put it in my pocket.

We genuflected as we walked past the church and under the shady poinsettia trees that led to Father Gattang's house. Father Gattang greeted us on his front steps with colorful rosaries for each of us. Father blessed us as we knelt before him and prayed over us in

Latin. He sprinkled us with holy water saying, "Go in peace and remain in peace."

As soon as the door shut behind him, I began enumerating to the others the multitude of things I was going to buy with my shillings. Lucinda laughed at me. "Mary, you're really stupid! Do you know what a new pair of shoes costs?"

"How should I know? This is the first money I've ever had."

"One pair of cheap plastic *ndala* flip-flops costs twenty-seven shillings. The red leather shoes Heini bought for me in Tanga cost ninety-six shillings."

My heart sank. I wondered where Lucinda, who had no parents, got her money. I'd heard that Heini gave her money for taking care of his needs and running errands. What needs? And what errands earned so much money?

"You can only buy little things like soap and chewing gum."

"We can buy bananas and mangos and Coca-Cola on the way to Mhonda," Mary Jameson added. I'd heard of Coca-Cola but never tasted it. But I wasn't going to use my money for food.

"I'll save my money until I have enough to buy new shoes."

"You'll never have anything new," Lucinda declared, enjoying my dismay. "You don't have friends who can give you money. But 'Little Fat Mary, you're very clever,'" she said, mimicking Sister Silvestris. "Let's see if your cleverness brings you a job and money someday. Until then, you have to get what you want out of the boxes from Germany."

I hated Lucinda. In an instant she had robbed me of so much pleasure.

I couldn't sleep that night. I wondered what an African government school was really like. Maybe what the Kongei girls said was true, that we would be persecuted because of our race, or lack of it. But I told myself once again that nothing could get in the way of my pursuit of an education.

I thought about Elizabeth. It was inevitable that we'd go our separate ways because her destiny involved parents and a family, while mine involved only me and the nuns. I had given up the idea of being adopted. I knew that once I left Kifungilo, I would be solely responsible for myself.

I needed to have a final conversation with my friend. We had shared a bed in the first small dormitory near *nyumba ile*, but since we moved to *nyumba mpya*—the new house—we each had our own metal bed. I crept through the dark room to her side of the dormitory and crawled into her bed. "Mary, you'll be punished if you're caught."

"I don't care. I'm leaving tomorrow."

Elizabeth was silent for a few moments, then said, "I'll miss you so much. What will life in Kifungilo be without you? Maybe I'll see you before I go home for Christmas, and when I return, you'll still be here for your two-month holidays."

"Aren't you going to Lushoto to help out in the dentistry?"

"I hope so. When the dentistry moved, I decided to be a helper there so I can watch the *wazungu* who live in Lushoto and learn to dress, walk, and talk like them. I think of myself as a *mzungu*. Even though we are African and European, I choose to be European. When Lizzy returns from her training to be a nun and a dentist, she'll ask Sister Nerea to let me help there."

"I hope Lizzy won't turn into a mean nun when she's in Germany. Don't you wish we could go to Mhonda together?"

"I'd rather stay in Kifungilo forever than go to an African school."

"But with an education, I think I could get a job in Tanga or Dar-es-Salaam and earn money to buy my own new things. My two dresses from Germany have to last the whole year. Sister Silvestris gave us needles and thread to mend them."

I recounted the contents of my suitcase for her—two Sunday dresses, two panties, one pair of shoes, two pairs of socks, a petticoat, nightgown, a sweater, four red hair ribbons, two needles and thread, two *merikani* sheets, twenty shillings, holy cards, and a rosary. "I packed the doll your mother gave me, too. The head is gone but it still has both arms and one leg. In the morning, I'll tie my blanket on top of the suitcase."

"When you went to say goodbye to the nuns, I put a few things in your suitcase. You're always cold, so I gave you the brand new sweater my mother bought me for Christmas."

"New? A brand new sweater?" I couldn't keep my voice to a whisper.

"Quiet!" a voice yelled in the darkness.

"I also put in some jasmine hair oil, my old toothbrush, and two pairs of panties—the ones you love to borrow."

"Oh, Elizabeth, you're a good friend. I feel bad because I don't have anything to share with you."

"You've shared your life in Kifungilo with me. When I'm grown up and think of my childhood, you'll be the most important part of it." We hugged each other for a long time and Elizabeth cried.

"Goodbye, my friend," I said.

"Goodbye, my forever friend."

Back in my own bed, I had a strange pain in my stomach as though a thick rope was being pulled tighter and tighter around my middle. I knew I would never see her again. I searched for Fat Mary and when she appeared, I asked her to safeguard my memories of Elizabeth. I had a hard time swallowing the lump in my throat. When I finally did, I felt ready to face life in an African school without my friend. I would be fourteen.

29

First Bus Ride

 At five o'clock in the morning, Sister Silvestris shined a flashlight in our dormitory and lit a kerosene lamp because the electric generator didn't come on until six. We cleaned up, got dressed, grabbed our suitcases, and marched down to the garage where Sister Fabiana was waiting for us with the baby blue Volkswagen van. Kiondo was holding open the huge garage door. Kiondo was the mailman and took every opportunity to ride to Lushoto so he wouldn't have to walk the thirteen miles back and forth to fetch the day's mail. He loaded our suitcases in back and we piled in. Mary Jameson, Stefana, and I sat in the rear. Kate and Lucinda were in the middle. Sister Silvestris climbed in the front, and Kiondo shut the door and sat among the suitcases as Sister Fabiana started driving.

I watched the lights of the van illuminate the stately cypress trees one by one and admired how Sister Fabiana steered our vehicle along the narrow, bumpy, homemade road with precision as she chatted in German with Sister Silvestris. I dozed until we arrived in Lushoto a half hour later. The dainty little town, built to feel like home to the Germans, was still sleeping as our van pulled in front of the dentistry belonging to the Precious Blood Sisters of Kifungilo. The dental office had been moved to Lushoto in 1953 where it became a good source of income for the Sisters as patients from around the country came to the renowned dental clinic run by Sister Nerea. The red brick two-story building, set on the main street in the center of town, included a residence for the Sisters and a garden with flowers, fruits, and vegetables.

Sister Nerea switched on the outside light and came to greet us. We stayed in the van while the Sisters went in for breakfast. After a while Sister Silvestris brought us sandwiches and a bottle of fresh passion fruit juice to share. "Sister Nerea said that you can use the W.C. but don't make a mess," she warned us. We all declined because we didn't know how to use a European toilet. The Sisters hurried back to the van and we took off. "The bus leaves at seven o'clock from Mombo and we can't be late."

"Now children, you must sing for me," ordered Sister Fabiana. I resented her calling us children because I felt very grown up and in charge of my destiny, especially on this, the first day of my new life away from the orphanage. The others sang church songs in Latin, English, and German, but it was getting lighter outside, and I was more interested in watching the terrain and the road.

I'd never been further away from Kifungilo than Lushoto and the surrounding mission stations. The road to Mombo was winding and precipitous and hardly wider than the dirt road from Lushoto to Kifungilo. The huge eucalyptus trees that lined the steep drop-off filled the crisp morning air with their nose-tingling scent. The entire fifteen-mile length of road was cobblestone with decorative brick and cement arches over water ducts, streams, and tunnels. The German colonizers chiseled and carved this road from Lushoto to Mombo, following the path made by torrential rains that flowed from the high mountain peaks in the Usambara Mountains through narrow gorges between steep ridges all the way down to the river deep in the valley. If a vehicle skidded or swerved even a foot, it was certain death for everyone.

I could feel the air getting heavier and warmer as we descended into the elegiac valley, strewn with skeletons of burnt and rusted cars, trucks, and buses. This beautiful valley, dotted with car disasters, was jarring and foreboding, but the natural scenery was compelling. The Usambara Mountains rose green and serene from fertile, cultivated valleys where clusters of Sambaa villages nestled among the foothills. Around every other bend on the road, thundering waterfalls emptied into dark, mysterious lakes. Cheerful rivers lay waiting for the rising sun, but this beauty was wasted on drivers whose eyes were glued to the treacherous road. Our well-seasoned

driver, Sister Fabiana, drove slowly and carefully. If a car came toward us, she'd have to back uphill until she found a spot wide enough
for it to pass. There was no chatting in German on this stretch of the
road. With a collective exhale, we safely reached the hot and humid
Mombo valley and had enough time to dash into the bushes behind
the petrol station to relieve ourselves.

The bus was at the station. It was a sickly mustard color that
had *Umeme* (Lightning) scrawled across both sides in huge fuchsia
letters. Most buses had names or sayings written on them like "God
Bless" or "Nearer my God to Thee" in English. Other buses carried
sayings like *Polepole ndiyo wendo* (Slowly but surely), *Kila jambo na
wakati wake* (To everything there is a season), while some buses
used their owners' names like *Lyimo Express* or *Fly with Abdullah*, or
were inscribed with words like *Upepo* (Wind), *Mapenzi* (Love), and
Sadaka (Sacrifice).

A large sign on our bus in the front window announced MORO-
GORO as its final destination. The dirty and dust-coated windows
were shut tight. Enormous back wheels, higher than the front ones,
lifted the rusty rear end of the bus a full six feet off the ground. A
short wooden railing encircled the roof, and a pair of thick sisal ropes
hung over the railings on both sides. At the rear of the bus, a narrow
metal ladder with several rungs missing, went to the roof. There was
no driver in sight. A few goats tethered to an old solitary jacaranda
tree peered at us from behind its large trunk as they ripped off and
chewed chunks of the bark. Kiondo gave us our suitcases and we sat
on them under the tree near the goats. The nuns were getting anxious about the timely departure of our bus. "Where's the driver and
where are the passengers?" Sister Fabiana asked Kiondo as though
he should know.

"They'll come," Kiondo answered with typical Sambaa faith in
everything. "They sleep to the last minute."

"Africans will never understand the importance of being on
time," Sister Fabiana complained to Sister Silvestris. "They come late
to work, and when the morning is cloudy or rainy, they sleep until
they see the sun. Why do they bother to wear wristwatches?"

"Most can't tell time, but they love their watches," said Sister
Silvestris with a chuckle. "European items signify progress and

prestige. Many women ask me for ties and belts for their husbands to wear when they go to town even though they don't have shirts or trousers."

"Get your suitcases and line up at the back of the bus," ordered a young man dressed in old khaki shorts and a light blue, short-sleeved shirt buttoned only at the top. Within minutes, the bus stop was buzzing with hundreds of people. We pushed our way toward the bus with the rest of the chaotic crowd. The five of us were the first in line with our suitcases on our heads. Climbing up to the roof, the young boy motioned for us to give him our suitcases. I didn't want to part with my suitcase, but Sister Silvestris told us to do what he said. I heard a loud thump as he threw all my worldly possessions to the far end of the roof. We moved away and huddled near Sister Silvestris and Sister Fabiana.

The crowd of Africans proceeded to throw their bundles up to the conductor, with almost every other bundle falling and spilling its contents on top of the waiting passengers who were showered with corn flour, cassava, beans, sugar cane, green bananas, salt, cooked ugali wrapped in green banana leaves, guavas, pots and pans, coal, hoes, swatches of cheap fabric, and baskets of every shape and size. Even a few pangas—machetes—tumbled down from the roof.

It took over an hour to load the bus. We watched the chaos and listened to the Africans speaking Kisambaa and other tribal languages we had never heard. To our surprise and horror, a little boy dressed in rags untied the goats from the tree and brought them to be loaded on top of the bus along with the mountain of luggage. "No room for the goats today," the conductor said. "Come back next week."

"These are a wedding present for relatives in Korogwe. They must arrive today."

"I said there's no room." The little boy struggled with his goats as they went every which way among the travelers.

The conductor put a dirty piece of brittle plastic over the luggage and tied down the four corners with the sisal ropes. "Line up by the door and show me your tickets," he ordered as he descended into the mob. There was no way we could push our way through the crowd to get to the door.

All of a sudden we were deafened by the shrill of a loud police whistle. Total silence ensued. Sister Silvestris continued blowing her whistle, and the Africans made way for her as she walked to the head of the line with our tickets in hand. Seeing her, the young conductor bowed his head and said respectfully, *"Tumsifu Yesu Kristo"* to which Sister replied, *"Milele na milele. Amina."* He listened intently to what Sister was telling him, and then he motioned for us to come over to the bus and get on.

As we followed Sister Fabiana on the path opening in the midst of the people, we heard whispers from the crowd, *"Chotara, hafukasti."* Heads popped up as curious Africans strained to see us. The comments got louder and louder and included *kilokote* (gutter child), *wazungu weusi* (Africans acting like Europeans), and *matajiri* (rich ones).

Sister Silvestris walked to the third row of seats with me. Taking my hand, she held it in both of hers and shook it firmly without saying a word. She said goodbye to the other girls, then hurried out. Sister Fabiana waved at us and the two nuns in their sparkling white habits melted into the crowd. All five of us squeezed onto the seat for three that Sister had pointed out.

The conductor kept the other passengers from entering the bus until the Sisters were safely out of sight. Then all hell broke loose. Screaming and shoving people waved their tickets and climbed on the bus, four and five at a time, clutching huge bundles. There was an awful smell as they passed by. Soon the seats were packed with people and bundles, and the aisle became a solid wall, restricting air circulation. The conductor tried to count the passengers but gave up. We huddled together in our seat, hot and afraid. The bus windows remained closed.

The conductor entered the driver's compartment and began honking the horn. We held our hands to our ears as he honked for five minutes. He stepped out of the compartment and said that he hoped the honking would wake up the driver who was still sleeping down in the valley.

Mary Jameson turned to me. "I'm afraid we'll die from suffocation."

"I can't breathe," Stefana choked.

A loud bang caught everyone's attention. The bus driver arrived and shut himself inside the driver's protected cubicle with a slam of the door. He was a no-nonsense man of about fifty-five, whose first order of business was to check his salt-and-pepper goatee and adjust his red felt fez in the cracked rearview mirror. He started the engine and, without looking in the rearview mirror, backed up the weighted bus. We jerked and swayed so much that, if it hadn't been for the sardine-like packing of bodies, we might have broken our necks. He switched gears and we lunged forward onto the road. Seconds later, he slammed on the brakes, got out of the bus, and went back to talk to the little boy under the tree with the goats.

Returning, he stormed into the passenger compartment and ordered, "Show me your tickets!" We held up our tickets. "Everyone in the aisles, off the bus!" he ordered. "*Funga mdomo!* Shut up!" he yelled at the complaining passengers.

The passengers in the aisle reluctantly got off. The driver walked down the narrow aisle and every few seconds he shouted "*Toka! Toka!*" to get people out. At least half of the seated passengers had no tickets. When they left, the passengers with tickets came back on the bus, and the driver closed the door. I noticed an empty seat across from us so I nudged Stefana and we took it. Just as we settled in with smiles on our faces for the first time that day, the door opened again, and lo and behold, the four goats scampered onto the bus. They trotted with such assurance, you'd think they rode the bus to pasture every day. "Meeeeeh, meeeeeh," they commented before lying down in a pile at the center of the aisle beside their happy shepherd. The driver must have been a relative of the bride or groom in Korogwe.

I was busy watching this show when Stefana started to hyperventilate. Her face was changing color and her already protruding eyes were bulging. I rushed to the front of the bus and hit the driver's panel with my fists. "Could you open a window please?"

"Open a window? Open a window? *Shenzi!*" he shouted at me (*Shenzi* is a swear word meaning "pagan"). He steupsed at me several times. "What's the matter with you spoiled half-castes? You get special air in Kifungilo?" The passengers burst into laughter.

"Please open the window!" I begged. An African girl sitting behind us joined me and spoke in Kisambaa to convince the driver to do something.

"*Shenzi!*" the driver spit out. He braked, reached down to his feet and grabbed something. He came out of his compartment and into the bus. Suddenly there was a smashing sound and glass smithereens flew from our window in all directions. The driver pointed to the gaping hole he had just created with a short axe and said, "There, I opened the window for you. *Shenzi!*" he glared at me. He stomped his feet, spat on each of the four goats, steupsed at the passengers, went back into his cubicle, and slammed the door.

Throughout this entire episode, the other Kifungilo girls sat like statues, while several African passengers, young and old, left their seats, stepped over the goats in the aisle (the herder slapped their legs with his sisal whip every time they came near his animals) to stand directly in front of us and stare.

The driver took off, leaving behind a cloud of dust and smoke. Miraculously, the air rushing in from the broken window revived Stefana. As our crazy driver careened down the road, we managed to collect the pieces of glass and throw them out the window. Such was my introduction to public transportation in Tanganyika.

30

An African Guardian Angel

The first stop was a large town called Korogwe. Our bus lined up behind three other buses, and as they left the station, clouds of black, smelly diesel exhaust from the departing buses filled our bus. We didn't dare move before the goats left lest the fierce little herder strike our legs. The goats must have enjoyed the ride because they had to be pushed, shoved, and carried off the bus.

On the roof, the conductor listened to passengers describe their bundles, then tossed them down. Another mob of people carrying bundles waited to enter the bus. Our harassed driver collected the tickets and closed the door when the vacated seats were taken.

The remaining passengers on our bus rushed to the food sheds to buy bananas, homemade *pombe* beer, chai or Coca-Cola. My twenty shillings were in my suitcase on top of the bus, so I couldn't buy anything. Leaving the station, our bus skidded on a pile of banana peels and other rubbish. Huge puffs of black exhaust trailed behind us as the bus climbed the steep road.

We had gone a short distance when an old woman started shouting and hitting the panel separating the driver from us. "*Simama! Simama!* Stop! Stop," she shrieked. The driver slammed the brakes. The old woman with shriveled breasts hanging over her cheap, faded, black *kaniki*, pushed at the door. "What did you forget, Mama?" he asked, opening the door. His tone was now gentle and respectful. She hurried down the steps and ran back to the station. The driver backed up the bus. She disappeared behind the food sheds, and when she appeared again, she held three live chickens by their necks in one hand and a huge pod of green sugar bananas in the other. The driver helped her board then roared down the road again. The old woman sat with the chickens on her lap, and whenever they fussed, she talked to them in her tribal language, kissing them, and flashing a smile that exposed a single brown tooth on her lower jaw.

I was so busy watching the woman and her chickens that I didn't notice the girl sitting behind me looking at my braids and touching them. It was the same girl who spoke to the driver for me. "Is hair like yours hard to take care of, especially when it's so long?"

"Why is yours so short?" I countered. I was a little wary, but this young African woman was speaking easily to me.

"Mine's curly and coarse, and when it's long, it gets so tangled that I can't get even a wide-toothed comb through it. I wish I had soft hair like the half-castes."

"Soft, fine hair can get tangled too."

"You and your friends are going to Mhonda?"

When I nodded yes, she said she was too. "I just finished primary school in Lushoto. I've never left Usambara before."

"So you are a Sambaa?"

"My father is, but my mother is Pare. What about your tribe?"

"I don't have a tribe. Half-castes don't belong to a tribe."

"But at least one of your parents has a tribe."

This was the first time anyone assumed that I belonged to a tribe. It was also the first of many times that my tribal identity had to be established before I could carry on a conversation with an African stranger. Such questions initially reminded me that I didn't belong, but eventually I understood that asking about your tribe was the African way of getting acquainted.

"Have you heard of Kifungilo?"

"Of course. That's where German nuns take care of children whose mothers are ashamed of them. We hear that you live just like *wazungu* there." Her eyes were full of concern and genuine interest. "I'm afraid you'll have a hard time in Mhonda," she continued in a serious tone. "People tell me that Mhonda is primitive and the headmistress is a devil."

"Why are you going there then?"

"I'm one of the few girls from my tribe and the only girl from my little village who finished primary school. My father is a teacher, and he wants me to continue in school even though it's not our custom to educate girls. Mhonda is the only middle school for girls with an opening this year. Boarding school is hard for everybody. The better your life is at home, the harder school will be."

"Well, life wasn't easy for me in Kifungilo, so I should be fine in Mhonda."

She told me her name was Paulina Yahana. I liked her openness and I sensed someone who was also curious and wouldn't be put off by my endless questions.

The bus stopped at Handeni and Paulina got off to buy a mango and a Fanta. She motioned for me to get off the bus and offered her Fanta bottle to me. I couldn't believe that a stranger would buy a drink with her own money and share it with me. I ran down the steps and took the bottle of orange drink from Paulina.

"Let me wipe it for you first." Paulina took a clean green handkerchief from the small basket she was carrying and wiped the mouth of the bottle.

I took a greedy mouthful of Fanta, but the sharp tingling sensation paralyzed my tongue. I spit it out. "I've never tasted anything like this. The stinging hurts my tongue."

"Have some of my mango then." As I attacked the ripe mango, I felt that I was the luckiest person on earth to have found an African who didn't treat me like an outcast who had "child of sin" written across my forehead. I handed what was left of the mango back to Paulina and shamelessly licked my fingers.

"I thought they taught you manners in Kifungilo," she teased.

Back in my seat I felt wonderful. I had made a friend. The other Kifungilo girls were sleeping except for Kate. "Mary, remember Sister Silvestris told us to stick with each other and not mix too much with the Africans." Kate, as the oldest of the Kifungilo girls, felt she had to set us straight when we strayed.

The bus roared off again, this time without incident. Paulina dozed off and I found myself looking out the window with the shattered glass. How different the terrain and the vegetation were from that of the Usambaras! We had snaked in between the Usambara and Pare mountain ranges and had now entered the Uluguru Mountains. The soil on either side of the black tarmac road was as fine as flour and as red as the blossoms of the flame tree. Baobabs and acacia trees were scattered all over the landscape and the tall grass beneath them was scorched from the bright, hot sun.

Here I was seeing real baobab trees instead of pictures in Sister Theonesta's story book. She told us why the baobab looked so strange with tiny leafless branches on top of its thick trunk. According to the story, it all began with God creating heaven and earth,. As he admired his handiwork, Lucifer, one of his angels, boasted that he could create a tree that was more spectacular than any God had made. His tree would not only have different colored flowers, fruits, and leaves on the same tree, but would be big enough to feed and shelter all the birds and animals that God had created. God listened as Lucifer continued to sing his own praises while making his tree. In order to teach him a lesson, God snatched up Lucifer's tree by the trunk, shook it, and stuck it back in the ground upside down. That, Sister Theonesta explained, is why the golden-brown baobab tree has its twisted and knotted root-like branches on top of the tree instead of under the ground. I could almost see Sister Theonesta in her black and white habit shuffling across the red-dust terrain.

Our bus made three more short stops before we arrived in Turiani where the driver woke us up by loudly announcing the town. It was almost dark and the food stands were closed. The young conductor who loaded our suitcases that morning climbed on the roof and threw them down to us. The bus rushed down the road on its way to Morogoro leaving us in a cloud of dust and exhaust.

Three girls in orange mid-calf school uniforms ran up to us and shook our hands. "Are you the half-castes from Kifungilo?"

Before we could answer, Lucinda grabbed the arm stretched out to her and twisted it. The girl screamed as Lucinda snarled, "Don't call us half-caste. I'll smash your head next time."

"Don't hurt the girl," Kate said, "How's she supposed to identify us?"

"She can see that we're half-caste, can't she?"

I reached out and stroked the girl's arm.

"Don't side with the Africans, Piggy!" Lucinda snapped at me. "We don't like being called half-caste, but no one does anything about it. If anybody in Mhonda calls me half-caste or *chotara*, I'll kill them, the bloody fools."

I gave Paulina a hand putting her large suitcase and a big basket wrapped in *khangas* on her head. Then I balanced my suitcase on my head, and holding on to it with one hand, I helped her carry another bundle also wrapped in *khangas*. We walked in front, right behind our escorts and listened to Lucinda swearing and steupsing a while longer before she calmed down.

The sun was setting. Golden rays pierced through the branches of the tall trees and flickered on yellow and brown leaves covering our path. It felt good to walk after sitting in the hot bus all day. Our strides were long and determined now that we had almost reached our destination.

"How much farther do we have to walk?" Paulina asked our leader.

"Look way up there in the clearing between the brown mountains. That's Mhonda."

Although it was pitch black when we arrived, we could see the typical manicured entrance that announced a German settlement. The path became a road and the road got wider. Hibiscus bushes lined the remaining quarter mile, ending at the silhouette of the church. After we passed the church, girls carrying kerosene lamps came to meet us and led us into Sister Florestina's office, which had electricity from a generator.

The headmistress welcomed us and said we would sleep in the infirmary. Her accent was harsher than that of any of the nuns at Kifungilo. She was thin, and her elongated, angular face appeared cut in half by the Precious Blood headdress that extended from the top of her head to the tip of her eyebrows. With a sweep of her long bony hand, she instructed one of the students to show us where we would sleep. The infirmary was a few yards into the school compound, and the beds were just like the old wooden ones we had in the sleeping room next to *nyumba ile*. We crawled into bed without bathing or washing. In the morning the white sheets were orange and brown from the soil that clung to us from the long bus trip.

The heavy, pungent air prolonged my getting out of bed. It was quite a change compared to abruptly rising in Kifungilo's crisp morning air. When I did get out of bed, I saw that only Paulina was up. We were drawn to each other like magnets, and without saying a word we opened the infirmary door and went outside. I took a good look at her for the first time. She was short and solid and her face was rounder than the usual long, thin faces of the Sambaa. A bright yellow and green *khanga* was tied under her arms and over a red short-sleeved cotton dress. On her feet she had purple flip-flops which were brown from the bus trip and the five-mile walk to Mhonda. Multi-colored plastic bangles clinked and clanged as she gestured. She was quick to smile, and when she did, her whole face lit up reflecting the brightness of her white teeth. The intensity and sincerity of her gaze gave the impression that she was wise beyond her years.

I wondered why this lovely person would go out of her way to make me feel comfortable among the Africans. Didn't she know that half-castes were often ridiculed and their character prejudged? Or could it be that she, like me, acknowledged another human being first and then noticed the distinguishing attributes? We easily launched into the first of many satisfying and meaningful conversations we would have during our time together at Mhonda. I was relishing this expansion of my limited world and sensed that this African girl had much to tell me.

"Did you sleep well, my friend?" she asked.

"Very well, and you?" We sat on the cool cement steps outside the infirmary.

"I was thinking about Mhonda all night and couldn't sleep. Leave it to the German nuns to build a school in remote mountains just like your orphanage in Kifungilo."

"From living with German nuns, I've learned they want to make everything as difficult as possible." I figured I needed to enlighten her about the nuns we'd be dealing with. "They don't like anything that looks easy. A Sister once boasted that Germans were the toughest and smartest people on earth and that one day Germans would rule the world. They think they are superior to everyone."

"Baba has an old newspaper that tells how the Germans lost the Second World War," Paulina said with disdain. "It shows pictures of the people they had killed just because they weren't Germans. Baba said that Germans were the cruelest race of people on earth."

"I don't think they're the cruelest, but they must believe that suffering and pain are the way to the Kingdom of God."

"Even though I'm a Christian, I don't believe in heaven or hell."

"Sometimes I don't believe in heaven, but I definitely believe in hell. If I go to hell, it won't be so hard for me because I'm used to pain and suffering."

"What do you know about suffering, Mary? You have clothes, food, and shelter while people in my village struggle to survive."

"I don't know if what I feel is suffering, but I always carry a heavy load. I feel alone. I was sent to the orphanage because my parents didn't want me. I always think about that."

"Mary, of course you feel alone if you don't have family. But I know people in families who are unhappy."

I had always felt the reason I was unhappy was because I didn't have a family, but here Paulina was telling me a family is no guarantee of happiness. I remembered being happiest with my friend Elizabeth and my Fat Mary. Could Paulina be right?

"Paulina, do you promise not to laugh or say I'm crazy if I tell you something about me?"

"I promise."

"I have a special friend who lives inside me. Her name is Fat Mary. She loves me all the time, no matter what I do. She helps me and advises me. Even when I forget her, she's with me."

"We all must find ways to make our lives bearable. When I'm unhappy, I remember my grandmother. My Bibi used to tickle me and make me laugh until I cried. I really miss her. When I'm upset or sad or scared, I think of her and I feel better. She always said that laughter and tears are medicines from our gods, and we should use them when we need them. Fat Mary is your medicine. Don't be ashamed of her."

How could Paulina so easily understand this secret side of me when she had just met me? I resolved to seek her opinion on everything no matter what it was. Hadn't she just opened the door of unconditional love and acceptance for me? I knew then that she was brought to Mhonda to be my African guardian angel. Who could better educate me about African life and teach me what I would never learn from my German nuns? She would guide me in my new life away from the orphanage.

31

Welcome to Mhonda

What struck me most about Mhonda and the Morogoro District was how hot it was compared to the Tanga Region where Kifungilo was located. It was the first morning in my life that I wasn't cold.

The school compound was much larger than Kifungilo, but the buildings weren't as well built. Instead of the lively, German-looking red-tiled roofs, the buildings were covered with ugly gray sheets of corrugated metal. Only the Sisters' residence was two-storied. The rest of the buildings were long and narrow with boring beige cement walls.

A student knocked loudly and told us to follow her to the laundry shed to wash up. It was heaven to be outside so early in the morning, wearing only my nightgown instead of huddling under a woolen blanket trying to get dressed. We walked past a plain gray building which looked very much like the long rectangular slaughtering shed in Kifungilo. A few paces up were three cement troughs, just like the ones our farm animals drank from in Kifungilo, with brass taps along one side. "Here is where you wash," the student said.

We looked at each other and made faces—how primitive! But when we opened the tap, the warm water made us forget how backward and basic these toilet and washing facilities were. It was outright hot compared to what we were used to. As long as I didn't have to clench my teeth and shiver from the cold in the morning, everything would be all right. We were still cleaning up when we heard wooden doors bang, and pails and *makarai* basins clanging. Students came running in our direction and quickly swarmed around the other two washing troughs and ours too. They pushed and shoved as they hur-

139

riedly sprinkled water on their faces and then rushed back to the dormitory to dress for church. It took them three minutes to wash up in total silence.

Back in the infirmary I put on one of my Sunday dresses, brushed off the red dust from my shoes, put on my socks, combed and braided my stiff, dirty hair, and followed our student leader to church. It was much smaller than the one in Kifungilo, and the statues of Jesus, Mary, and Joseph looked crude and out of proportion compared to the ones Mother Ancilla made for our church. It had no stained glass windows, lace altar cloths, brass candelabras, waxed and polished communion railing, or the Stations of the Cross on the walls. This church looked unfinished and neglected. By the time the students were in their benches in front of the two pews reserved for nuns and teachers, the church was packed. The five of us squeezed into a bench in the back. It was Sunday, so everyone had on their Sunday best. I had never seen so many beautiful, shiny dresses. They all looked new. Once again I wondered if I would ever own a new dress.

Mass was celebrated by a young Holy Ghost Father who seemed impatient. He went so fast that I didn't recognize or understand the prayers, even the Latin ones. By communion time, most of the students had heard, via nudges and whispers, about the five of us in the back. There was so much murmuring and so many stares when we walked up for communion that the miserable statues, and even God himself, must have felt the competition for attention.

After Mass I said to Mary Jameson, "Don't the girls have the prettiest dresses you've ever seen?"

Before she could reply, Lucinda, the all-knowing consumer, said, "Those are cheap dresses! They're not cotton like ours. They're made out of slippery, hot and uncomfortable nylon, and the colors run when you wash them. Mary, are you sure you aren't a full-blooded African? You like their cheap clothes, their food, their hair, their strange dances, and you talk to them as if they're your relatives."

I didn't answer. I could never win an argument with Lucinda.

"Sister Florestina wants you in her office after breakfast to give you your uniforms and school supplies," the student in charge of us said.

I had studied the uniforms worn by the girls who met us at the bus. They were made of light cotton fabric with short sleeves and a flared skirt.

"You rich *hafukastis* might not like them, though."

Lucinda grabbed her arm and twisted it so hard that she screamed. "Don't call us *hafukasti* or *chotara* or *kilokote* or any of those names. Are you better than us because no one calls you names? Listen, you ignorant, dirty, smelly, primitive, superstitious, and stupid African. The *wazungu* call you monkeys. When you call us nasty names, we'll call you baboons."

The poor girl was speechless. "I didn't mean anything bad when I called you *hafuca*—." *Wham!* Lucinda slapped her across the face, then grabbed her. The girl cried out loud and started hitting back. Before we knew it, the two were in a full blown fist fight. As was my custom whenever there was a fight, I disappeared. I did not enjoy watching or being dragged into a fight and being beaten up. Gentle Kate, Stefana, and Mary Jameson tried to pull Lucinda away, but she punched them too. As I walked away from the crowd that had gathered, two Africans students grabbed my braids, threw me to the ground, and started hitting me.

"Stop it! Stop it!" I heard someone shout. "She wasn't fighting!" But they continued kicking me and calling me every name under the sun. *Thump!* One of my attackers fell to the ground. *Thump! Thump!* The other one fell. "Are you all right, Mary?" It was Paulina.

"I'm OK except I can't stand up. I think they would have killed me if you hadn't come."

"What did you do? Why did they beat you?"

"I didn't want to get into Lucinda's fight, but I guess when they heard there was a fight between an African and a half-caste, they assumed it was me."

My head felt as though an angry elephant was stomping on it. I hobbled along with Paulina to the dining room. The other Kifungilo girls were sitting alone in silence at a long table. When Lucinda saw me, she came over and looked at me. I was so intoxicated with pain that I didn't care what she might say or do to me. To my surprise, she held my battered head in her hands and started to cry, "I'm sorry I started that fight. I never thought you would defend me. I'll take care of you from now on."

"Thank you very much," I mumbled, wondering how she'd feel if she knew what really happened.

32

Half-Caste Teacher

Sister Florestina had heard about the fight when we appeared in her office. She looked at us with a stern, brick face. She spoke to us all, but focused mostly on me. "I told Mozher Rufina zhat having your kind here among Africans could only cause *matata*—problems. Now tell me, vhy vere you fighting?" No one answered.

Since she didn't take her eyes away from me, I felt I should say something, "Because they were calling us *hafukasti* and *chotara*."

"Eez zhat a reason to get into a fight your first day here? Vhat should zhey call you? You vill alvays be called such names."

"Not if I can help it!" Lucinda said. "I'll beat up anybody who dares call me anything other than my name."

"Eez zhat how you handle problems in Kifungilo—by fighting? I vill not permit fighting in my school. Next time you fight, you vill get *adhabu*—punishment. Do you understand?"

"Yes, Sister," we all said together.

She went on in her buzzing accent to tell us that the school rules must be copied into our notebooks and obeyed. Then she announced special rules for the five of us. "You are no better zhan Africans no matter how zee nuns at Kifungilo raised you. In fact, you are vorse— you have no family, no home, no tribe. You shall not vear shoes in Mhonda. Your hair must be cut short like Africans. You vill participate in tribal dances. No German valtz here like in Kifungilo. Our school eez for Africans and everyone here vill be treated as African."

My mind was reeling. I was happy about the tribal dances, but I didn't want to have my hair cut. I resented Sister stripping us of whatever dignity we had by reminding us that we were worse than the Africans because of our birth.

She gave us each one uniform, even though Mother Rufina had paid for two. The Africans only have one uniform, she informed us, and so our extras would be given to girls who couldn't afford them. Our beds were in the section with a half-caste teacher, *Mwalimu* Agnesi, who, Sister Florestina emphasized, was brought up by her African mother in a village and knows how to be African. "She's not proud and she's a hard vorker. I guarantee when you leave Mhonda you von't feel superior to Africans. I vill show Mozher Rufina how to raise bastard children."

Maybe I should have waited until there was an opening in Kongei. At least there, Sister Ignatis, the headmistress, was more like Sister Silvestris. She was very strict, but not cruel. Sister Florestina definitely didn't like us. Was it my lot in life to forever be punished for my parents' sins? Was I doomed to more years with another Sister Clotilda? Was getting an education worth this constant humiliation?

Then she singled me out. "You. Come, sit here! I vill cut your hair now. The rest of you can go because your hair is short enough."

It had taken several years to grow my hair long. Because it was the only part of me that people liked and admired, I resisted every attempt to even have it trimmed in Kifungilo. I saw the determined look on Sister's face and watched the menacing black scissors flutter in her hands. She didn't undo my pigtails, but grabbed one and started sawing at it with her blunt, rusted scissors. She pulled and tugged as she tried to cut through the braid, but finally had to undo the braids. Then she chopped away at my once beautiful hair, leaving it strewn about in soft clumps on the cement floor.

"Pick it up," she said, stepping over my curls.

I knelt down and gathered handfuls of my soft curly locks into my skirt. I felt as though my head had also been chopped off. I was light-headed and sadness filled my heart. Sister told me to get out of her office. I left with both hands clutching the large ball of hair in my skirt. After dark I would undo the seam of my pillow and tuck my hair into the sisal filling. I could hug it at night and relive pleasant conversations about my hair to help me hang on to what dignity I had left.

We brought our suitcases to the dormitory. It was three times larger than the one in Kifungilo, but the beds were very different from what we were used to. Two hundred beds were arranged side by side in several rows with only a foot between them. Each bed was covered with a different patterned *khanga*. Some had pillows but none had mattresses.

At Mhonda, all the lay teachers were addressed by the respectful term *Mwalimu* meaning teacher. "Come over here, you spoiled girls," ordered *Mwalimu* Agnesi, the half-caste woman in charge of us. She looked at us from a raised platform on the opposite side of the dorm. "Put down your suitcases and set up your beds." She pointed to a wall that had several wooden planks, each about a foot wide and six feet long, leaning on it. I didn't see any beds. "What are you waiting for? Take two planks and put them at your assigned places." I still didn't see any beds. "Get two iron rods and make your bed like this." She removed a *khanga* from one of the beds behind her and to my horror I saw how the beds were constructed. Two U-shaped metal rods, about three feet high faced each other, forming the head and the foot of the bed. The upside-down U-shaped rods stood, not too steadily, on their bent "feet." On top of them lay two unpolished and warped wooden planks. That was the bed.

We got our rods and planks and set our beds in a line against the wall near *Mwalimu* Agnesi's proper bed, which was separated from ours by a curtain made of *khangas*. Hers was just like the beds in the infirmary with mattresses, pillows, blankets, and mosquito nets. A matching set of small wooden chests stood on either side of her bed, and a kerosene lamp hung from a rusted nail at the center of the wall above a wooden headboard. Thank God it was warm in Mhonda, I thought as I folded my blanket to use as a mattress and laid it directly on top of the wooden planks. I put one sheet over the blanket and the other I used as a cover.

I found myself missing Kifungilo and wondered how I would sleep on a bed made of two planks of wood. Wouldn't it be better to sleep on the floor? I looked down at the uneven cement floor and noticed that the wooden windows were only a few inches from the ground, so a snake or anything could crawl in at night.

During the entire bed construction exercise, *Mwalimu* Agnesi kept looking at us critically and making comments to the African students around her about the spoiled Kifungilo half-castes. I put my suitcase under my new bed, dreading nightfall. To distract myself, I decided to walk around the school. Although school wouldn't start until the next day, many students were reading and studying. Some sat in groups behind the kitchen, braiding their hair, and still others were gathered in little groups singing, chatting, and laughing. They had changed into old dresses or blouses over which they wrapped *khangas*. Most had no shoes, though some wore flimsy flip-flops that made loud, flapping noises when they walked. I went to sit with the hair braiders hoping one of them would corn row what was left of my hair, but when I approached them, they got up and left.

Back in the dorm I saw the other Kifungilo girls sitting on their beds quietly arranging and re-arranging the contents of their suitcases. "What do you think of my haircut?" I asked. They were so engrossed in their own worlds, fearing the unknown life ahead of them, that they scrutinized me as though I were a stranger.

Stefana finally said something. "I don't think I can take a whole year of this place. It seems they've decided—Sister Florestina, *Mwalimu* Agnesi, and the students—to be as mean as possible to us."

"Maybe they're trying to help us fit in better?" I offered. "I'll do anything to fit in, but I didn't think I'd have to lose my hair."

"You and your hair!" Kate looked at me shaking her head.

I remembered how Elizabeth admired my hair and how Zami once told me that if it weren't for my half-decent hair, I'd look like an overweight chimpanzee. "My hair was the only good thing about me. Now I feel one hundred percent ugly."

"You could never be as ugly as some of the Africans here," Lucinda butted in. "Do you see how they pierce their noses and wear those cheap, rusty nose-rings that make their noses even blacker?"

"Lucinda," Kate said, "stop making fun of the Africans and calling them ugly. You'll get us into more fights and expelled from school."

Expelled? Never, I thought, but I could see the others were already savoring the idea.

"I'm telling you again, no one's going to act like they're better than me. They're jealous of us, no matter what they say."

"How could anyone be jealous of someone without a home, parents, or tribe?" I asked.

"Despite their families and tribes, they are backward and live in miserable mud huts. They can never become *wazungu,* but they hate us because they think we can."

What Lucinda was saying I'd heard before, and sometimes it seemed to be true, especially in the Usambaras. Yet I felt the need to identify with a race. It was clear to me that I was more African than European, if for no other reason than that Europeans treated me like they treated Africans—with outright contempt or by patronizing us. But I often met friendly Africans who made me forget that I was half-caste. Lucinda was one of the many half-castes from Kifungilo who really believed that we were better than the Africans, and she wasn't going to let anyone tell her otherwise.

"Why are you sitting in here?" *Mwalimu* Agnesi asked. "It's lunch time. Go get lunch and tell me how it compares to your fine Kifungilo food." I couldn't understand why she, a half-caste, could be so harsh and make fun of us. Tall and slender, she was yellow-skinned with brown nappy hair rolled in a bun at the back of her neck. She wore a full-skirted yellow dress with a heart-shaped black leather belt that pressed into her narrow waistline and enlarged her small breasts. She would have been very pretty except that her dark soul pierced through her tiny black eyes and made her face look chiseled out of stone.

Lunch was the driest *ugali* I'd ever encountered. When *ugali* is well cooked, it is smooth, but the corn flour stuff we were served from a big aluminum bowl sat in large dry clumps surrounded by half-cooked kidney beans in watery gravy. It had no taste. The other Kifungilo girls didn't eat, but I closed my eyes and swallowed the food.

After lunch we went to look at the four large classrooms across from the dormitory. Each had twenty double desks arranged in four rows. There was a large blackboard in front and several storage cabinets along the side walls. Maps of Tanganyika, Africa, and the world covered one wall, and posters announcing the subjects to be taught hung on another wall. I sat in a desk and, forgetting about my guaranteed hard life in Mhonda, imagined absorbing the vast knowledge of the world that my teachers would impart.

"Mary, I've been looking for you all morning." It was Paulina who wanted to share the food she brought from home. "We have to eat it today, otherwise it will spoil. Come on."

I happily followed my friend to the small, dark kitchen. The only light came from the glow of orange coals underneath two petrol barrels filled to the brim with the simmering evening meal. She grabbed a small bundle tied in *khangas* and we sat behind the building. She offered me rice pilau, *sambusa*, fried plantains, and *mandazi*, deep fried, sugary pastries. We ate with our fingers making appreciative sounds, but otherwise didn't speak until we'd polished off everything. I had never eaten such spicy and tasty food.

"You must be feeling better. Listen, my friend, I heard that *Mwalimu* Agnesi makes the life of half-castes who come to Mhonda so miserable that they don't return. No matter what she does to you, remember she's the bad one. Sister Florestina depends on *Mwalimu* Agnesi to maintain strict discipline and gives her a free hand to punish us," she continued. "I just met a girl from the Bondei tribe of Tanga. She said that students form cliques according to their tribe, wealth, or parents. Some girls are daughters of chiefs, ministers, or government employees. Since you and I are from Lushoto and she's from Tanga, we'll hang out together and take care of each another. We'll be like your 'Fat Mary' here."

I realized that Paulina had genuinely listened to me when I told her about myself. "Paulina, you're so good to me. Will I ever be able to do anything for you? You see that I don't even fit in with the Kifungilo girls. In the orphanage, Sister Silvestris used to tell me that I thought too much, and no one had all the answers for my questions. There are so many things about my life that I don't understand. I don't know what's wrong with me. Why would *Mwalimu* Agnesi and Sister Florestina single me out when they don't even know me?"

"Something about you makes them uncomfortable. Maybe it's because you're the prettiest of the half-castes."

"That's not true! You don't have to invent things to make me feel good."

"I already admired your hair and even now I love the way your short ringlets shine with so many colors in the sun. You also have the largest and darkest eyes I've ever seen."

"I was told I was fat, stupid, and ugly, but I remember an old Sambaa woman who said I was pretty. I didn't believe her then, and I don't believe you now, but it means a lot to me that you're not ashamed to be my friend."

"I don't have any relatives here and not a single member of my tribe either. We'll be each other's family."

If only Paulina knew what those words meant to me.

33

The Bed

Paulina and I walked around the school compound checking out what would be our home for the next ten months. Mhonda was surrounded by the smaller peaks of the Uluguru mountain range whose fertile slopes boasted colorful patches of cultivated corn, sugarcane, vegetable terraces, and cashew trees. Beyond the church, the land was settled in clusters of dense villages with the dome of a white mosque at the center. But Mhonda was closed in. I couldn't see for miles and miles across valleys and to the horizon like I could in Kifungilo. Except for the withering flower beds filled with stunted marigolds in front of the church, convent, and the approach to the office, there was no effort to beautify the school grounds.

We could smell the toilets behind the dormitory and the washing shed. They were housed in a long, narrow cement building with four red corrugated iron sheets that served as doors. Without a way to lock these doors from the outside, they banged all day long against the cement walls in the wind when no one was holding them shut. Inside, instead of a simple hole in the ground, a narrow cement ditch ran along the bottom connecting all four chambers. Outside, a large water pipe cut through the walls of the toilet shed releasing a steady stream of water which carried the deposits from the first toilet to the last, and then into a cesspool down the hill. That explained the lines in front of the first and second toilets, even though the third and fourth stood empty. I took the free fourth toilet and Paulina took the third. Most African toilets were simply a hole in the ground surrounded by tall dried reeds or rudimentary mud walls for privacy. I preferred them to this piece of engineering. At least everybody's refuse didn't parade sluggishly under your buttocks in little piles as you did your business.

We walked back to the dormitory and sat on Paulina's bed in the lower section of the dorm. Apart from the church and the classroom, we were told that the dormitory was the only other room we could use if we wanted to be inside. Paulina's bed was covered with a beautiful pink and green *khanga*. Her suitcase and two large baskets took up all the space under her bed.

I stretched out on her wobbly bed. "I'm sure these planks will spread apart at night and leave us suspended on our suitcases."

"I'm more worried about the *kunguni* that infest the planks. Did you see bugs in the wood when you made your bed?" I sat up. Paulina continued, "Every Saturday, we have to take the planks outside, scrub them with Dettol, and set them in the sun to kill the bugs."

"I was prepared for almost everything in Mhonda except for the beds."

"Many Africans sleep on mats on dirt floors in their huts. As awful as these beds are to you, they're an improvement for many students."

"I took a lot for granted in Kifungilo. Do you think that the children from Kifungilo who went home with their African mothers for holidays slept on mats on the ground?"

"Not if their *wazungu* men lived with them, which is seldom the case. The *wazungu* are very strange people, I tell you. They despise us, but they have African mistresses in the villages and love to sleep with black women, especially young girls."

"I wonder what village my mother was from and why she sent me to the orphanage. No matter how poor life in her village was, I would have been happy knowing that she loved me enough to keep me with her. At least I'd belong to a family and could proudly name my tribe and speak a tribal language instead of the mix of languages I learned in Kifungilo." I stretched out on the bed again, forgetting about the bugs we would be sleeping with that night. "Besides being poor, I have the heartache of being abandoned by those who should have loved me. Although I'll always be grateful for what the orphanage did for me, I can't help the way I feel."

"Why not concentrate on enjoying what you do have rather than longing for what you don't have?"

"That's easy to say, Paulina. But I have to believe that I'm okay no matter what. Like I told you, in order to survive in Kifungilo, I learned to love myself even though I was told over and over that I was fat and ugly and a child of sin. I don't understand how those nuns could do so much for us when they thought so little of us."

"It's the Christian thing to do. They come to Africa to convert us because they believe we'll go to hell unless they try to send as many Black souls as possible to heaven. What they do, they do for God and for themselves. They need countries like Africa to redeem themselves."

"Where did you hear that?"

"Baba dislikes missionaries, and he hates hypocritical Africans. Most Africans, especially educated ones, don't like missionaries, but in their presence they act like they revere them. Baba didn't want me to go to a mission school, but government schools are only for boys. It was the missionaries who started the middle and secondary schools in the country to educate girls."

"I'm glad your father let you come to Mhonda."

"His parting words to me were, 'Don't let the nuns brainwash you with their superstitions and force you to give up your culture and beliefs to attain everlasting life or whatever it is they teach you. You have only one life, and it's this one. I'm sending you to a mission school to help you prepare for it. Work hard and make your family and the Wasambaa proud.'"

"I've often wondered about the everlasting life we're supposed to have after we die. I'd rather be happy in this life than spend my time earning merits for an afterlife."

Paulina lowered her voice. "Remember that this is a Catholic School and we could be expelled if the nuns heard our conversation. Pretend you agree with everything they teach. That's what most thinking Africans do. Then the missionaries can go back home and boast about the number of heathens they've converted. Imagine when they arrive in heaven and see how many African souls prefer to be with their ancestors rather than with the Christian God."

"Speaking of God, we'd better go to church for Benediction. I don't want to get into any more trouble my first day of school."

Just like Mass, Benediction was over so much faster than I was used to. I figured it must be because the priest wasn't between eighty and death like our Father Gattang. He was middle-aged with a full head of dark brown hair, and he was in a hurry. I wondered what *wazungu* priests in the middle of Africa did besides their religious duties. They could live in Africa as long as they had what they considered basic: a house five times the size of an African hut with several rooms, indoor plumbing and running water, beds with mattresses, sheets and pillows, a stove, furniture for the sitting room, and a servant to run errands, another to clean, another to cook, one to do the wash, and several servants to grow and harvest their food. But most of all, they needed Africans who believed they needed the *wazungu*. Yet it must be hard to be a missionary, I thought, even though Paulina's Baba said that we're doing them a favor. They must miss their families, their land, and their strange customs and dances. Priests and Brothers must be the loneliest of all, because they usually don't have any of their kind living within a hundred miles of their scattered mission posts. That must explain why many of them are alcoholics, grossly overweight, and generally somber and disagreeable.

Supper was the same *ugali* and beans as lunch. I sat with the Kifungilo girls at our assigned table. I wished we were not lumped together as if our identity was determined solely by the color of our skin. I made up my mind to move around once I got accustomed to the place and found out which rules were enforced and which ones weren't.

There was no outdoor lighting, so we walked in the dark to the dorm to fetch our toiletries and wash up before going to bed. How few students cleaned up in the evening surprised me. In contrast to the morning, when we had to squeeze our hands through the crowd to reach the water tap, we had the entire shed to ourselves. When we got to the dorm, it was buzzing with activity. Students banged their planks to get to their suitcases and bundles from under the beds and took out their uniforms, hair oil, and hair picks, and whatever else they needed for the morning. Pairs of girls braided one another's hair, and groups of three or four sang softly in various languages as they huddled on beds in different areas of the room. *Mwalimu* Agnesi sat on her bed behind the *khanga* screen looking at her watch every few minutes.

Shreeeeekk! She blew a silver police whistle. Silence fell in the dorm and everyone scurried back to her own bed. Before I could get into my nightgown, *Mwalimu* Agnesi had turned off the one light bulb hanging from the ceiling and began talking to us in the dark.

"I know there are many new students this year, and if you haven't come to greet me yet, see me right after Mass in the morning. I'm in charge of everything that goes on outside the classroom—from your chores to your appearance. I say things only once. The most important rule is that I do not tolerate breaking the rules." She stopped for a second to let that sink in. "If you're caught talking after the lights have been turned off, if you're caught stealing, not doing your assigned chores promptly and correctly, wearing any cheap accessory that isn't part of your uniform, not going to church, being tardy, or saying anything bad about the Sisters, teachers, or Mhonda in general, you'll be punished. The most severe punishment is expulsion from school. I am ruthless in matters of discipline. There's a reason Mhonda has the reputation of producing the most proper young women in the country. No student will interfere with that hard-earned distinction. Do you hear?" No answer. "I said did you hear me?"

"*Ndiyo, Mwalimu*," we all answered.

"Tomorrow is the first day of classes. After Mass, Mother Majellis, the mother superior at the convent, will come to the main courtyard in front of the office to address you. Sister Florestina, your headmistress, will assign your teachers and classrooms, and I shall assign your chores for the month. We have no servants in Mhonda to grow and prepare our food, clean for us or do our laundry like the half-castes in Kifungilo have. We do everything ourselves and we do it well. Is that understood?"

"*Ndiyo, Mwalimu*," we hastily answered. She went to her bed in the corner and disappeared under the mosquito net without saying good night.

Whoa! My firm conviction that education was worth any price was shaken to its core. I lay still on my hard planks, hoping they wouldn't separate. I thought about my bed in Kifungilo and pretended I was hugging the new soft down pillows that the retired nuns had made for us a few months ago. I thought about Sister Silvestris saying good night, praying, and blessing us with holy water before she locked us in. I wondered if punishments from *Mwalimu* Agnesi would be as dreaded as our regular childhood beatings by Sister.

I found myself thinking about Elizabeth, but I quickly decided not to dwell on her. I'd left my childhood two hundred miles away and school was where I wanted to be. Our choices in life would most surely send us in different directions. I prayed for Elizabeth and for myself. I prayed that our growth would be as strong and determined as the seeds of coconut palms, boldly reaching skyward toward the sun, diligently boring deeper into the earth to secure a firm foundation for the beautiful, durable, fruit-bearing trees they would become.

For me, Mhonda was the place to continue the growth of the still young but strong roots of my tree planted in Kifungilo. This was my life now, the life I'd prayed for, the life that would provide me with an education and would open doors. I wanted this life very much. I told my wavering spirit to bear with me because, just like the coconut palm, I would sway and bend and bruise, but I would survive. I would have to become the tree in the African saying: "The tree that bends with the wind does not break."

I slept all night without incident. I couldn't fall off the planks if I tried. There was no room between the beds for them to slide, and they couldn't separate since I'd wrapped them together tightly with my blanket. My guardian angel must have been hovering above me because I had pleasant dreams of Elizabeth and Rosa and Sister Theonesta.

34

Mary Two

 Mother Majellis was a short, plump, pleasant-looking nun who reminded me a little of Sister Theonesta. She smiled a lot, nodding and turning her head back and forth as she addressed a crowd of attentive girls in orange uniforms and warmly welcomed us to Mhonda. Next, Sister Florestina assigned forty students to each class and announced that the half-caste girls would be tested to see if we were ready for Standard Seven. *Mwalimu* Agnesi stepped forward to dish out the chores. Five others and I were to clean the toilets. I couldn't believe my bad luck.

Even though our test was in Swahili, a language we Kifungilo girls spoke badly, we all passed. The five of us were put in the same class and assigned seats together. That bothered me. Did Sister Florestina want to know where we were and what we were doing at all times? Or did she want to rub in how different we looked and how we didn't fit in? One by one, our teachers introduced themselves and their subjects. We had three nuns who taught English, Religion, and Domestic Science, a male teacher who taught Math and Current Affairs, and two lay female teachers who taught history and geography.

Each day we had to greet the African teachers with a greeting of respect reserved for elders, "*Shikamoo Mwalimu*," and "Good Morning, Sister" for the nuns. The first week we had to stand up and introduce ourselves by name and tribe.

I noticed that everyone had a surname and some girls had two or three. For the first time I heard Kate say "My name is Kate Lychnaris." Had she found her father and not told us? Mary Jameson always had a last name, but Stefana, Lucinda, and I just said our first names. On the fourth morning, Sister Florestina walked into the classroom. Whenever she did this, we had to stop whatever we were doing, stand up and greet her. We then continued with our self-introductions: *Jina langu* Nanadi Pauli. *Jina langu* Lydia Mwema Simbali. *Jina langu* Fatuma Ali, and so on.

Then it was my turn. "*Jina langu* Mary."

Sister Florestina asked, "Vhat eez your zurname?"

I hesitated for a moment, wondering what to say. Then I answered, "I don't have one."

"Everybody has a last name. Vhat eez yours?"

"I don't know it."

"Vhy don't you know it."

"I don't know why I don't know it."

"Vhat do you mean? You must know vhy you don't have a zurname."

"I think it's because I don't know my parents."

"And vhy don't you know your parents?"

"Because I was brought up in an orphanage."

"Kifungilo is a home for children whose parents didn't vant them. Vhy didn't your parents vant you?"

"I don't know."

"Vell, you do know. It's because you are a child of zin. You are born from a European and an African zinner."

Sister then proceeded to lecture the class about children born out of wedlock. She told us that when we commit the big sin, we have to live with many bad consequences. All men are evil when it comes to the big sin, she emphasized, then went on to say that for Africans born in sin, life would be easier because they all have the same skin color. But, she said pointing to the Kifungilo girls, it's obvious that their parents have sinned.

"Look at her," she said, signaling me out as a concrete example of how much they should fear men and the big sin.

Because I didn't have a last name, she continued, I wouldn't be able to sit for the Territorial Exams that were given at the end of the Eight Grade. The government wouldn't accept my examination, I would automatically fail, and this would give Mhonda a bad name. "I vill have to send you back to Kifungilo."

"Please don't send me back. I want to stay in school."

At that moment something in her demeanor changed as she realized I could be a useful teaching tool. "I'll see vhat can be done for zhis miserable girl."

"Thank you, Sister"

She listened while the rest of the students introduced themselves, but said nothing when Lucinda and Stefana introduced themselves with only their first names. Then Mary Jameson introduced herself.

"Ahh, zhis Mary eez also a child of zin," Sister Florestina interrupted. "From now on, your name vill be Mary One," she said to Mary Jameson, and to me she said, "You vill be Mary Two."

"Thank you, Sister," I said. I was confused. First she called me a child of sin because I didn't have a surname, and then she said that Mary Jameson, who had a last name, was also a child of sin. Are all half-castes children of sin whether they have loving parents or not?

When she left, no one moved. Silence descended upon us like a heavy blanket. Its weight crushed everyone in the classroom. *Mwalimu* Haule, the math teacher, left the room without dismissing class. He leaned against the wall near the door, holding his head and swaying. He was a good man and I hoped he wasn't ill. The Kifungilo girls were weeping softly. The other students sat stone-faced. They couldn't look at us. The dull thump thump thump of Lucinda banging her head on the desk kept pace with the beating of my heart. I watched her body distort with anger and pain. I was grateful that she could weep because I was numb.

35

First Bra

"I heard what happened in class today," Paulina said to me at lunch. We met after our usual inedible *ugali* and bean meal and walked together to our next class. "Baba was right about these German nuns. They're frustrated, escaped Nazis who want to impose their beliefs on Africa." I didn't know what she was talking about. "The Nazis are the Germans who lost the Second World War to the British and other Europeans."

"How do you know this?"

"My father discusses what he reads in the paper with us at dinner. He explains what we don't understand and then asks us questions."

"Why were *wazungu* fighting other *wazungu?*"

"Maybe the German tribe wanted to conquer the other *wazungu* tribes. Baba told me that the Nazis were trying to create a pure race of people and they killed everyone who wasn't like them. Think about it, Mary. Why does the sight of a half-caste like you drive Sister Florestina crazy enough to humiliate and crush you in front of everyone? A girl in your class told me that the African students felt terrible for you. How could you just sit there?"

"Kifungilo prepared me for this kind of pain. I told you that I was used to suffering."

"And how do you feel about having 'Two' as a last name?"

"What's a name? It won't change me, but one day I'm going to make up a name for myself. I don't have parents, so no one will care what name I use. Having 'Two' as a last name is just one more thing I have to accept to get an education. Although when Sister

Florestina used me as an example of sin, I felt the black mark I've been carrying in my heart since I was born is now stamped on my forehead."

"That woman is evil."

"At least she's not a teacher. I'd fail her classes and then be sent back to Kifungilo, which is already looking like heaven compared to Mhonda!"

"I told you so, didn't I?"

To my surprise I was good in most subjects especially in math. *Mwalimu* Haule started calling me *Mwamba*—the rock, usually used for brainy people. I felt warm inside every time he called me that. After a few weeks he stopped calling me Mary altogether. Several students in my class had trouble with math, so I helped them with their homework in exchange for a dab or two of the sweet-smelling perfumes and powders that they bought from the market in Turiani. Although I wrote Mary Two on top of my notebooks, assignments, and tests, neither *Mwalimu* Haule nor the other students ever called me by that name. They simply called me Mary or *Mwamba*.

Almost all students spoke at least two languages—their tribal language, which they used outside of class, and Kiswahili in which subjects were taught. I felt left out not only because I didn't understand their tribal languages, but also because I didn't have a language of my own to show off. However, I really impressed the Africans when I recited bits and pieces of Latin prayers and songs, and spoke our Kifungilo mix of German, English, Kisambaa, and Latin. The only problem was that I didn't always understand what I was saying and I got mixed up when I translated my nonsense. I had to give up that idea, so I decided to learn proper Kiswahili instead and hoped that someday I could speak at least one language correctly.

I did enjoy learning songs in Kiluguru for feast days and I enjoyed dancing the *mnenguo,* a Luguru dance. We celebrated birthdays and feast days by performing and singing for Mother Superior and the headmistress, and then dancing in the courtyard until bedtime. I was the only Kifungilo girl who learned the tribal dances.

One day, after we'd been in Mhonda about six months, we were dancing in a circle and taking turns showing off and challenging each other, when Sister Florestina came to watch. I hadn't seen her arrive when I entered the circle, so as usual I danced my heart out. Everyone was clapping and laughing when all of a sudden I was yanked out of the circle by my arm.

"*Schwarzer Teufel!*" Sister's face was red and contorted. "Isn't it enough ve accepted you bastards in our school? Do you have to show us zhe filthy minds of your parents?"

"What did I do? I was just dancing like the others."

"Zee ozher girls do not shake and touch zheir breasts, laughing and giving zinful suggestions. Go to the infirmary at once!"

"But I'm not sick."

"Don't talk back to me, evil girl!"

I entered the infirmary and stood against the far wall. She rushed in and locked the door behind her. Was she going to beat me? At this stage in my life I was no longer afraid of any beating, no matter how bad. She opened a metal cupboard and took out a four-inch bandage roll. "Come here, you vicked zinner! Remove your dress!" I hesitantly removed my dress while keeping an eye on her. "And your petticoat too!" I removed my petticoat and covered my sprouting breasts with my hands. "Put your hands down!" I put my hands at my sides. "Turn around!" I turned my back to her. She anchored the edge of the bandage under one arm, stretched it across my breasts and around my back. "Breasts are temptation to men to commit zin," she lectured, wrapping my breasts tightly with the bandage. "Vhy aren't you vearing a bra?"

"I don't have a bra. I'll ask Sister Silvestris to sew one for me when I go to Kifungilo for holidays."

"It's four months before you go to Sister Silvestris. You must wrap your breasts every morning, do you hear?" She fastened the end of the bandage in the back with a huge safety pin.

"Yes, Sister."

"If you don't, I'll send you back to Kifungilo."

"Yes, Sister." I left the infirmary and ran to the toilets. The bandage was very tight. I tried to remove the safety pin on the back, but couldn't reach it. I went to look for Paulina who was still dancing.

"Paulina," I said. "Please come with me."

"What's the matter?"

I pulled her from the group. "Come with me to the toilets. I need your help." When we got there, I pushed the reluctant Paulina inside the stall and removed my dress and petticoat.

"*Mungu wangu wee!* How did you get hurt?"

"Please remove the safety pin. The bandage is so tight I can't breathe." Paulina tugged at the pin and removed it.

"Are you hurt, Mary? What are you hiding?" She helped me unwrap the long bandage. I turned around and looked her straight in the eye.

"Please don't ever tell anyone about this. I'm not hurt. Sister Florestina pulled me from the dance, took me to the infirmary, and bandaged my chest because she said my breasts were sinful."

"What?"

"Sister said that if I don't wear this bandage every day to prevent my breasts from dancing when I do, she'll send me back to Kifungilo."

"But your breasts are hardly larger than gooseberries. My breasts are twice as large as yours, and she didn't say anything to me when I danced."

"My gooseberries must seem sweeter than yours and maybe she was tempted to pick them. Just imagine how much more sinful they'll be when they become like mangos."

"How can you joke about this?"

"I can't cry, so I have to laugh."

"Are you going to wear that silly bandage every day?"

"If I want an education, I have to."

"I'm going to find you a proper bra."

Paulina couldn't find me a bra. Most girls had only one or two, and they weren't willing to part with them. Every morning I locked myself in the toilet and wrapped my chest with the bandage, pinning it under my left arm where it was easier to reach. After a while I got used to it, except it took longer to get dressed and I couldn't change in the dorm like everyone else.

36

Delirium

 Toward the end of the school year, Standard Eight students started preparing for the Territorial Exams they would take in the beginning of December. Because they would be tested on everything they had learned from Standards Five to Eight, they remained in the classrooms studying until ten o'clock at night, while we younger students went to bed at eight. They came into the dorm whispering and yawning as they looked for their beds by the glow of their flashlights. I had adapted to my bed and usually fell asleep as soon as I hit my pillow, but on these nights bodies silently moving around the room often awakened me. I listened to the students and to the many sounds of a tropical night.

I heard the cries of crickets and frogs and the quiet maneuvering of snakes and other creepy, crawly things. On some nights, I heard the wailing of Lugurus at a wake or the *thum thum* of their drums as they danced funeral rituals. The unfamiliar songs and cries of sorrow, which might have intrigued me in daylight, were haunting in the dark. My mind magnified the distant sounds until I felt I was in the village participating in the rituals. Each night they became louder and stronger, sadder and more desperate. In my imagination, students around me turned into ghosts, left their beds and moved toward me, but when I opened my eyes, they retreated and slowly dissolved into the darkness.

For several weeks I had been staying in bed and not going to Mass because my head and stomach ached and my whole body was sore, but I always went to class. At night I felt as though my muscles were separating from my bones.

162

The Luguru funeral chants and ghostly images continued haunting me night after night. Then one night, when there was a wake in a village near school, the mournful chanting voices came right into the dorm, and I thought I saw the ghost of a dead woman poke out of her funeral shroud. Her fingers grabbed me by the throat. I woke up trembling and hollering, "No, no, I'm not ready. I want to finish school." I tried to sit up in bed, but the planks had separated and I was wedged between them with my buttocks on top of my suitcase.

"What is going on?" *Mwalimu* Agnesi was at my bed. "You've woken up the entire dorm."

"She wakes us up every night," a student down the row said. "She talks to herself and her bed rattles."

"Come with me." *Mwalimu* Agnesi tried to drag me to her corner of the dorm. My body was heavy and didn't budge. "See this?" She held up a leather whip in front of my face. "You will sleep on the floor beside me and if I even hear you breathe, I'll use it. Do you hear?"

"*Ndiyo, Mwalimu.*" It took all the strength I had to stand. I took inch-sized steps to get to her bed where I stretched out on the cold floor and fell asleep.

At breakfast I was the subject of conversation. I wanted to find Paulina, but we were in different classrooms and our assigned chores took us to opposite corners of the school.

Just before supper, Sister Florestina called me to her office. *Mwalimu* Agnesi was also there. "*Mwalimu* told me zhat you disrupted zee entire dormitory last night and you make diabolical noises vhen you sleep. Is it true?"

"I think so, but I've never heard myself."

"What do you mean you think so?" *Mwalimu* asked. "We all heard you screaming. You scared everybody with your devil sounds."

I apologized, but that wasn't enough for Sister. Her deep-set eyes narrowed and pierced through me like razor blades as she reminded me that the students needed their sleep in order to prepare for exams. As my punishment she told me to hoe the cornfield every day after lunch for a week. If it happened again, I would be expelled. "From zee moment I saw you, I knew you vould bring *matata* to Mhonda."

The next day during study hour, while the other students were in their classrooms, I was hoeing the hard, dry soil barefoot in the hot sun when Paulina appeared.

"Mary, why are you hoeing at this time of day? You shouldn't work in this midday heat."

"It's my punishment for waking up the students at night. Were you looking for me?"

"I am always looking for you, or I know when you're in trouble. I heard that you had a terrible nightmare. Students say you're possessed by evil spirits."

"I've been dreaming of death, and ghosts haunt me when there's a funeral in the village. I get so frightened. I try to run from them and cry for help."

"You were having a scary nightmare. Come out of the sun. You'll get a headache!"

"Get one? My head hurts so much I can barely see you."

She took my hand but dropped it. "Mary, your skin is burning. You're sick!" She touched my forehead. "*Mungu wangu wee*, you're boiling!"

"It's because of the midday sun. I'll cool off when I'm done. I'll be fine." Paulina took off and I began hoeing again. She came back in a few minutes with a wet rag, grabbed the hoe from me, threw it on the ground, and told me to lie down. The cold rag against my skin felt wonderful.

"I'm taking you to *Mwalimu* Agnesi. No matter what she says, I know you're sick. I don't want to scare you, but I think you have malaria. I've seen people with your symptoms die."

"Did they wake the whole dormitory up at night too?" I tried to laugh.

"Mary, this is no joke. If you don't get medicine soon, you'll die."

It had been a long time since I'd wished for death, but I started imagining a life without pain and said, "Death will end the pain."

Just then *Mwalimu* Haule, who was on duty that afternoon while the Sisters and teachers took their siesta, appeared. "Why aren't you two in study hour?"

"*Mwalimu*, please help. Sister Florestina made her hoe the field as punishment for having a nightmare. I think she has malaria."

Mwalimu touched my forehead, looked into my bloodshot eyes, and mumbled something to himself. Then he told Paulina, "Take her to bed. I'll tell *Mwalimu* Agnesi and Sister Florestina." Paulina and I went to the dorm. Without saying a word, she undid my breast bandage and helped me get into my nightdress. I fell asleep instantly.

When I woke up, it was about midnight. The bed planks were hitting the metal rods, my teeth were chattering, and I was drenched with perspiration. My blanket and sheet were soaking wet. I must have cried out and woken the dorm again. I was shivering and jerking so much that I was being held down on the bed by the other Kifungilo girls and Paulina.

"She's going to die!" Mary Jameson sobbed.

"Shut up, you stupid girl!" *Mwalimu* Agnesi yelled at her. "Get out of my way."

"If she dies, I'll tell everybody that you and Sister Florestina killed her." Paulina was crying. "You must have known she was sick. Haven't you seen anyone with malaria before?"

At that moment Sister Florestina walked into the dorm with a flashlight and Paulina turned on her. "How could you make her work in the hot sun just because she had a nightmare? If anything happens to her, I will personally go to Kifungilo and tell the Sisters that you killed her." Sister Florestina slapped her across the face, but Paulina didn't stop. "If she dies, it will be your fault. She wants to die because of you." I heard Paulina's words like echoes from the distant Usambara Mountains. Although I could hear, I couldn't see her or anyone, only distorted shadows.

"Get out of the way!" *Mwalimu* Agnesi commanded again. The Kifungilo girls moved back but Paulina didn't budge.

"She must go to the infirmary. She's very sick," Sister said.

Mwalimu Agnesi and Sister Florestina leaned over the bed to lift me, but Paulina screamed at them, "Don't touch her! We'll carry her."

Sister backed off. Paulina, Mary Jameson, and Stefana carried me, and Sister Florestina and *Mwalimu* Agnesi walked behind them. The tiny procession slowly wove through the aisles of the now fully awakened dorm and out toward the infirmary on a path lit only by the moon.

Sister took some rubbing alcohol from the same cupboard from which she'd taken the bandage for my breasts, poured several capfuls in a basin of cold water, put in cloths and had the girls rub me down with the cool cloths to lower my fever. She gave me a bitter yellow quinine tablet and some aspirin with a cup of water. Paulina held the cup to my mouth because I was shaking violently. The cool alcohol cloths lowered my fever and calmed me down enough to keep a thermometer in my mouth. Sister took it out after a few minutes and looked at it.

"What's her temperature?" Paulina demanded.

"One hundred and four," reported Sister and left.

I slept throughout the night and most of the following day. I was awakened by an excruciating headache and felt I had to vomit. My body was boiling again. I lay there with my eyes shut, not daring to open them or move my head. Any motion intensified the pain to the point that it felt like my brains were seeping out of my skull.

I didn't know how long she'd been there, but when I opened my eyes, I saw Mother Majellis sitting by my bed, her trademark smile reassuring me that there were good nuns on earth. She was busy cooling my naked body with wet washcloths, replacing the ones from my upper body just as soon as she had covered my lower body.

"Good morning, Mother," I struggled to say.

"Shhhhhhh!" was all she said. My headache quieted down a little and my fever gradually lessened.

"Mary, you have one of the worst cases of malaria we have ever had to treat. If you don't get better by tomorrow, we'll take you to the hospital in Morogoro, though I'm sure you'd get better care here." The word hospital evoked all sorts of memories for me. I thought about the mother who mourned the death of her son in the African hospital when I had typhoid. I remembered how I envied the dead boy because he had relatives who mourned him.

"I shall take care of you until you're well," Mother said, squeezing my hand. She seemed determined to keep me out of the hospital. "You have a very good friend in Paulina. She told me that Sister Florestina hates you. Of course that's not true."

"It is true, Mother."

"Sister Florestina is very strict. We need her to discipline the girls. Many boarding schools have sanitary issues, delinquency, vandalism, burglary, and even pregnancies. Since Sister Florestina has been here, we've been almost a perfect school. I get good reports about your work from your teachers, and Mr. Haule says you're the best math student he's ever had. Next year when you take your exams you shall make Mhonda, and especially the Sisters of Kifungilo, very proud. You must get well soon. It's only a few weeks before holidays, and we can't send you home until you're completely well." The thought of not going to Kifungilo for holidays seemed like the greatest punishment of all. "I shall pray for you every day."

"Thank you, Mother. I shall pray for you too."

Mother pensively held both my hands, looked into my eyes, and said, "No student has ever said she would pray for me. We all need prayers. I'll be especially grateful for your prayers because I know God listens to you."

"Not as much as he should." She must have thought that was funny, because she left the room laughing.

While I was recuperating, the Kifungilo girls and Paulina came to visit me in the infirmary every day, but Sister Florestina never came. One day when I was feeling much better, Mary Jameson came. "And how eez my Fett Mary?" imitating Sister Silvestris.

"Fat Mary is missing her Sister Silvestris," I replied.

"I know, so I have something special for you," Mary Jameson said as she leaned over and stroked my hair. "Can you sit up?"

"I think I can."

She took a jar of Vaseline brilliantine hairdressing from her pocket, dabbed a tiny amount in the palms of her hand, and spread it into my hair. "Your hair is as tangled and matted as Julitta's hair. Remember her?"

"Who can forget Julitta and how she used to beat us up when we fought. Poor Julitta. She suffered a lot because of bedwetting. Maybe that's why she was angry all the time."

"Mary, this is the most you've said since you got sick. You look so much better today and your skin isn't hot."

"I'm better because Mother Majellis herself cared for me with a lot of love. Why are some nuns so good and others so bad—angel nuns and devil nuns. Sister Florestina and Sister Clotilda must have gone to the same training school for devil nuns."

"They all go to the same Motherhouse to become nuns," my friend laughed. "Mary, I came to tell you that we've decided not to return next year. We want to go to Kongei instead. What about you?"

"I like Paulina and my teachers, and I'm learning a lot."

"Is school the only thing that matters in your life? You almost died! You must have been sick for a long time, because no one gets deathly ill from malaria suddenly. Why didn't you tell anyone?"

"I tried to tell Sister Florestina that I wasn't feeling well, but she accused me of wanting to get out of my chores."

"The way she treats you makes me want to cry, but you act like you're not afraid of her."

"I'm not. What can she do to me besides torment me for being born? If I do well in school, obey the rules, and do my chores, she can't expel me. That's the one thing I'm afraid of."

Mary Jameson was quiet for a moment and she looked a little sad. "Sometimes I wish I believed in something as much as you believe in education."

"Since my first day of school with Sister Theonesta, I knew that education would save me. I know I'm right."

"I hope so. I'm so glad you're better. That night you talked so much nonsense, we feared you'd gone mad. But your brains are back. We've missed the way you make us laugh. I have to get back to class, now. Think about transferring to Kongei next year."

Mary Jameson was the quietest and most sensitive of the Kifungilo girls. She didn't mix with the Africans as much as I did, but wherever she was, her calm presence was felt. She always looked peaceful. If her soul was as tormented as mine, she didn't show it or talk about it.

That same evening Paulina came to see me after supper. "I heard that you're better and I had to see for myself."

"Maybe I can go to school tomorrow."

"Not a chance! Recovering from malaria takes a long time. One day you're feeling good but the next you're sick again. Mother Majellis told me that she'll decide when you're going back to school."

"You talked with her?"

"Yes. I told her how Sister Florestina is cruel to the half-castes, and especially to you. I told her about giving you 'Two' as a last name and binding your chest with that bandage."

"Then that's why she brought me this. Open it." I handed Paulina a manila envelope with "For Mary" written on it. She pulled out two beautiful satin bras, one light blue and one pink. They were very different from the ones students use. Although they had tiny cups, I knew my breasts wouldn't fill them.

"They're so pretty. They must be from Germany." Paulina felt the smooth satin fabric and pulled the elastic straps.

"I'm tempted to wear them on top of my uniform and visit Sister Florestina in her dreams to perform a special heathen dance just for her."

"She'll never hurt you again. Mother Majellis promised me that. She found out about everything because Sister Florestina wanted to expel me for talking back to her the night you were so sick. When I explained what happened, she thanked me for telling her and for taking care of you."

Tears came to my eyes. Paulina had risked being expelled for me. "Your friendship means everything to me. I'll always remember your kindness."

"Yours means more to me. You share everything with me. You help me with my homework. Our classmates envy me because we study together. You never say a bad word about the Africans, even though the other Kifungilo girls do. You don't think you're better than anyone else. You're strong and tough and sensitive, yet so funny. Your words are as deep and wise as those of an elder. You feel everything and aren't afraid to express yourself or ask questions. I'm so happy I was on that bus with you."

Paulina's face was animated and full of conviction. Did she really see me as strong and tough? I knew that large chunks of my dignity had been systematically chipped away, but I always hoped that I would have enough left to keep me from crumbling or giving up. Based on Paulina's words, I had succeeded so far.

37

Missing Anatomy

 Three weeks later I was back in school, and I didn't have too much trouble getting caught up with the work I'd missed. Sister Florestina didn't bother me again and soon the long holidays started. I counted the days until we left Mhonda for Kifungilo. During the last week of school, while those in Standard Eight sat for their Territorial Exams, we prepared to go home. Paulina and I always did our laundry together, and this day we washed everything we owned, from our blankets to our panties, which by now had only threads for crotches. One by one we took items from our wash pile, dipped them in the trough of water, rubbed a three-inch bar of blue detergent soap over them, and scrubbed them against our knuckles.

"I haven't been this happy in a long time," my friend said as we scrubbed away, "and you survived your first year at an African School."

"I'm really looking forward to going home to Kifungilo and seeing Elizabeth and Sister Silvestris."

"I missed my village more than I thought I would. I missed Baba lecturing me and my busybody aunt talking and fussing with friends and strangers. I missed my little brother hiding in a tree frightening girls by cackling like a hyena. I missed my three-year-old sister trying to imitate me. I missed the village women chatting and flirting with passers-by on market day. So often I imagined sinking my teeth into our luscious Usambara Mountain plums, custard apples, peaches, and pears."

As we sloshed our clothes through the tepid water, I reflected on what I missed too. Paulina listened attentively as I told her I missed a lot of what I took for granted at Kifungilo—my soft sisal-filled mattress covered with clean flannel sheets that caressed my body when I turned on the metal spring bed, real down pillows that the nuns made from the poultry they raised, and the heavy woolen blankets donated by Germans. I missed the slice of dark, dense bread on Sundays. I missed Sister Silvestris' stories and walking with her to the villages to visit the sick and baptize her pagans. I missed having running water in the dormitories. And I especially missed my friend Elizabeth.

"I told you your life in Kifungilo was heaven compared to life in an African school. Remember I said you were spoiled? Do you believe me now?"

"My life in Kifungilo was easier in some ways than life here, but harder in others. Life is hard for different people in different ways at different times. Kifungilo prepared me for that."

"Is it true that the Kifungilo girls won't be returning to Mhonda?"

"I'm coming back. Are you?" I asked.

"Of course I am. Baba believes that the only intolerable things on earth are those indignities, injustices, and prejudices that destroy the soul. When he hears about you, he'll want to write something in the paper."

"No, don't tell him. I might be expelled from school. But please tell him about our friendship and how you made my life in Mhonda easier."

"I felt lonely being the only Sambaa girl here. I'm glad you'll be coming back, Mary. I can't imagine life in Mhonda without you.

"You can't imagine life in Mhonda without an orphan, half-caste girl?"

"What can I say? I liked you from the day I met you."

"Thank you, Paulina. I think I like myself a whole lot more because of you. You don't see anything wrong with me. You just love me and you don't need a reason."

She was struggling to wring out her huge brown blanket, so I grabbed one end and she took the other and together we twisted it to squeeze out all the water.

"I'll miss the Kifungilo girls. They're the only family I've known.

Even though we didn't do much together, they stood by me and we took care of each other. "

"Mary, you haven't talked about your parents. Not all half-castes are born out of wedlock, no matter what Sister Florestina says. I know several half-castes in Lushoto who have parents, at least mothers, and their families are proud to have children with *mzungu* blood. They believe that lighter skin means a bigger dowry and a good chance of marrying a *mzungu*, who would probably treat them better than an African man."

"I can't answer any questions about my parents except that I no longer believe that I came from a pumpkin." Paulina's concern turned to laughter. "I used to explain my birth to myself by saying that one day God was carrying me along with several other children, but I was fussing and asking questions and dancing so much that I slipped and fell from the sky into a pumpkin patch. When a farmer heard the loud 'thump,' he rushed to his field, picked me up, and decided to take me to his wife to raise. No one in the village believed that I'd burst from a pumpkin, and his wife refused to take in a child she figured he'd had with a *mzungu* woman, so he brought me to Kifungilo, the home of other half-caste children found in pumpkin patches."

"You have quite an imagination. That shows intelligence."

"I don't think I'm that intelligent because I still can't figure out how babies get born, although I heard some stories in Kifungilo."

"The nuns believe making babies is sinful, so of course they wouldn't tell you anything. Let's hang up our laundry, and I'll tell you all about it."

"How do you know?"

"Remember that I'm older than you. Babies are made when men and women do the forbidden act that Sister Florestina is perpetually preaching to us about. My cousin is already a mother at fourteen. Her father gave her to an old man as a third wife because he needed the dowry money. Old men love having very young wives. They want to be the first one to break her skin."

"Her skin?" I stopped draping our clothes over the line.

"The man puts his penis into the woman's vagina and screams with pleasure while the woman usually cries with pain. The man has to push very hard to tear the skin that covers the vagina for the first time. When he gets inside, he deposits boy seeds and girl seeds and then those seeds make a safari to the stomach where there's plenty of room to settle down and grow."

"Who told you that?"

"My grandmother. When a young girl becomes *mwali*—a woman, usually her grandmother will prepare her for marriage. The Luguru tribe has elaborate rituals for young girls when they become *mwali*. The young girl stays inside her grandmother's house for several months where she's taught to do things to satisfy her husband so he will give her lots of children."

"Paulina, I saw a man's penis with my own two eyes when I was younger, and it couldn't rip or tear anything. It looked exactly like a limp, decaying banana, with white, fuzzy hair."

"Don't tell me the old priest in Kifungilo showed you his penis! Baba doesn't trust any man who abstains from doing the act."

"The penis I saw belonged to the old woodcutter in Kifungilo. And he didn't show it to us. We peeped at it when he was sleeping."

"The only penis you've seen belonged to a gray-haired old man?"

She stopped spreading wet clothes on the grass. "Mary, I'll be your grandmother today." I was eager to listen, but also a little frightened.

"Men have different sized penises, just like women's breasts are different. Although size doesn't matter, younger men can do the act more often than older men. When the man is ready to do the act, his penis becomes very big, hard and strong."

I imagined a huge arm made out of iron prodding a woman's soft private places without mercy.

"And when it gets like that, he has to get it inside a women and get rid of all the juices that make it hard, and—"

Now I became skeptical. "How can juices make it hard?"

"You know how those long thin balloons they sell at the Indian *duka* get hard when you fill them with water? It's a little like that. And after he empties his juices, the penis becomes like a deflated balloon—short, soft, and wrinkled. My grandma told me never to forget that the main thing men want women for is to empty their seeds in their vaginas—nothing more, no matter what they say."

I decided to take Paulina's word, though I didn't fully understand the whole process. "Imagine putting what he pees with into your body."

"I agree, but that's the way babies are made. Now you know the whole story. No matter what the nuns or others have told you, this is the truth about how babies are made."

Paulina went to the dorm and I sat down on the grass by the clothes. There was no way any man would get his big, iron penis near me, I vowed. I started appreciating the fact that I didn't have a grandmother to teach me how to subject myself to such awful things. The Kifungilo nuns were right. Men are evil. Why would they want to rip into and tear a women's vagina? Yet now, in spite of myself, I was fascinated with the whole idea of men and women, and why babies were made that way.

The very next time I went to the toilet, I decided to check things out. Crouched over the open trough, I felt very carefully for my hole. I couldn't find it. I found the big one for doing number two and the tiny one for number one, but that was all. I felt all over my bottom, front and back. I poked into my navel and checked every crease from the waistline down until I almost tipped over. There was no hole to be found. Maybe I didn't have one. How lucky! Without a hole, I was guaranteed to be safe from men! But what if they came looking for it and they didn't find it? Would they beat me and empty their seeds someplace else? All of a sudden, I wanted a hole so they wouldn't go poking every inch of me. I resumed feeling myself all over again. Nothing. I definitely didn't have one.

Later that evening when most of the girls were braiding their hair on the steps, I had to find Paulina to ask more questions. She was in the dormitory packing her suitcase.

"I'll never have children," I blurted out.

"Why don't you want to have children? When you grow up, you'll get married and have children. That's what all women do. My grandma told me."

"I can't have children because I don't have the hole you told me about. I checked myself very carefully and didn't find it."

"Don't tell me the nuns sewed you up?" Paulina looked horrified. "Some tribes sew up their young girls' holes just after they become women so they can't do the act with anyone except their husbands who tear them open. I'm grateful the Sambaa don't do it, because it's very painful for those women during their periods, when they do the act, and give birth."

"When do girls become women?"

"When they get their period for the first time. Haven't you gotten yours yet?"

"Is that when you bleed for three days like some of the students here?"

"Yes. I got my period when I was fifteen. That's when Bibi took me inside her hut and taught me about being a woman and a mother and about men."

"I wonder if the nuns teach the big girls about all this when they prepare them for marriage."

"The nuns will never teach you any of these things not only because they believe it's sinful, but they really don't know much themselves!"

38

Back on the Bus

 When I packed to return to Kifungilo, I found my twenty shillings in the bottom of my suitcase—I had forgotten to use the money! I tucked it in my satin bra from Mother Majellis. The morning after exams, we loaded our belongings on our heads and marched the five miles to Turiani to catch the bus, singing and laughing the whole way. Everyone was excited to be heading home, and I felt truly happy to be going back to Kifungilo. As I danced along the way, I imitated students' facial expressions and little mannerisms. "Do me! Do me!" they begged, so I set down my suitcase and mimicked them, but when a few students tried to imitate how I danced, they weren't very convincing.

"No one can imitate you, Mary—you dance like you talk, mixing English, German, Latin, Swahili, Kisambaa, and now Kiluguru," they laughed and cheered. "We don't know what you're doing when you dance, but we love it!"

The bus station in Turiani was jammed with students and their belongings. There were three buses, each going to a different destination. Our bus said MOMBO, and it was every bit as full as the first time I rode a bus. At least this time there were no goats. The attendant loaded the bus and we piled in after saying our goodbyes.

The other Kifungilo girls were already on the bus. After I recovered from malaria, I spent less time with them, but they still came to my aid whenever I got into trouble. I sat in the row in front of them with Paulina who was going to Mombo with us. They were bubbling with joy about going back to Kifungilo and talking about not returning to Mhonda no matter what Mother Rufina said. I thought how different our moods were on this second bus ride. Ten months ago I was full of hope, and getting an education was an end in itself. Now I was still committed to an education, but I wondered if I could survive another year in Mhonda with Sister Florestina.

"You're so quiet, Mary," Paulina said. "What's on your mind?"

"I worry that Sister Florestina will find an excuse to keep me from taking the Standard Eight Territorial Exams next year, and then my hard work will have been in vain."

"Mary, you must ask the nuns for your full name. They're secretive because they're protecting the identity of the *wazungu* fathers."

"I'll ask, but if they don't tell me, I'll make one up. Sister Florestina gave me a number for a name. I can do better than that."

We talked and sang school songs all the way to Mombo, at which point only the Kifungilo girls and Paulina were left on the bus. As we began our ascent on the famous white-knuckle road to Lushoto, we saw a speck of light blue and two tiny white dots far away in the mountains. The convent van coming to take us home was a comforting sight. We ignored the driver's orders to sit down and instead danced in the aisle singing *"Dereva, endesha mbio mbio!"* to the driver to go faster and faster, knowing full well that he had to crawl up the hill in order to get us to Lushoto in one piece.

I pulled Paulina into the aisle and swung her hips back and forth until she joined in. "I'm so happy to be going home I could cry," she said. "Seeing the Usambara Mountains with their halos of clouds and feeling the cool air on my face is almost more than I can bear!"

Just then we smelled the eucalyptus trees that signaled the approach to Lushoto. As soon as we rounded the corner, we spied the van. Sister Silvestris and Sister Fabiana were waving at us. As soon as the bus stopped we ran to them, all of us trying to shake their hands at the same time.

"*Mama yangu!* Mary, you've gotten taller," said Sister Silvestris, looking us over. "And all of you are so thin. I'll fatten you up again before you go back."

"We're not going back! We're never going back to Mhonda," the others told her.

"Oh no! Don't start that again," she said almost with pleasure. "After a few weeks you'll be ready to go back to school. Now get in the van and let's go home." Before I got into the van, I took Sister's hand again and shook it with joy at seeing her and sorrow because I had missed her.

"Welcome back! Welcome back!" she said over and over as we piled into the van. "It's getting dark, but we will stop at the dentistry to eat before we leave for Kifungilo."

I was already in the van when I saw Paulina waving goodbye, standing alone surrounded by her luggage. "Can I say goodbye to my friend?" I asked Sister Silvestris.

"All right, but hurry."

"How are you getting home?" I asked Paulina.

"Baba is coming for me. He'll be here soon."

"Here, take my twenty shillings and buy something for your little brother and sister. You said they expect presents when you return."

"No, I can't take the only money you've ever had!"

"Please buy them something and say it's from someone who loves their sister very much."

She accepted it and gave me a huge smile. As we hugged, I felt our hearts connect with love and gratitude. Lucinda was wrong. My twenty shillings did buy me something of immense value—the feeling of making someone happy.

Don Bosco Home at Kifungilo. Left to right: Children's quarters, dentistry, convent, church, priests' house, and guest house. Cypress trees line the mile-long road to the orphanage.

Mary at age three.

Sister Theonesta
who took care of
Mary as an infant.

Sister Silvestris
who was in charge of
raising the children.

Mary at age 7.

Zahabu, the wood-cutter who worked at the orphanage.

Father Gattang, the priest in residence at Kifungilo.

Mary after typhoid.

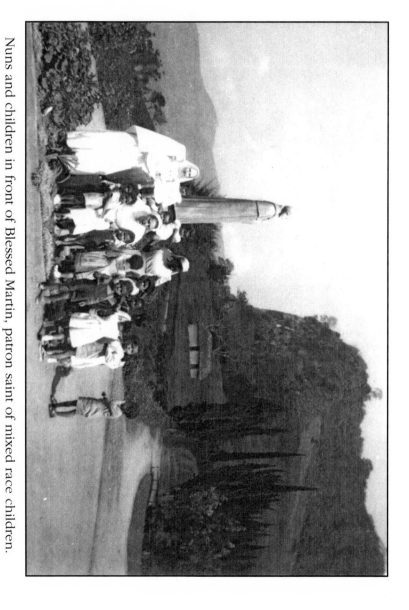

Nuns and children in front of Blessed Martin, patron saint of mixed race children. Visiting African mothers stayed at the house in back. Main entrance road.

Rosa's Wedding. Mary (to Rosa's right) and Mary Jameson, flower girls.

Sister Silvestris with her children. Mary is to her lower right (arrow).

Cathy and Mary (at far right) with Kifungilo nun and girls. Convent VW van in back.

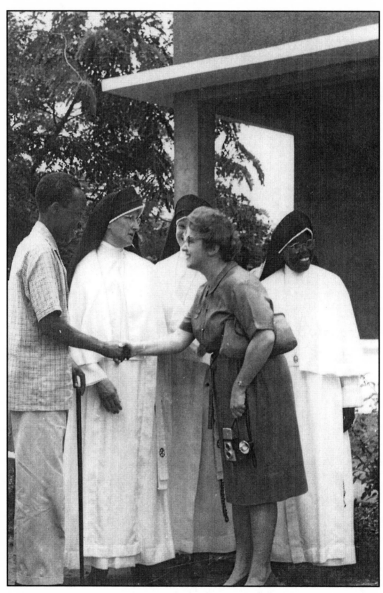

Cathy Murray greeting President Julius Nyerere.
Sisters Dolores Marie and Martin Corde.

Mary with Cathy Murray when Cathy asked
her to come to the United States.

Cathy and Mary at her graduation from Marian College.

Mary and Cathy at the Dar-es-Salaam airport leaving Africa
for the United States.

39

Home

 By the time we finished eating the sandwiches and drinking the tea that Sister Nerea gave us at the dentistry, it was already dark and Sister Fabiana was anxious to get going. All the way back to Kifungilo we didn't speak.

I don't know if it was because we were exhausted, or because we had so much to say we didn't know where to begin. So much had taken place in Mhonda, not just educationally, but socially, culturally, and personally. I decided I wouldn't mention the vendetta Sister Florestina had against me. Would anyone believe in hate at first sight?

It was very late when we arrived, and Kifungilo was asleep. Sister Fabiana dropped us off in front of the dormitory and Sister Silvestris told us to go straight to bed. We quietly climbed the steps to the sleeping room, left our suitcases outside the door, washed up, and found our glorious beds with the aid of a flashlight. As soon as my head hit the pillow, I started thinking about Elizabeth. The beds for us Mhonda girls were on one side of the dorm, so I had no idea where she was sleeping. Anticipating the morning made my heart beat faster and kept me awake. It was still two weeks before the start of Kifungilo Christmas holidays, so she must be here unless her parents took her away as they had promised.

It made me sad that once someone left Kifungilo, the only way to stay in touch was to return in person. We didn't write letters because we had no paper or stamps and had no way of getting to Lushoto to post them. Besides, the nuns read all incoming and outgoing mail in Kifungilo and Mhonda. I thought about all the letters I'd written to Elizabeth in my head and imagined our conversations in which

I told her what I'd learned in school and from Paulina. She'd be the only one I'd tell about the pain of being used as an example of the big sin, and how insignificant I felt because I had no last name. She'd understand, but then she'd say, "Forget about Mhonda. Let's play and laugh and be happy and pretend we never grew up!" And I'd tell her that I didn't know how to pretend anymore.

I was up before anybody else. I walked between all the rows of beds looking for my friend. I could tell what bed she was in because she slept wrapped in her blanket and curled up at the bottom of the bed. I couldn't find her. The same feeling of nausea I had in the pit of my stomach the night we said goodbye engulfed me again.

"Mary, you're back." It was Julitta. "Why are you up so early?" she whispered.

"I'm looking for Elizabeth. Where's her bed?"

"Elizabeth isn't at Kifungilo."

"Where is she?"

Julitta pulled me into the hallway by the bathroom so we didn't wake the others. "Mary, Elizabeth ran away."

"Ran away from Kifungilo? What happened?"

"She became interested in boys. Remember how she used to powder her face, fix her hair, and make eyes every time a man came around, and how she even flirted with the priests?"

"I don't remember that. Are we talking about Elizabeth? My Elizabeth?

"Listen, Mary," she said as we huddled together in the hall, "Elizabeth really changed after you left. She began talking back to the Sisters and the big girls and even attacked them when they beat her. She didn't speak to anyone and refused to go to class."

"I can't believe it!"

"When her mother came to visit the last time, she wanted to leave with her, but her mother said she had to stay in Kifungilo a little longer. Well, Elizabeth put on a mighty tantrum and even bit her mother's arms and cheeks."

"You're talking about my friend Elizabeth?"

"Her mother managed to calm her down and promised she'd take her home soon. Elizabeth couldn't wait. She ran away from Kifungilo several times but someone always found her and brought her back."

"Where is she now? Lizzy had promised her she could work at the dentistry."

"No one knows where she is. Elizabeth turned into a rebel overnight. Doris, who works at the dentistry, told Sister Silvestris that Elizabeth stayed there for a few months but then ran away with a German boy she met. I heard she's living in Moshi now, but I don't know if that's true. Every night Sister has us pray for her to Blessed Martin."

I was crushed. My Elizabeth was lost. Tears started swelling in my eyes, but I struggled to keep them there until I could swallow them. I swallowed again and again. For the first time since I was twelve years old, I really felt like crying with my whole body and soul. But I couldn't and I wouldn't cry because I didn't want to disappoint my lost friend.

"Thank you for telling me, Julitta."

"I knew you'd miss her, so I tried to remember all that happened to tell you when you returned. The nuns never tell us anything. I don't think the others knew the deep friendship you two had. To me, you were more than friends. You were like twins. Except for praying for her, no one in Kifungilo has mentioned her name."

I went back to bed and found myself wishing I were far away from this suddenly painful place. Elizabeth told me we would see each other before Christmas. What made her change her mind and act so bad? I was lost in thought when I heard a faint knock on my heart.

Who is always here when you need her? I recognized Fat Mary's delicate, quivering voice. "Come in, Fat Mary. I am glad to see you! Look at you. You haven't changed at all. Come, get into bed with me." She was chubby and warm, and her long brown pigtails ended in tiny yellow ribbons. She was wearing the Christmas dress I choose when I was six years old.

I came to tell you that you will be all right, she assured me. *Mhonda was a tough test and you survived it. I will keep and treasure all your memories of Elizabeth forever. Now you must be even stronger and continue with your life. Nothing is lost.*

Having Paulina in Mhonda, I hadn't had many conversations with Fat Mary. I had almost forgotten how soothing she was. I hugged my little girl and thanked her for coming to me when I needed her even though I hadn't paid much attention to her for the whole year. Would she come to me only in Kifungilo or would she follow me wherever I went, and no matter how old I got?

By the time Sister came to wake us, I was again happy to be in Kifungilo. Although we were not permitted to talk in the morning until after church, the dorm was buzzing with excitement. All Sister said was "Shhhhhhhh!" and told us not to be late for Mass. Curious girls anxious to hear about life far away from Kifungilo surrounded us. Right after Mass we started answering their questions: Why were we so thin? What did we eat? Were there other half-castes? Were we called names like the Kongei girls were? Was it fun to ride the bus? What did we learn? What could we buy in Turiani and were the shops there bigger than the ones in Lushoto?

I listened to the other girls describe our life: the food worse than what our pig in Kifungilo eats, no bread or sugar, or butter, or biscuits, or pears, only tiny portions of rice once a month, and dry *ugali* and cassava every day. I told them about fruit that students bought in Turiani and shared with us—big juicy, sweet mangos, and sweet, slippery breadfruit. We told them about *Mwalimu* Agnesi, the only other half-caste, and her mean ways, and how Lucinda threatened anyone who called us names. With a mix of pride and solidarity, they discussed my malaria and how they tried to protect me from Sister Florestina. Were they boasting a little when they said I was more African than the Africans and that I learned dances and customs from many tribes? I think so, because then they mentioned that the math teacher called me *Mwamba* and that when I corrected homework for him, I fixed their wrong answers.

"We were our own tribe and we helped each other like the other girls with their tribes," said Mary Jameson.

Life at Mhonda was harder than Kongei, we insisted. It was clear that each of us had re-evaluated our relationship with Kifungilo and decided it was the best place for us. I added that we learned a lot about our country, the world, and the possibilities that education would give us. Only Lucinda and I wanted to go back to Mhonda.

Lucinda talked about her friendship with *Mwalimu* Clara who treated her like family and bought her presents. I was glad I wouldn't be alone there and told her so.

"Mary, I have only one good friend, but besides Paulina, you have dozens of students who love you."

"That's true, Mary. Several girls told me they were worried you might not return, and they wondered who would entertain them and make them laugh next year," Mary Jameson said.

The five of us had several similar conversations throughout our vacation, but surprisingly, Sister Silvestris didn't care to hear much about Mhonda. She was only interested in how well we did in school, and she didn't fuss much when the others told her that they weren't going back. Sister did ask me what I liked most and I told her I loved learning about all the African tribes, their customs, and especially the dances. She thought we all had learned tribal dances and wanted to see us perform, but I told her only I danced with the Africans.

"I should have known. I knew you used to run off and dance with the Wasambaa. Why do you enjoy dancing like them?"

"Because it's the only thing I can do that is always right. When you dance with the Africans, unless it is a ritual dance like a wedding or harvest or rain dance, there's no right or wrong way to dance. There's only movement. And the more you express your feelings as you move, the better you feel when you're done. But with the German waltz, the steps never change and you have to follow or lead your partner. How can you show what you're feeling? When I dance the African way, I show my feelings with my body instead of hiding them in my heart. When I dance, I know I'm alive here and now. My body and soul are in harmony. You should try it sometime when Mother Rufina isn't looking."

"You funny girl. I can't even do the German waltz! But as long as you don't dance sinfully, dancing is good. Now, will you teach the children a dance for Christmas?"

I had to demonstrate the dance I chose to Sister Silvestris first. It wouldn't be an African dance, but I knew the "Hokey Pokey" which we danced at school would win her approval. I demonstrated the entire song and acted everything out, putting my feet, arms, and knees in and out, and shaking each part as much as I could and turning around and around.

Of course, I didn't do the special African version we did when the nuns or teachers weren't around. Then we sang the song in Swahili, fancied up the footwork, and put all parts of our bodies in and out, including each hip, breast, and buttock. We extended the shaking it about part while we made our entire bodies tremble freely, and we scrunched up our faces trying to put our eyes and ears in and out of the circle as well. I would shake my body pretending to loosen up all the parts until they fell off. Then I'd pick them up one by one and reattach them. But in my dancing frenzy, and to the delight of the other dancers, I often attached a foot to my chest or an eye to my knee. It was really unfortunate that I had to clean up the "Hokey Pokey" for the nuns.

Christmas Eve, the dance was a hit. The children loved performing it, and I foresaw how this song and dance routine could replace "Trim the Tree" as the most requested encore.

Before we left the recreation hall, I went over to the Nativity scene to talk to Baby Jesus. I looked at the statue that held so much life and promise for me as a child and wondered if the reason I couldn't talk to Baby Jesus as easily any more was because I had grown up and he hadn't. He knew everything anyway, since he was the Son of God, and as long as I didn't completely forget him, he would always listen to me.

"This is for my Fat Mary, the teacher," Sister Silvestris said affectionately as she handed me a red nylon duffle bag with a shiny silver zipper. "I know you will use your education to help others." I took the bag and thanked her, but it was customary not to open a gift in front of the giver, so I had to wait until she left. The most important part of a gift for me was guessing what it was. I poked the bag and felt a soft area, but also several solid, heavy items and something rolling around loose. I imagined a dress, a petticoat, a nightgown or sweater, and maybe shoes and soap and candy. When I was satisfied with my guesses, I went to the attic where we stored our suitcases to open it.

I found two Sunday dresses, a pair of shoes which were too

small, two panties with elastic and lace, Maclean's toothpaste and a new toothbrush, a bar of Lifebuoy soap like the Africans in Mhonda used, a jar of Lady Lavender brilliantine for my hair, and an old German prayer book with several holy cards tucked in the pages. These gifts were the most and best I'd received from her. As I transferred them to my suitcase, I found something heavy tied in a handkerchief. I tried to guess what it was but gave up and carefully undid the knot.

I held up a sparkling red, green, and yellow rhinestone necklace with a huge forest-green stone in the center and alternating crimson and yellow stones that tapered to a silver clasp. The way the stones caught and reflected the light almost blinded me. Nestled in the handkerchief were also a matching bracelet, dangling earrings, and a brooch whose reflections danced on the floor, ceiling, and on my clothing. I closed my eyes and put the necklace around my neck where it fell just above the spot where my cleavage would eventually be—assuming Sister Florestina's bandage hadn't stunted the growth of my breasts. It felt heavy and rich. I put on the rest of the set. If Sister Silvestris hadn't shown me in the past that she loved me, she certainly did now.

This was such a special and exquisite gift and had such meaning for me that I knew I would give it to Paulina to show her how precious she was to me. That idea made me flush with delight. I locked my suitcase and went to thank Sister Silvestris.

"I don't know how to thank you for your gifts. They make me feel rich and spoiled and loved. It's so good to feel this way. I shall never forget today and your gifts."

"Fat Mary, you deserve it. I am happy when you are happy."

Vacation seemed to fly by and before we knew it, it was time for Lucinda and me to go to the sewing room to get our supplies for the year. Sister asked us if there was anything special we wanted to take to Mhonda from Kifungilo.

"I'd like to have a Kifungilo pillow," I said. "It's the best pillow on earth." Lucinda, whose friend *Mwalimu* Clara had given her a soft foam pillow, asked for the tasty *vushti* sausage made in Kifungilo.

Sister told me to take the pillow from my bed and promised

Lucinda she'd have the sausage in the morning. We finished packing and went to say goodbye to Mother Rufina and Father Van Leer. Dear old Father Gattang had died while we were away and was probably still chuckling in heaven about our confessions.

Mother Rufina again gave us each twenty shillings and reminded us that we had to pay back every cent she'd spent for our education—from school fees, uniforms, notebooks, and bus tickets to the twenty shillings in our hands. Father Van Leer simply said "Be good Christians." We said goodbye to the girls that same evening with special hugs and wishes from Kate, Stefana, and Mary Jameson.

There was one more person I had to say goodbye to—Elizabeth. Before I finished packing, I took my broken doll from my suitcase. I hadn't looked at it even once since I left Kifungilo. Holding the doll brought back many happy memories. I longed to see Elizabeth again. I longed to hear her laughter and her jokes and to make delicate designs with her rough hair and feel her fingers rearrange mine.

Carrying my doll wrapped in an old German newspaper, I went behind the statue of Blessed Martin. Sitting on the grass, I relived the hours Elizabeth and I spent in our hideaway near the statue of our beloved half-caste friend. With a stick I slowly dug a hole. I recalled how we buried the dead grasshoppers, lizards, chameleons, and frogs that we gathered in our wanderings. When the hole was big enough, I placed my doll in it with all the love my heart held for her. I picked some dandelions and carefully placed them beside her. I covered her with the fresh black dirt. As each handful of dirt left my hand, I let Elizabeth go. When I was done, I smoothed out the mound of earth and covered the grave with dried spongy grass that grew among the dandelions. "Goodbye, my forever friend. Goodbye."

40

Terror

 At 6 o'clock in the morning, Lucinda and I got into the Kifungilo van along with Sisters Silvestris and Fabiana, Kiondo the mailman, and a sick nun I'd never seen before. Sister Fabiana was taking her to the doctor in Tanga, a large city on the Indian Ocean. We drove up the hill past the cemetery, past the newly constructed teachers' house, the school, and the custard apple orchards. We went up the road bordered by cypress trees, along the meadows with wild gooseberry patches, past the waterfalls, over the log bridge in Mkuzi, along the river where Wasambaa were already washing their clothes and laying them to dry on the short grass, and on to Lushoto. The nuns were silent most of the way, except for the sick nun who had us stop on the side of the road periodically.

I was excited about seeing Paulina who would be waiting in Mombo, so I was pleased that we didn't stop at the dentistry for breakfast. As we descended into the tiny town of Mombo, I could just make out the unforgettable *Umeme* bus that slept at the station.

"As soon as we arrive, get out quickly because we still have several hours to drive to Tanga," Sister Silvestris said. She gave us our tickets. "Get in line before the crowds come."

"But last time the mob arrived before the driver collected the tickets, and if it weren't for you, we wouldn't have had seats," I said.

"You won't have any problem this time. The new driver of *Umeme* walked miles through the bush to Kifungilo carrying his sick child to me. I instructed Juma to take good care of the half-castes who get on the bus in Mombo. I said that you were all my children, and he should get you safely to Turiani." We were near the center of the station when Sister pointed out the bus driver. Juma was a short, skinny fellow with laughing, beady eyes and a mischievous attitude.

"Jambo, Sista," he said as he helped her out of the Kifungilo van. He was probably a Muslim and had never learned to greet nuns and priests with the traditional *Tumsifu Yesu Kristu.*

"Hurry, hurry. We can't spend more than a minute here," Sister Fabiana reminded Sister Silvestris. "Today I have only two children." Juma looked at us as he tightened the belt of his khaki shorts. "Make sure they get to Turiani safely."

"I'll guard them with my life," Juma said.

We shook Sister's hand and she hurried back into the van. Juma took our suitcases, climbed on top of the bus, and secured them on the roof.

"Are we the only passengers?" I asked.

"The bus doesn't leave for another hour, and it's always full. I came early because I promised the good Sista to take care of her children. I'm going back home for breakfast." He unlocked the door. "Go inside and choose any seat you want. I'll lock you in so you'll be safe." He got in first and watched us climb the three short steps and walk down the narrow aisle.

"*Asante sana,*" we said and sat by the same window the driver had broken for Stefana a year ago. Apart from having more clumps of dirty sponge filling on the seats, and more rusted iron bars and springs where seats should be, and several new holes in the floor through which we could see the road beneath us, the bus was the same.

Juma turned to Lucinda and as an afterthought said to her, "I have a son who's looking for a third wife. Come with me to meet him."

"You're joking!" Lucinda said. "That's not what Sister had in mind when she asked you to take care of us."

"I'm in charge of you beautiful half-caste girls. I like your light skin. You should come to my house." He adjusted the belt of his shorts again. "Come to the village with me, and for one hour my son and I will treat you very well."

"Shall we go?" I innocently asked Lucinda.

"Mary, have you lost your mind? You can't trust this man."

"I haven't visited an African village since we used to go with Sister Silvestris. Why don't we see what it's like?"

"You'll come back pregnant."

Pregnant? Lucinda knew how to scare me. Girls left Mhonda because they were pregnant and they never returned. In spite of conversations with Paulina about penises and vaginas, seeds and making babies, I was still in the dark about how the act actually happened. If someone told me that I'd get pregnant from a man just looking at that part of my body, I'd believe it.

"Are you coming?" asked Juma. "I'll give you some of this if you come." He flashed a thick wad of twenty-shilling notes in front of our faces. It was the most money I'd ever seen. I started thinking of what I could buy when Lucinda yelled, "You'll become pregnant and then you won't finish school."

"No, we're not coming with you. We'll wait here," I said.

"You are refusing me?" Juma's mood suddenly changed. "I'll show you what happens when you say 'no' to a man. Take your clothes off!"

"You crazy old man," Lucinda shouted. I had flashbacks to when Sister Florestina ordered me to take off my clothes so she could bandage my budding breasts. That day I vowed no one would ever force me to take my clothes off again.

Juma grabbed my shoulder, pulled me off the seat, and threw me down in the aisle. "Take off your clothes, you bloody *chotara!*"

"No! Never!"

He straddled me with his skinny legs, reached down and lifted my skirt as I tried to sit up. He wrapped my skirt around my head. I kicked and screamed, but he overpowered me. He pushed me towards the window in between two seats. I kept screaming and managed to get my skirt partially off my face. Then he unbuckled his belt, pulled down his pants, and right there in front of me, I saw my first erect penis. I noticed he wasn't wearing underwear. No doubt, had it been under different circumstances, I would have had lots of questions, but at that moment I saw a disgusting and feared weapon. It looked like the heavy wooden handle of a machete.

As I lay there screaming and trying to kick him, I saw Lucinda's big furious eyes bulging from her face. She was beyond angry. She pushed Juma forward, reached in between his legs from behind, and grabbed his penis with both hands. She pulled it back towards her with all her might. Juma let out a loud, long roar and then cursed and groaned as he fell over me with his hot sweaty face landing on my stomach. Lucinda held onto Juma's organ until he begged her to stop. Before she obliged, she kicked him in the buttocks and rolled him off me, slapping every part of his writhing body. She took her shoe off and continued smacking the squirming Juma's hands which were trying to protect his penis. Juma managed to turn around and sit up still clutching his penis. He swore that he was going to kill us. I hadn't lost sight of his dreaded weapon from the moment he lowered his pants. After Lucinda hit it with her shoe, it deflated and shrunk into his crotch. When I could no longer see it, I felt safer.

"Get off the bus. Quick, let's go!" Lucinda said. We pushed the still moaning Juma under the seat and ran out of the bus.

"Get our suitcases," I said to my savior. Lucinda raced up the steps to the roof of the bus and threw them down. We sat on them behind the flame tree, hoping other passengers would arrive soon. My body was shaking and I was disorientated and nauseous. I put my arms around Lucinda and hung on to her.

We were silent for a long time. I was terrified. Then I slowly realized something. What Juma did to us on the bus was frightening, but underneath that fright, was another sharp anxiety about what Sister Florestina might do to me in Mhonda the coming year. I feared I could die in the pursuit of an education—and I was beginning to get the idea that an education probably wouldn't protect me from evil men. Gradually I came to see that it was not Juma or Sister Florestina or even evil men that I was afraid of. For the first time, I saw the bigger picture. I was fearful of life itself.

"The nuns are right. All men are evil," I managed to say between shivers.

"Don't talk. Yes, men are evil." Lucinda continued holding me in her arms like a baby.

"Imagine, attacking me just because I'm a girl!"

"Hush! Try to calm down before the others come."

"Thank you for what you did for me."

"Did for you? When he was finished with you, he would have done it to me too."

"What will Sister Silvestris say when we tell her?"

"Did you see how he acted so nice and concerned in front of her? She wouldn't believe us, and she would blame us if we got pregnant. When it comes to the big sin, the nuns say men are evil, but they believe women are responsible for tempting them."

"We'd better keep this to ourselves. I know Paulina and *Mwalimu* Clara will believe us."

Crowds of people began appearing around the bus. Shouting and shoving began as soon as the conductor started loading the roof and people piled into the bus.

"We'd better get a seat. We're safe now. He wouldn't dare do anything to us with people around." We managed to get our suitcases loaded on the roof, but the vehicle was so packed with passengers, we had to shove and push along with everyone else to get on.

"Mary, Mary," I heard Paulina calling my name. "Over here. I saved you a seat."

"Paulina, is it you? I'm coming." Lucinda and I remained glued to one another as we inched our way toward Paulina. We squeezed in next to her.

"I was worried when I didn't see any half-castes, but I was sure at least you would show up. What's the matter? Your hair is messed up and your dress is torn."

"It seems like such a long time since we parted," I told Paulina, trying to control my shaking voice. "You look rested. I like your red dress and *khangas*."

"My holidays were great. Are you okay? It was hard saying goodbye to my family, but Baba kept reminding me that I had only one more year at Mhonda." She looked me over. "Mary, something's the matter."

"Something did happen. I'll tell you later." My nerves started to calm as I listened to my friend. I borrowed her hair pick and rearranged my short hair. I tied the large tear in my skirt with a knot and Lucinda attached it to my petticoat with a safety pin.

Before the bus left, we had the now familiar checking and collecting of tickets, with the unloading and reloading of passengers. The bus conductor honked the horn. I felt anxious until Juma was safely in his compartment. Lucinda and I prayed that he wouldn't see us and throw us off the bus.

"Now, calm down and tell me about your holidays," Paulina started. We exchanged small talk through Korogwe and Handeni, getting off the bus to buy a Fanta which we drank with some sweet *mandazi* that Paulina shared with us. Finally, I could tell her what happened. When I did, anger and hatred swelled in my heart and throat choking me, and I started to shake again. I hated Juma more than I'd ever hated anyone or anything before. I hated him more than I hated Sister Clotilda or even Sister Florestina or my big girl Zami—my three yardsticks for measuring evil on earth.

"*Mungu wangu wee!* The driver tried to rape you and Lucinda?" She had to explain to me what rape was.

Then I wanted to know, "Can a women rape a man?"

"I've never heard of a woman raping a man, but maybe *wazungu* women do it. Men like women to entice them to do the act, and as long as both like it, it's not rape. The problem is that men believe that women are lying or teasing when they tell them they don't want to do it."

"Are men so stupid?"

"Men who rape are. A friend of mine who's only twelve was raped by her uncle. She cried about it every day but didn't dare tell anyone except me."

"She's pregnant?"

"I don't think so. Women don't always get pregnant right away.

"Do all women want to become pregnant?"

"Most married women do. Of course, an unmarried girl who gets pregnant brings shame to her family, even though it happens all the time. Sometimes she's banished from the village or the mother takes the girl to a medicine man who gives her herbs to kill the baby. Sometimes the girl dies too. Each tribe handles this its own way, but in general it's taboo to get pregnant outside of marriage."

"And the men? How are they punished?"

"Punished? Men? *Mungu wangu wee!* Never! If the girl discloses his name, which she seldom does, her family might demand compensation or marriage or settle it some other way."

"I hate men. All of them!"

"You feel bad because of what Juma did. But someday you'll fall in love with a man, and you will marry him."

"I'm serious. From now on, I hate all men." I wondered how I could hurt so much when Juma hadn't even hit me.

"You can't live with hate in your heart. It's okay to hate Juma, but try not to hate all men. Baba is a good man. I don't want you to hate him. But tell me, did you find out your real surname?"

"One of the big girls who cleans Mother Rufina's office discovered where she hides the book with the *wazungu* names of the children at Kifungilo." I explained to Paulina that some children had surnames but most did not, probably because the *wazungu* fathers didn't want it known that they had an out-of-wedlock, half-caste child. But Mother Rufina was very shrewd. Before she accepted a child at the orphanage, she insisted that the mother reveal the identity of the *mzungu* father. Mother Rufina recorded as much information as she could gather from the mothers, who were usually sworn to secrecy by the fathers. She then used this information to solicit donations for the orphanage in exchange for keeping their identities secret. Many *wazungu* supported their children this way.

"I finally figured it out," I told Paulina, "because whenever the nuns had us pray for money, a *mzungu* from somewhere in Tanganyika came through for us."

"So the nuns know your last name."

"Well, the big girl cleaning Mother Rufina's office found out several children's names, but she couldn't remember mine although she recalled that it started with an 'r' and had an 'i' and it was short. An advantage to not having parents is that I can choose any name I wish, so this year I'll use Ryme, and when I'm tired of it, I'll invent another."

"You can't do that!" exclaimed Paulina. "Once you have a name, it's official."

"Who can stop me? Parents should name their children, even if they invent a last name. I've never been mad at my parents for anything, but I am angry at them for not properly naming me. Speaking of parents, why don't you ever talk about your mother?"

"She died giving birth to me. I was raised by my grandma." A look of deep sadness passed over my friend's usually calm face.

"I'm sorry. That's why your Bibi was so important to you."

"Yes, but I missed having a mother. Even though my stepmother is good to me, I don't feel I belong to her the way I belonged to Bibi when she was alive."

"I was told that I'm an orphan, but I wonder if my parents really are dead. When I was little, I prayed so hard for my mother to come, but I haven't even thought about her in the last year. If she's alive, it's too late for her to start loving me. I don't need her as much anymore."

41

Proof Positive

 We bought refreshments in Turiani before we began the hike to Mhonda. The Indian shopkeepers were happy to see us because students bought supplies from them. During the school year students often went to town to purchase small necessities at the Indian stores, and I'd tag along with Paulina or the Kifungilo girls. By the end of my first year in Mhonda, I knew every item and its price in each *duka* in Turiani.

When we arrived, we went straight to the dormitory to make our beds. I noticed that *Mwalimu* Agnesi's bed and furniture were gone. Our whole section was now filled with beds and in the front right corner was a proper teacher's bed with a mosquito net. I was thrilled not to have to see *Mwalimu* Agnesi first thing every morning. I no longer had to sit on my bed and listen to her chat and laugh with her chosen students as they ate heavenly smelling food, braided their hair, and talked about us.

There were several other changes in Mhonda for my Standard Eight year. Sister Florestina had been transferred, and Mother Majellis was now both Mother Superior and headmistress. *Mwalimu* Agnesi left, I found out, when Sister Florestina did.

Although the Catholic Precious Blood Order ran Mhonda, the government dictated the curriculum to prepare us to take the Territorial Exams. Teachers at the school were certified, while in missionary schools like Kifungilo, nuns and priests could teach whether they had teacher's training or not. A staff of five lay teachers—three women and two men, supported Mother Majellis, the only nun teacher this year. One of the teachers was Lucinda's friend, *Mwalimu* Clara, and another was *Mwalimu* Agnesi's younger sister,

195

Mwalimu Rosy who was the exact opposite of her sister. She was darker, her hair was coarser, and she dressed more like the Africans than her older sister did, but she was soft-spoken and kind and smiled a lot. We loved her as much as we loved our math teacher, *Mwalimu* Haule.

On the very first day of school, *Mwalimu* Haule told me to see him after class. The teachers were in one big room where each had a desk and a small metal bookcase. He was sitting on a cheap, gray metal chair with a wide seat that was too big for his thin frame. His trademark cotton, blue short-sleeve shirt was buttoned all the way to the neck and he had a beige sweater draped over his shoulders. "Tell me, did you find that things changed at the orphanage while you were away?"

"Everything was different because my childhood friend ran away, and no one knows where she is." *Mwalimu* Haule's face expressed concern. "When I left the first time, I had this strange feeling that I wouldn't see her again. Kifungilo wasn't the same without her."

"I'm sorry." He reached for my hand and held it in his. "It is always hard to lose a childhood friend." He was so sincere. I felt he really understood me. "As you grow up, you'll find out that life is a series of *jambos* and *kwaheris*—hellos and goodbyes. You cannot prepare for all your *jambos*, but you can and must prepare for your *kwaheris*. That way you'll be ready for your next *jambo* without the sad taste of your last *kwaheri*. When you part with a loved one, say your *kwaheri* as though it's the last time you'll be together. Then when you see that person again, it will be an unexpected feast day." I sensed that his words would guide me throughout my life.

He continued, "How many from your orphanage thirst for an education the way you do? How many have the intelligence necessary to fulfill that desire? How many would return to Mhonda after your experience last year? You have faith and perseverance. After many *jambos* and *kwaheris*, you will have a feast day that will last a long time—a feast day you will have earned because perseverance is the most rewarded of all virtues."

"*Asante, Mwalimu.*"

He let go of my hand and was quiet for a while. "I see you have a surname this year. How did you find out your name?"

"I chose it myself. I have no family and I knew I couldn't sit for the exams without one, so I made one up."

"That's brilliant!" *Mwalimu* Haule stood up and hugged me.

"I want to say *asante sana* for telling the students not to call me Mary Two last year. It was very kind of you. I still remember how you left the classroom that day. Were you ill?"

"No one there could ever forget that morning. Yes, I was ill." *Mwalimu* Haule crossed his hands over his heart. "In my heart. The students were horrified at the drilling you got about your name. It was shameful, cruel, and unnecessary. I took the matter to Mother Majellis and she too was very upset and quite angry at Sister Florestina. That day I decided I would always watch out for you." *Mwalimu* Haule was smiling now. "Little did I know that you're a *mwamba* and can take care of yourself."

"I may be a rock on the outside, but inside I'm made of sand. As long as I keep the sand in and don't let it seep out through the cracks, I'm all right."

"Just don't let the sand inside turn into rock, okay? You're a brave girl." He gave me a hug and I left his office. I realized as I walked into the courtyard that *Mwalimu* Haule did keep the promise he made to himself that day. I always felt that he had a special place in his heart for me. When I was sad or worried or scared or upset, his many words of encouragement would carry me through.

Life in Mhonda during the second year turned out to be a hundred times better emotionally, but physically it was just as hard as the first year. I found the chores quite difficult. The soil we had to prepare for planting was as dry and hard as always, and my hoe just bounced off when I tried to dig. If Paulina didn't help me every time it was my turn to plant maize, I'd never have finished. In spite of this difficulty, hoeing wasn't my worst chore. That was being in charge of meals, especially the midday one. Cooking the stiff *ugali* in the huge five-foot-tall petrol barrels built into elevated cement platforms was the toughest job for me. I didn't even know how to cook *ugali* with a regular wooden spoon in a small earthenware pot squatting on the ground like the Wasambaa. Much less could I do it standing on a narrow ledge pushing a heavy wooden ladle that was taller than

I was inside a giant barrel of boiling, steaming water. I dreaded that chore. I was so afraid I would fall into the barrel and boil to death before anyone found me.

I had already performed that chore a few times when one day my meal preparation partner happened to be Paulina. She usually helped me and did most of the stirring herself, but this day she had a cold and did only her share. I was stirring the *ugali* with all my strength while perspiration rolled off me in streams, mixing with the flour in the barrel. I couldn't remember perspiring that much except when I had malaria. Rivers of thick, hot perspiration flowed from my face, down my neck and stomach, in between my thighs where the heat became unbearable, and continued down my legs to my feet, where a tiny pool of hot sweat accumulated. When I was done, I was exhausted and got off the platform feeling like my body was as heavy as a petrol barrel.

"*Mungu wangu wee!*" Paulina screamed. "Mary, what's going on? Your legs and feet are covered with blood. How did you hurt yourself?" I was just as surprised as she was.

"I don't know. I've been feeling funny for a few days. Cooking today took every bit of energy I had."

"Let's go to the washing shed." All I could do was to put one foot in front of the other and pray that I'd be able to get myself to the shed. "Are you in pain? Should I take you to the infirmary?"

"I'm just tired. I want to lie down."

"Let's clean you up first. Then you can rest in the shade behind the shed." She helped me walk to the shed. "Pull up your uniform so I can clean your legs to see why you're bleeding. Oh, I know what it is. You just got your period!"

"My period? From my legs?"

"It's not from your legs. It's from your vagina. Remember I told you about it last year? I don't believe you're just getting it now. How could you stand there and cook and just let the blood flow?"

"I didn't know it was blood. I thought I was just perspiring more than usual today."

"Couldn't you feel where it was coming from? It's a lot for the first time. Well, maybe it came out all at once, instead of coming slowly for three or four days."

"Three or four days? Am I going to be sick for that long?"

"You're not sick, though I swear you look as if that barrel of *ugali* rolled over you."

"What am I going to do? I don't have any of those cloths the girls use for their period."

"I'll give you some of mine until you get your own."

"In Kifungilo, Sister Silvestris saved old flannel sheets and night-gowns and gave them to the big girls to make their period cloths."

"If we get our periods at different times of the month, we can share my cloths, otherwise maybe Lucinda can give you some."

"You're right. Over the holidays she made new ones for herself and for *Mwalimu* Clara. I didn't prepare for this. I guess I thought I'd never get my period because I didn't have a hole."

"Your period is positive proof that you have a hole. That's where the blood comes from."

"Now I can get pregnant?"

"That's right. No sleeping with men from now on," Paulina teased.

"Do you automatically get pregnant when you sleep with men?"

"'Sleeping with a man' is a saying that means doing the act. You can do the act with a man anywhere—under a tree, on the bus as Juma tried, by the river, or in the kitchen. You don't need a bed."

"Paulina, I must be the most ignorant person you've ever met! Who would tell me these things if you didn't?"

Paulina showed me how to use the rags, then Lucinda kindly gave me her old ones that were softer than Paulina's and much easier to use. I tied them on with a string instead of jamming them into my panties like Paulina. I had lots of questions about my period and its role in pregnancy and birth that Paulina couldn't answer to my satisfaction. One thing I did learn: I hated how my period interfered with my life. My stomach hurt, it called attention to "that part" of my body all day long, it took time to attend to, and every month I was afraid it wouldn't stop and I'd bleed to death. And I couldn't understand why students announced their periods by saying, "My friend has arrived." My period could never become my friend.

42

BBC News

"I am walking to the door." Mother Majellis super-enunciated the phrase and the entire English class stood up and repeated the phrase loudly as we walked to the door. "We are looking out the window." Jostling each other and laughing, we chanted that phrase on our way to the window.

My first year in Mhonda, Sister Florestina taught English. I remembered little, except that I couldn't understand why she taught the class when she spoke English with such a strong German accent. My second year, Mother Majellis was the teacher and we all loved her. We looked forward to her daily class where we could talk and be noisy. She told us we had to act out everything we learned because that way we would imprint the words on our brains. When Mother said, "I am standing on my chair," she had us repeat the phrase and climb on our chairs. My favorite was "I am dancing on the table."

Unfortunately, I was so tired from acting and vocalizing in English class that by the time I got to Domestic Science, I couldn't concentrate. We were mostly taught how to cook *wazungu* food. I found the class boring and irrelevant, so I daydreamed. Consequently, I was never able to bake a cake, make custard pudding, potato soup, or any of the *wazungu* foods the teacher demonstrated. My food turned out lumpy and nobody wanted to be my cooking partner.

The teachers in Mhonda were certified and received a salary from the government. We had a set of government-issued textbooks in each classroom and two students shared one book. Books had to be returned in perfect condition at the end of the year so we made sturdy covers to protect them. Students also shared a desk that had an attached bench and a compartment for school supplies. Most of us had only one pencil and one ballpoint pen. We cut our pencils in half to give to friends who had lost theirs.

Our subjects were English, mathematics, geography, history, Current Affairs, Domestic Science, and religion. Muslim girls at the school didn't have to attend religion class or go to Mass. *Mwalimu* Clara, one of our Standard Seven teachers, taught most subjects and was as gentle and kind as *Mwalimu* Haule. She took our side and defended us half-castes against false accusations by other students.

My favorite class in Mhonda was mathematics, not only because I was good at it, but because I knew that *Mwalimu* Haule had a soft spot for me. *Mwalimu* Haule also taught Current Affairs where we studied the countries of the world in depth. We learned everything from the heads of state to per capita income. In geography class, we had studied the names, capitals, mountains, and rivers of all the countries in the world along with their major tourist attractions, but now we probed the inner workings of each country, especially England and the United States, discussing the American constitution, memorizing the states and their capitals, and the names of their senators and governors. *Mwalimu* Haule made it so interesting we didn't mind learning about the industries and populations of each state, the universities and other institutions of higher learning. We even studied American prisons and how they operated. *Mwalimu* Haule used well-worn books, old newspapers, clippings from international magazines and read us articles from the paper, then had us discuss what we were learning. We felt smart gaining so much knowledge about other countries, though we knew little about our own. To remedy that, *Mwalimu* Haule brought a little radio for us to hear the day's local news in Swahili. For most of us, it was the first time we'd listened to a radio. We were very attentive even though the static hurt our ears.

At noon on Sundays all two hundred students and teachers gathered in the dining hall to listen to the BBC World News in English and a half hour of East African Weekly News broadcast by *Sauti ya Dar-es-Salaam*—Voice of Dar-es-Salaam—in Swahili. Sitting on the cement floor, we concentrated on the news coming from the small black radio perched on the shelf and tried to memorize the broadcast in order to discuss it.

One Sunday he had us listen to developments in our country. Tanganyika was requesting independence from Britain. We had heard rumors about neighboring Kenya's fight for Independence and how their leader had been imprisoned by the British for demanding that right. In Tanganyika a schoolteacher from the Lake Victoria Region, Julius Kambarage Nyerere, was leading the quest for independence.

We crowded as close as we could to the little radio to hear every word. I studied the faces of my schoolmates as we listened to Mr. Nyerere's forceful voice. He urged people to join the party working for independence, TANU, the Tanganyika African National Union. He told us that independence did not simply mean freedom from the power and grip of white people. It meant freedom but also hard work to develop ourselves and our country, self-reliance, and self-determination both locally and internationally. He spoke of freedom for every citizen to not only have a part in the wealth and resources of Tanganyika, but also to take care of our neighbors the way our tradition dictated.

My own heart was beating hard, and my imagination was soaring. I saw hope and excitement on the faces of some companions, while others looked puzzled and even a bit fearful. Mr. Nyerere, a Catholic, finished with a prayer. "We beg you, God in heaven, help us take back the dignity and equal rights that are our birthright."

We barely took a breath after the radio went off. "What does this mean?" several students asked, then everyone chimed in. "What about our tribes and our families?" "Will there be trouble like in Kenya?" "Does this mean we won't have cars anymore? Will we go back to our primitive ways?" "This seems too risky. Maybe it's better to remain a British Colony." "Who will maintain the schools, hospitals, and railroads if the British leave? Are there enough educated Africans to run the country?"

Mwalimu Haule listened to our questions and discussion then raised his hand for silence. After a long pause he said, "You are right. There are many risks and many difficult issues that independence will bring. Challenges will come from within and from outside our country. But this is why your education is so important. You will be the ones helping Mr. Nyerere make Tanganyika an African nation. You each will have a part to play."

We all sensed the seriousness of this effort, but felt that Mr. Nyerere would keep his promises as our president and were excited about becoming an independent nation. Even though we were aware that the transition from being ruled to ruling ourselves would be difficult, we understood that we would have our dignity. We would no longer be second-class citizens in our own country. We knew that Africans were not perfect and that our tribal customs reflected the same British social class hierarchies that Mr. Nyerere said would be abolished if we got independence. No matter the hardships, we all agreed it would be better to have one of our own as head of our country. And we pondered what roles we might play in the new nation.

43

Territorial Exams

 By the first week of December we were preparing full time for the Territorial Exams. These exams were given throughout the country to all Standard Eight students on the same day, and they covered everything taught from Standard Five through Eight. How we did on the exams determined our further education. Mother Majellis urged us to study hard to make Mhonda proud. If we did very well in the exams, we would be selected to continue to secondary school. When we took our exams, we listed preferences for teacher training, secretarial college, nursing and vocational schools or secondary school. Only a handful of students would be selected for secondary school, she warned us, because there were very few such schools in the country, and the available spaces were usually given to boys. But she encouraged us to list what we wanted and had us repeat after her a favorite expression from English class: "Nothing ventured, nothing gained." I knew that I wanted to go to secondary school and that my second and third choices didn't matter. But I put down teacher training and women's vocational school as my second and third choices.

The next afternoon *Mwalimu* Haule got me excused from chores because he wanted me to help correct math papers. While working with him, he asked me if I wanted to go on to secondary school.

"Yes! I want to go to school forever, but even if I do well, I'm a girl and probably won't be chosen."

"I want to talk to you about that," *Mwalimu* Haule said. He told me about Marian College, the first secondary school for girls, founded two years ago in Morogoro by American Catholic nuns. "I'll write a recommendation for you. I'm sure you'd be admitted." A government committee controlled higher education, and he said that if I wasn't chosen, he'd personally investigate why not.

"I'd be the happiest person on earth if I could go there. Two girls from Kifungilo went there after they finished in Kongei. When they returned for holidays last year, all they talked about was the American nuns who acted like ordinary people."

"All nuns are ordinary people, you know."

"No, they're not. I know two nuns who came straight from hell. And I've known other nuns who were so good, you'd think they came straight from heaven."

"I heard that Sister Florestina was sent back to the Motherhouse in Europe."

"Good. Maybe they can retrain her to do God's work."

"She never broke your spirit, though."

"When I was young I cried a lot, but then I decided that no one would make me cry against my will."

"And your mind controls your will. Continue to use your mind and you'll go far. You must have faith that anything is possible."

"Thank you, *Mwalimu*. You made a big difference in my life here."

"It's my job. Some students need guidance, others understanding, but all need love."

"If I don't get into secondary school, I'll become a teacher like you. I might forget everything you taught me about math, but I'll never forget you."

"Thank you, *Mwamba*."

The exams were nearly upon us, and we studied day and night. On the day of exams, Mass was offered for us. I prayed hard and promised God that if I was chosen for secondary school, I would do whatever he wanted me to do, even become a nun.

At eight o'clock the morning of the exams, a forest green Land Rover pulled up in front of the office and two Africans dressed in leisure suits got out. Their driver brought several cardboard boxes into the office. I entered the silent classroom where the mood was fearful and expectant. We sat in our desks, clutching a ballpoint pen, pencil, and eraser. At 8:30 sharp, the proctor walked in. We stood up, "Good Morning, Sir."

As the driver brought the boxes in, the proctor gave us instructions. "The first exams will be Health Science and Swahili. If you finish before the allotted four hours, bring your papers to me and leave. In the afternoon you will have Math and English exams, and tomorrow morning Domestic Science and Geography." The proctor opened a box and handed out the exams written on pale blue paper.

Although they weren't as hard as I'd expected, many students were in tears when they left the classroom. They feared they had done badly and were petrified of repercussions from their parents, especially students whose families weren't convinced about the value of educating girls who would become mothers and homemakers.

After the last exam, Paulina and I, confident that we'd passed, discussed our plans for the future as she packed her things.

"Teacher's college is my first choice. Baba wants me to be a teacher. I'd be the first woman teacher from my village and that would make him very proud."

"I wonder where I'll be."

"At Marian College, of course. If you don't make it to secondary school, no one will."

I wasn't so sure. I had learned never to take anything for granted and never to believe anything was going to happen until it did. Paulina said we'd see each other when I returned to Kifungilo for holidays. Again, I wasn't so sure. Up to now in my life, every time I said goodbye to someone I loved, it was a last farewell. I told Paulina I looked forward to seeing her, but I didn't fully believe what I said. I recognized the feeling I always had when I said goodbye.

The day before we left Mhonda for good, we celebrated by dancing and singing until midnight. I danced so hard that when I finally went to bed, pleasantly exhausted, I realized that no matter what scars Mhonda had left on my soul, it also provided me a way of healing myself through dance and that was something no one could take from me. That was middle school's unexpected and invaluable gift. I knew that I would always have dance in my life.

It was hard to say goodbye to *Mwalimu* Haule. His kindness and understanding broke all the rules of being male. In English class we learned the expression "the exception to the rule," and we had to use it in a sentence. My sentence was: "We know that all men are evil, but kind and considerate *Mwalimu* Haule is the exception to the rule." Mother Majellis declared that it was a very good example.

He shook each of our hands on the last day of class and left before the exams. When it was my turn to say goodbye, my stomach tightened up. He was the first man I ever got to know and he was a good man. I held his hand for a long time and simply said, *"Asante sana, sana, Mwalimu."*

"Mwamba, Mwamba, Mwamba," he said instead of saying *kwaheri*.

We sang and danced as we walked to the bus at Turiani, holding hands and promising to stay in touch with friends. Paulina and I didn't speak much during the trip. Every time I wanted to tell her what she had meant to me and how often I thanked God for sending her my way, I felt that familiar heavy, dull pain of loss. When we got off the bus, I saw her father walking toward us and the Kifungilo van waiting on the side of the road.

I tried to put my feelings into words. "Paulina, I'll never forget you. You were my father, my mother, my brother, my sister, and my tribe. We might never see each other again, but you will live in my heart forever. I love you, and I thank you for being my friend." But Paulina headed toward her father. "Please, Paulina, look at me for the last time." She kept walking. "Goodbye, Paulina. Paulina!" I turned and went toward our blue van with a crushed heart. But then I remembered I wanted to give her the beautiful green rhinestone necklace set from Sister Silvestris. I had put it in my pocket that morning for her. After telling Paulina on our trip to Mhonda that I had a present for her, I had forgotten about it and left it in the corner of my suitcase all year.

I turned and saw her running towards me. We wrapped our arms around each other without saying a word. When we let go, I put my gift in her hand. She hugged it to her chest, saying, *"Asante sana rafiki mpendwa."* Yes, she was my beloved friend. Paulina's eyes were swollen with tears and mine were filled with love, gratitude, and pain of loss.

"She was your good friend?" Sister Silvestris asked me when I got into the van.

"Yes. Without her, life in Mhonda would have been unbearable."

On the drive back with Lucinda, I realized the two of us had rarely been together during the year at Mhonda. She spent her free time with *Mwalimu* Clara and didn't dance and hang out with the African students like I did.

Sister Silvestris had plans for us. "Next year, you'll stay in Kifungilo and help me with the children. We have twelve new children, and several big girls have left. Mary, you can teach dances and what you learned in school. Lucinda, you will help me in the sewing room."

I took a deep breath. "I can't wait to teach the children new dances and songs to perform for the old nuns at Christmas time. But if I pass my exams, I won't be in Kifungilo next year. I want to go to the new girls' secondary school run by American Sisters in Morogoro."

"American Sisters? How can Americans run anything?" she said with disdain. "The Americans nuns are worldly and soft. They know nothing about discipline. Africa is not for them."

"Mother Rufina will never allow any more of our girls to go to that American School," Sister Fabiana warned. "They become spoiled and lazy just like the nuns."

I was in trouble. Even if I passed the exams and was selected for Marian College, I probably couldn't go because Mother Rufina disapproved of the nuns who ran it.

The two months of waiting to find out if I'd passed the exams would be an eternity. Maybe it would have been better if I hadn't had a taste of school and been exposed to a world of possibilities outside of Kifungilo. If I couldn't continue with school, I was sure I would resent the Sisters of Kifungilo.

"I'd prefer to have you stay with me in Kifungilo," Sister Silvestris said after a long silence, "but if Mother Rufina thinks it's all right to send you to an undisciplined American school, that will be her decision."

The conversation turned to Lucinda who planned to become a teacher. Sister explained that Kifungilo was becoming a proper, government-accredited school up to Standard Four and that they would admit African students in the future. Lucinda was assured of a teaching position.

I thought about these changes as the van wound its way along the narrow road to Kifungilo. Would I ever be able to stop worrying about my future? Was there such a thing as a secure, predictable future? Maybe the future seems so attractive because it is unknown—and my past left so much to be desired. If I couldn't go to secondary school, what should I do? Marry the first man I meet, run away from him, get a job, earn money for school fees, and then go to secondary school? Would they accept me? Where would I go for holidays? Would the nuns take me back, or should I find Paulina's village and live with her family? If I had parents, would they be making these decisions for me? Would having parents solve my problems? Questions and more questions crowded my mind assuring me that I'd have plenty to think and worry about while I awaited the results of the Standard Eight Territorial Exams.

44

Flashback

Another plan Sister Silvestris had for me during my two months of vacation, or forever, as she hoped, was to take care of little Monika, a five-year-old new orphan. At first I was excited to have someone in my charge even though I was only fifteen. When I was Mary *Mdogo*—Little Mary—the big girls seemed very old to me. I was happy to be a big girl and promised myself I would be kind and gentle like Rosa.

Monika was not a precocious, scared, lonely, and fat crybaby like I was. Thin with pretty green eyes, golden kinky hair, and very light skin, she was full of mischief and knew that she could get away with anything because I treated her like my little doll. She refused to let me comb her hair and would literally roll in the dirt after I had bathed her and changed her clothes.

One day I was thoroughly annoyed with her, so I sat her down to recite the rules of behavior toward her big girl to avoid beatings. She listened carefully and then laughed and dared me to touch her. Sister Silvestris had already told me several times how disappointed she was that I had learned nothing from my big girl Zami about taking care of little children. "You might be clever and want to go to secondary school, but your primary role in life will be to get married, have children, and take care of them."

Despite constant flashbacks of Zami beating me, often for no reason except that I was in the wrong place at the wrong time, I became so frustrated with Monika that one day I found myself cutting a flexible green twig from the passion fruit vines behind the laundry room and waiting for her to talk back or disobey me. Monika had told me that she wasn't afraid of me.

"Monika, please come and help me fetch water for washing your clothes."

"I can't carry a heavy pail of water and I don't have to help you."

"Look, when I was little we had to carry water from the river, but now there are two taps in the laundry room. You don't have to fill up the pail. Just carry as much as you can."

"Make me do it!"

With that, I grabbed her left arm and pulled her close. "Today I will show you who is the big girl and who is the little girl. I'm in charge here." I ordered her to stand in front of me. With my stick in hand, I told her to put one hand out, palm up, for me to hit it just like Sister Clotilda did in class.

She pulled away from me and started running, saying, "You can't catch me."

I ran after her and caught her by her dress without too much difficulty. Angrily I said to her, "Stand in front of me and put out your hand. From now on, you will get two sticks every time you disobey me. I should have done this the first time you were naughty." To my surprise Monika put her right hand out to me and I hit it hard.

She started crying and screaming and tried to run. I stopped her and stood her in front of me. I raised my arm to hit her again. As she put out her hand for me to strike, I saw a little stream of blood trickle down her fingers. I saw droplets of blood on her yellow dress. I saw a barefoot little girl with two long braids trembling as she gingerly put her hand out for Sister Clotilda to strike. I saw Fat Mary's face covered with tears as she fixed her eyes on the cement floor, bracing herself for the next blow. My arm holding the stick stopped and trembled in midair. Fear, pity, and shame overwhelmed me as I dropped the stick and let out a cry that was louder than Monika's. Tears that were denied for years came pouring out as if from a bursting dam. I pulled little Monika to me and held her tight while I sobbed. Her crying became soft, evenly paced whimpers and my own sobs quieted down.

What was I doing? Why was I beating this child? What was the matter with me? Was I beating her because it was expected of me? Was I beating her to see what it felt like to be a big girl?

"I'm sorry for beating you, Monika. Please forgive me. I'll never do it again."

"But you're supposed to beat me when I misbehave. The other little girls were jealous when I was assigned to you because they said you were kind, and you always played with them and helped them with their chores. Now I can tell them that you tried to beat me."

"Please tell them that it's wrong to beat a child. Tell them it won't happen again, and that it hurt me more than it hurt you."

"I don't believe that, but I do believe you won't ever beat me again."

"That's a promise. Now you have to promise never to give me a reason to beat you. Can you do that?'

"I'll try."

I didn't touch little Monika again and her behavior improved. Mostly.

45

The Americans

 I passed my exams and Mother Rufina arranged for me to go to the secondary school in Morogoro. If Kifungilo had done the required job of building my character, then no undisciplined American Sisters could spoil me. She told me that I ranked at the very top of eighth graders who took the standardized tests that year in Tanganyika and that she was willing to pay for my next four years of school. The only requirement was to pay her back.

Morogoro was only about twenty miles further on the same bus line from Mombo to Turiani, but being the only Kifungilo girl to make the trip on the bus was scary. There was no Paulina or Lucinda, and I was the only schoolgirl on the bus for that day-long trip. Sister Dolores Marie, the headmistress, met my bus in Morogoro and drove me in a huge, luxurious sea-green Chevrolet to Marian College, my new boarding school. Her long white robe, with a black veil that came to a sharp point at the center of her forehead, made her look like a crow stretching its beak to the sky.

"You must be Mary Ryne," she smiled as she reached out a warm hand to greet me. "Welcome to Marian College." She said my last name wrong, and I was about to correct her when I realized that Ryne sounded better than Ryme so I decided to use it. I wondered if she knew anything about me, or if she would ask me a million questions that I did not want to, or could not, answer. Sister Dolores Marie took me to the convent, which was a far cry from the stately burnt-brick and red-tiled roof convent of the Precious Blood Sisters of Kifungilo. Even though the Maryknoll Sisters' convent was just as big as the one in Kifungilo, it was made of cement and had a plain

213

corrugated iron roof. Sister took me to their receiving room and another nun brought us some Coca-Cola and Marie Biscuits.

These were no German nuns! Both of them sat with me and smiled the entire time as though they were interested in what I had to say. I was shy and afraid. Their English was different and smooth, and I didn't understand much of what they said. Although I answered most of their questions in monosyllables and looked at the floor throughout this first encounter with Americans, they said that my English was quite good and they were happy to have me in their school. An African girl dressed in a green and tan uniform knocked at the door and said she'd take me to my dorm. From her accent, I could tell that she was from the Chagga tribe.

We walked a few yards past the classrooms and then further up to the dormitories. I heard students talking, laughing, and singing as they sat on steps braiding their hair or washing their clothes. I didn't see any other half-castes, but no one paid any undue attention to me. The buildings were smaller and much better constructed than the ones in Mhonda, but not as beautiful as the new dorm in Kifungilo. Instead of having one huge dormitory for all the students, there were several small ones, named after saints, each housing twenty-five students.

The student took me to Saint Joseph's Hall and showed me my bed. A small varnished wooden cupboard for my belongings stood near the head. The beds were like the metal ones with springs in Kifungilo. I sensed right away that life at Marian College would be much better than in Mhonda. My bed was against the far wall next to the small room where the dorm prefect slept. There was plenty of space between the beds. Some students had straw mats on the floor and all the beds had mosquito nets. I finally understood why Sister Silvestris searched far and wide to find one for me to bring. Kifungilo was too cold to have mosquitoes but here nets were a necessity.

I emptied my suitcase and arranged my belongings on the cabinet's two shelves, placing each item inside with pride and satisfaction. I put the lock that Sister had given me on the latch, locked it, and put the key in my bra. I put my new *merikani* sheets on the sisal mattress and spread out the hand-knit woolen blanket that a generous German had sent to Kifungilo in the Christmas boxes. I put the dainty pillowcase that I had embroidered with daisies a few weeks earlier on the wonderful down-filled pillow I had taken to Mhonda and attached the mosquito net to the corners of the metal frame above the bed. Most of the other beds in the dorm had raggedy blankets and mismatched *khangas* for sheets.

Each cabinet was marked with the name of its owner, and I noticed that the girl next to me was Henrietta Selemani. I wondered if we would be friends, or if she would hate me because I was half-caste. As I rested on my bed, I wondered what was ahead for me. I didn't know anyone here. I felt physically and emotionally isolated. Would my lifelong habit of analyzing and searching for answers within myself serve me here too?

The ringing of a very loud bell returned me to boarding school routine. Students appeared from everywhere. I followed them into a huge dining room that had about twenty long rectangular tables with narrow benches on each side of a wide aisle. Students at the tables were laughing and speaking extremely broken English. Another bell rang and the hall was silent. A Maryknoll nun with a very red face and small eyes that darted around the room from under her pointed headpiece stood at the center of the dining room and led us in saying grace. It was the same prayer we said in Kifungilo and in Mhonda, except it sounded like the nun was singing. Her English was smooth and melodious. I wondered how it could be the same language, and if American English sounded so fluid and relaxed because they lacked the discipline to pronounce all the letters. I liked it right away and made a resolution to learn to speak like them.

Sister told us that after dinner we could finish unpacking and preparing for church the next day. As soon as she left, the room grew noisy as students ate their *ugali* and beans and spoke in many tribal languages. Getting ready for church on Sunday turned out to be a big deal. Back in the dorm, the girls ironed their dresses and polished their leather shoes and cleaned their canvas ones. They braided their hair into elegant designs adding shiny hairpins, beads, and ribbons.

The church, which the Americans called "chapel," was tiny compared to those at Mhonda and Kifungilo, and it was very simply decorated. Mass was also very basic with little rehearsed singing. I hoped that the spontaneous harmonizing, characteristic of most African gatherings, would please God just as much as formal rehearsed songs. The nuns didn't seem to care whether we knelt upright or sat down during the service. It felt like they aimed for a direct path to God and didn't want to put obstacles in our way like the German nuns did. They actually looked around during service and smiled and nodded as we entered the church and when we went up for Communion. They seemed to accept us as mostly good girls rather than sinners who should constantly be begging for forgiveness every minute we were in church.

As for me, I prayed very little that first Sunday at Marian college. I was too busy trying to understand these American missionaries. Why were they so different from the Germans? Wasn't Catholicism the same everywhere in the world? Why did these Maryknoll nuns act as if religion was something you could like and even enjoy? They also didn't put on saintly mannerisms when in church. It seemed they were true to who they were in front of God.

That day I felt that God could be as loving, caring, and attentive as Baby Jesus had been in the Christmas Nativity scene and that maybe God wasn't principally interested in punishment. Whenever I went to church, I first prayed for forgiveness for my sins before asking for anything. Although I often couldn't name those sins, I figured that God was keeping track, and even if I forgot, he knew all the evil things I'd done. But here at Marian College, I felt I could jump right in and pray for whatever I wanted and God would accept my prayers. Why did I feel this way? Was it the American Sisters' attitude toward religion and us, or had I matured enough to understand that religion was a personal matter and that, apart from the actual doctrine of the Catholic Church, no one could dictate what religion should mean to me?

We gathered in the recreation hall after breakfast and the Sisters and two lay teachers entered the hall after we were seated. Even the nuns' names were different. They each had two Christian names like Sister Dolores Marie, Sister Marian Teresa, Sister Antonita Rose, Sister Paul Mary, and Sister Martin Corde. To my great surprise, two of the four lay teachers were half-castes. Although I was proud to know that there were other half-castes who had made something of their lives, I expected nothing from them.

Sister Dolores Marie, the headmistress, had a very soft voice and smiled as she read us the rules and regulations. Her face was narrow and her long nose curved down at the tip, almost touching her upper lip when she smiled. As far as looks were concerned, I preferred the habits of the Precious Blood Sisters. As the Sisters nodded or moved in their chairs, which they frequently did, the pointed tip of the black headpieces and their flowing veils made them look like giant crows agreeing on the tastiness of a fresh ear of corn. It was hard to take them seriously. They seemed even more out of place among us than the German nuns did because they had no idea how to pronounce Swahili words, and the harder they tried, the funnier they were. Out of respect we didn't laugh. And to make sure that they would never learn correct Swahili, we always had to speak English. I was very happy with that rule because I had no tribal language, and even though my English was horrendous compared to the music of the Americans' speech, it was much better than the heavily accented, almost incomprehensible English spoken by most of the students.

Our headmistress said that our assigned classrooms would be posted on the bulletin board next to her office, and everything we were required to know each day would also be posted there. She explained that we were grouped according to our academic (another new American word) ability, so we would each receive instruction at our level of comprehension. I don't think most of us understood what that meant, but who would dare question our placement anywhere, for anything, for any reason by a teacher, especially by a *mzungu*?

Letters or packages from home would be set on the windowsill in the headmistress's office, and letters for mailing could be dropped in a box inside her office. When she had finished explaining all this, the other nuns spoke to us about tryouts for the glee club, drama club, and a Future Farmers of Africa Club. This last American-style club puzzled us. Why would we go to school and then go back to work in the fields? The club never attracted members.

Much to my relief, most students were very friendly. Upper level classmates, who were called "Pioneers" denoting their status as the first students to attend the only secondary school for African girls in the entire country, took great pride in showing new students like me around and telling us about our groundbreaking school. Everything was Pioneer this, Pioneer that, Pioneers first, Pioneers in front. Having never heard the word before, I thought that in American English it meant the color green because all Pioneers wore green uniforms. Each class, it turned out, had its own color. There were the Greens who were the Pioneers, the Pinks who came the following year, and the Blues, my class. The class after mine would be the Yellows. As each class graduated, the incoming students took their color.

Even though we wore the same color uniform for four years, each year we were labeled by the uniquely American terms Freshmen, Sophomores, Juniors, and Seniors. These terms sounded so much more sophisticated and prestigious than Standards Nine, Ten, Eleven, and Twelve. These Americans know a thing or two about self-esteem, or maybe this was an example of "calling things other than what they are" that Mother Rufina spoke about when she gave me her last words of advice before I left for school. "It's very hard to know if Americans mean what they say or say what they mean," she had warned me. "They seldom knowingly tell lies, but they give you the truth in bits and pieces, bits and pieces, bits and pieces. You must listen to them carefully and always ask questions."

In Mhonda I had to get used to the students, but at Marian College I had to figure out my American teachers. They used many new and big American words, which we couldn't find in our dictionaries. Tanganyika was a British colony and whatever little English we spoke was British English. The Cambridge Exam we would take at the end of Standard Twelve—I should say our senior year—would be in the Queen's English. And it was evident that they didn't know how to exercise authority or how to treat us. They explained everything and gave us reasons for their rules. The African way, especially for students under *wazungu* teachers, was always to obey and say "yes" and never to disagree with or question authority. Did our opinion really matter to them? And didn't they know that it's hard to take seriously someone in authority who smiles a lot?

I didn't know how to feel. On one hand, were these nuns really honest or did Mother Rufina's analysis of Americans in general apply to them? On the other, it was a relief to finally find such human nuns and to be at a school where what I thought mattered.

However, I found the American teaching style quite amusing. Instead of writing everything on the board and then having us memorize it for a test, they took forever to present a new topic, and even if it required the entire hour to get two words out of us, they insisted on "discussion." I hated that word. They were the teachers. Why did they want to learn anything about their subjects from us? Most of us were very shy, and the monosyllabic answers we gave to questions should have convinced them to abandon that style of teaching—but no. I truly wondered if any of them were "real" teachers, or if they were simply missionaries who did what missionaries do: teach their doctrine and culture to the less fortunate. And it was also odd that no matter how wrong an answer was, they smiled and said, "Not quite!"

So we presumed that because we could never be a hundred percent wrong, we would never fail any exams. We were wrong. Students did fail tests. Why didn't our opinions matter on paper like they did when we answered questions orally? I figured out that only the American teaching style was different. Just like the Germans, they wanted us to repeat exactly what they taught in class. The endless "discussions" were simply to make us practice speaking English.

There were several students we called *wafariseo*—Pharisees— because they did everything right. They obeyed all the rules and tattled on those who, like me, took liberties with the regulations. They became prefects of the dormitories and classrooms and represented the students in speeches to visitors. Their hands were permanently raised in class either to ask or to answer questions. They were seen reading in the library and studying in the classroom during our free time, and they spoke English loudly whenever a teacher was near.

Another innovation in this American school was the library. We were supposed to borrow books and read as much as we could for no reason at all. Imagine reading a book that wasn't a textbook! Most of the books were about saints, some of whom I had never heard of—like Kateri Tekakwitha, an American Indian. Maybe American Catholics had their own saints. How did the Sisters decide which saints' lives we should read? Did they play favorites with the saints as some of them did with the students?

The books not about saints were mostly called "classics." After reading some classics, I realized that they could only be written by *wazungu,* because all the classics in our small library were by American and European authors.

Apart from being confused half the time, I liked Marian College. Yet Mother Rufina's assessment of Americans made a lot of sense. Every time I was puzzled, I remembered her warning about the undisciplined Americans who never say what they mean or mean what they say and tell the truth in bits and pieces. I wondered where she had learned so much about the Americans. As I went through secondary school, which they called High School, this advice was very helpful. I understood them so much better than most of my classmates.

46

New Friends

 In the dormitory, the chapel, the classroom, and in most of what we did, we were in alphabetical order. I saw on the bulletin board that I was in Form IA along with Henrietta Selemani, whose bed was next to mine. I was anxious to meet her. She arrived late, and I explained everything I'd learned about the school to her, for which she was grateful. She wasn't as warm toward me as my African friend Paulina had been, but I hoped that she was only shy and not afraid of me as, for some reason, she seemed to be.

One night, I heard Henrietta crying. "Is anything wrong?" I asked her.

"I traveled a week by bus, train, and on foot to get here, and now I'm not sure I can be away from home for ten months. I miss everyone."

I went under the mosquito net on her bed and stroked her face as she cried.

"My mother didn't want me to leave. Morogoro is farther than anyone in our family has traveled before, but my father insisted that I come. He said that *wazungu* from America treated Africans much better than *wazungu* from Europe. That's the only reason I came. I hate the *wazungu*."

"Your father is right. These Maryknoll Sisters are far different from the German nuns at my other schools. They smile a lot, they sit right next to us, and they act like they want to help us, not just save our souls."

"Don't be fooled. All missionaries believe that their culture and religion are better than ours. And American *wazungu* don't learn our languages like the European *wazungu* do."

"But have you heard the Germans speak Swahili? They butcher the words and make up part-German ones."

"That's why your Swahili is so bad. I was afraid of talking to you. You're the first half-caste I've met. The ones I've seen are usually arrogant and they think they're better than Africans."

"Well, everyone is better or worse than somebody else in certain things. I'm better in English than you, but your Swahili is so beautiful! I want to speak just like you some day."

"You help me with English and I'll help you with Swahili, okay?"

"I've figured out something about these American nuns. Although I don't know if they always tell the truth, there are white lies and black lies, and I think they only tell white lies."

"I'll try to remember that. *Lala salama, rafiki.*"

I felt pleased she called me friend as she said good night. "*Lala salama,* Henrietta!"

Henrietta and I were together for everything in school, from study hall to chores to kneeling side by side in chapel. She wasn't a warm person, but she was very understanding. She didn't ask me embarrassing questions like why I never received letters from home, or why no one ever came to visit me on Sunday afternoons when almost everyone in school had a relative or boyfriend visitor, or why I never went to town to buy biscuits, *sambusas,* or mangos. And she shared whatever she had with me.

One Sunday after dressing up, she opened a jar of *Mono Snow,* a fluffy and pearly-white skin bleaching cream and vigorously rubbed it into her face. "You don't need to use this, but it lightens my skin and the longer I use it, the lighter my skin will be." I watched her rub her face, and to my surprise, the *Mono Snow* cream did work. Her skin was lighter, although it looked ashy and gray.

"Today, my friend, please come with me and visit with my guests in the recreation hall." Her guests were two young men. One of them started smiling and talking as soon as he saw me. "My name is Peter Mganga. It gives me much pleasure to know your name."

Henrietta and her male friend disappeared and left me alone with Peter. I wondered what I was supposed to do with him. Peter took a melted Cadbury milk chocolate bar from his pocket and put it in my hand. "Thank you," I said and started walking back toward the dormitory.

"Don't leave! I want you to be my girlfriend."

I froze. What did that mean? Did it mean that I might get pregnant soon? At age sixteen I had no idea what this young boy wanted or how to respond. This was another area where I didn't understand the American nuns. How could they allow boys to come and visit girls in school? Didn't they know that men are wicked and that the only thing they wanted with women was to do the act and make them pregnant?

"Are you all right? You look worried. Say something!"

How could Henrietta do this to me? Didn't she fear men? There was no way I could be someone's girlfriend. I was ugly. Why would any man want to be my boyfriend?

"Did I say something wrong? What's the matter?"

"I can't be anyone's girlfriend because I'm ugly and I want to finish school." It was Peter's turn to freeze.

"I...I don't, I don't want...to...marry...you. I also go to school. I just want to come and see you and have a friendship."

"Thank you very much, but please don't come to see me again. I don't like men and I am afraid of them." Peter lowered his eyes and tried to say something, but I left him standing there. He seemed hurt and sad. Maybe this was one of those moments where an American white lie might be better than telling the truth. But how do you lie about something you've always known is true? Henrietta was so angry at my behavior that she avoided me for a long time.

The American nuns forever endeared themselves to me because, in their great wisdom, they decreed that every Sunday after supper we all had to go to the recreation hall to learn each other's tribal dances. This requirement offset for me whatever was strange or undisciplined about them. In Henrietta's absence, I spent time with two other Blues, Stella from Dar-es-Salaam and Theresa from Muheza, which was in the Tanga district like Lushoto. They were the flipside of Henrietta in personality. Just like me, they loved to dance. We formed a threesome and called ourselves Happy (me), Sunny (Stella), and Smiley (Theresa).

Although there were less than two hundred students in the Pioneer classes of Greens, Pinks, and Blues, sixty different tribes were represented at our small school. The Chagga tribe from the Kilimanjaro area had the most students, so we had to learn their dances first, though their tame steps and singing were boring. Sunny, Smiley, and I pouted our way through their *Ooh-yay-eeh, wilele wilele wilele*, a very repetitive song and dance whose steps were simply tiny jumps to the right and left of a circle with our feet together and arms around each other's shoulders. We loved the dances of students from the Fipa tribe around Kigoma (Henrietta's tribe), the Hehe near Iringa, and the Nyamwezi from Dar. The Fipa had very clever footwork; the Hehe danced wildly, stooping over and keeping their bodies close to the ground while the Nyamwezi *sindimba* dance called for furiously rolling and shaking our hips.

I wasn't required to teach a dance since I didn't belong to a tribe, however I insisted on teaching the students the only authentic dance I knew—the German Waltz. Sunny beat a slow waltz rhythm on the drum as Smiley and I practiced the steps during the week, and by Sunday we were ready. Soon the entire auditorium was happily humming a song I learned from Sister Theonesta. Smiley and I each escorted a student to the center of the room, and while Sunny beat the drum, we sang *Wunderbar Wunderbar* and showed them how to waltz. They loved this stiff dance and from then on requested it almost every Sunday evening. One evening I taught them another of my "tribal" waltz songs, "Beautiful Girl on the Prairie." They loved it just as much, except we sang *Bee-you-tee-fool-gal-on-de-plaayly*.

Soon we realized that we could waltz to almost any song in English, so members of the glee club taught us American songs like "Home on the Range," "Yellow Rose of Texas," and "Git Along, Little Dogies" and we danced away. We performed dances for teachers' feast days and religious holidays.

Namesake days were very important to the American nuns. Our classrooms were decorated with flowers and we wore our best dresses. We made cards and read out loud our florid poems of praise and gratitude to the nuns for coming so far to teach us. We poured our feelings into those poems. Our tributes must have sounded quite sappy considering that we seldom differentiated between the expressions of love for our teachers and anything else we loved. I admired the American nuns because no matter how boring or repetitious our dances, or how often they had seen a particular routine, they stayed to the very end, clapping and cheering. This must be the American character trait that Mother Rufina talked about—not to tell the whole truth or show exactly how they feel.

I couldn't help comparing these "nuns from heaven" to my Germans nuns, who often told us to stop our singing and dancing because they were tired or because they wanted something different. The Americans respected African culture. Even though they couldn't pronounce African names, they tried much harder than the Germans did. In spite of their efforts, however, no other *wazungu* pronounced our names quite that badly. We imitated Americans saying Swahili words and wondered how they could be so much worse than the British who also spoke English, yet were even better with Swahili and Bantu names than the Germans.

Despite the social oddities and the newness of so much at Marian College, I had survived a whole year alone as the only half-caste from Kifungilo without any problem. There was a light-skinned half-caste from the southern region who, as a Green, was two years ahead of me. We didn't mix much, though she was friendly and smiled a lot. She had the prettiest freckles on her face and her hair was short and curly. I heard her speaking Kihehe fluently, a tribal language from the Iringa region, and wondered if she was raised by her mother in the village.

There was a half-caste teacher from the same area named *Mwalimu* Fliakos. She was gentle, warm, and shy. I enjoyed my sewing classes with her because she asked me questions about Kifungilo and about my life and plans in the most sensitive and caring manner. She was the first adult with whom I discussed my insecurities about being half-caste. One day she invited me to the teachers' house for lunch. Although I was very excited, I was quite anxious. I wasn't sure how to behave in a private setting with an adult and especially a teacher. My comfort zones were offices, dormitories, dining rooms, classrooms, and the maize fields.

"Tell me, Mary, why are you so serious whenever a teacher comes around?" she asked. "I see you laughing with the students, but when the nuns appear you become stiff and nervous. Are you afraid of them?"

"I'm used to being afraid of all nuns."

"I've heard that the German nuns in Kifungilo beat the children and remind you that you're unwanted."

After Mhonda I decided that no matter how horrible Kifungilo seemed to me as a child, it was my home, and I wouldn't discuss it with anyone who wasn't from there, so I responded with, "Who told you that?"

"It's not true? I'm relieved. I couldn't believe that nuns would do that. In Tosamaganga, where I come from, we have Italian nuns. Although they're very strict, they never made us feel responsible for being half-caste. They tried to help us fit in with the Africans."

"That's the big difference between your Italian nuns and my German nuns. In Kifungilo we learned that we're better than the Africans, but worse than the *wazungu*. The orphanage was surrounded by Wasambaa villages, and villagers came for religious instruction, medicine, clothing, and food, and to work for the nuns, but we weren't raised with Africans."

"So you grew up only with nuns and half-castes. You know that Kifungilo half-castes have the reputation of being proud and not wanting anything to do with Africans and even other half-castes. Do you speak Kisambaa?"

"Very little, but I can understand almost everything. I also understand German. I've always wished that I could speak a tribal language, and I'm jealous that the half-caste from your area speaks Kihehe so well."

"It's because we spent a lot of time with our relatives in the villages, and Mama Clementina encouraged us to respect our African families."

"Our Mama Clementina in Kifungilo was Sister Silvestris. She loved us very much, but I think she was more interested in keeping us from sin and getting us to heaven than in teaching us how to communicate with our neighbors, whom she lovingly referred to as 'my *washenzi*' and 'my *maskini*,' my pagans and my poor. The German nuns, with a few exceptions, seem angry."

We agreed on the reputation of the Germans in Africa for being organized, hardworking, and persistent, but also cruel and ruthless.

"You're lucky to be at Marian College," declared *Mwalimu* Fliakos, "because the American nuns seem happy to be in Africa, and they really care and want to do everything right."

"And Americans are undisciplined, superficial, naive, insincere—but very considerate, appreciative, and open-minded. I prefer Americans!"

"Italians are often undisciplined as well," *Mwalimu* Fliakos said, "and it seems to me they don't take their mission in Africa very seriously, but they don't have kalaba."

"Kalaba? What's that?"

"Color bar—when people of different races, especially Africans, are barred from participating in activities with *wazungu*. The Italian nuns in Tosamaganga mix with Africans, and Italian men often marry African women and take them back to Italy."

"Imagine being treated as an equal by a *mzungu*!"

We were so engrossed in our conversation that we had no time for lunch. As I left, she put a hand on my shoulder and said, "Please feel free to come and talk anytime, and if you need anything, don't be afraid to ask."

"Thank you, *Mwalimu*."

That evening as I lay in bed, I knew that I would always remember the first of many conversations with a very special friend. An adult friend. A teacher friend. A half-caste friend. Who cared if I had no friends or relatives to visit me on Sundays? What did it matter if no one ever wrote me a letter? I had a new friend who talked to me with gentleness and interest.

47

Sister Martin Corde

 By the end of the first year at Marian College I was quite used to Americans and their unconventional ways. When I returned to Kifungilo for holidays, I had to revert to acting subordinate to the German nuns and not expect them to have discussions with me or to be able to initiate a conversation with them. I had to remember the German words the Sisters used when they didn't know the English ones so I wouldn't be accused of becoming "American." Sister Silvestris was the only nun who enjoyed the Americanisms that, nevertheless, slipped into my speech.

"What is it they call the recreation room?"

"Auditorium."

"Ah-uh-dee-tor-rhee-oom," she tried to repeat after me, but ended up laughing as she butchered the pronunciation. "It sounds like a Latin word. I've heard that Americans cannot pronounce simple words like 'water,' 'butter' and 'matter.' Is it true?"

"Yes, they say 'war-dhur,' 'bu-dhur,' and 'ma-dhur.' They pronounce 't' only when they want to and only when it doesn't appear in the middle of a word. And they pronounce 'nut' and 'not' and 'hut' and 'hot' the same way."

"*Mama yangu*, even their language is undisciplined! Can you understand them? When American visitors come to Kifungilo, we go to church so we don't have to talk to them. But Mother Rufina likes to visit with them. She says they're happy people and laugh all the time. And when she corrects their English, they don't get angry. They repeat what she says but they never say the words right. Do you like the American Sisters better than us?"

I told her what I observed—they don't take themselves very seriously, they seem to enjoy being in Africa, and they like African culture and encourage us to learn tribal dances. They talk to us and ask our opinion. They admit when they're wrong and sometimes even apologize, and I wasn't so afraid of them. But, I told Sister, "It's easier to like them because they're only our teachers and they don't have to be our parents as well."

"I believe what you say about the Americans, but remember that we also love Africa. Our first mission is to convert the *washenzi* to Christianity. The Americans came after we'd done the hard work. We go out into the villages where no one has seen a European and find the people who need our help. The Americans wait for villagers and already educated people to come to them. It's easy to teach English and arithmetic and even enjoy African culture but hard to teach matters of the soul. Yes, we are like your parents, but we will have fulfilled our mission if we meet you in heaven someday."

I don't think that Sister Silvestris ever felt threatened by the American Maryknoll Sisters. She probably felt that at least spiritually, she was much closer to God than they were because of the many souls she sent to heaven and the hardships she endured in order to fulfill her mission. She thought that Americans were spoiled and was more amused than threatened by them. But for further information, she referred me to Mother Rufina who had travelled to America when she was younger. "Mother Rufina tells us that many Africans were brought to America as slaves long ago and were treated badly. Even now they aren't treated as real Americans."

"How can that be?"

"Maybe if you do well in school, your American teachers will send you there to study, like we send some girls to Germany, and then you will see for yourself."

Sister's comment reawakened a lifelong desire in me. From that day on, I was obsessed with the idea of going to America. But whenever the thought entered my head, I pushed it away because it seemed too good to be true. How could something that great happen to me, a person wanted by no one except herself? The idea of going to America was a secret I shared only with God. It was so far-fetched that I knew I couldn't tell another soul. I did tell my secret to Fat

Mary though, and she reminded me how I used to answer the priests who came to Kifungilo for retreat when they asked me, "What's your name, little girl?" I always replied, "I'm an Amelican gal." Fat Mary said, *Maybe you will one day become an Amelican girl.*

During my next three years at Marian College, I saw everything in a different light. For the first time a future outside of Kifungilo seemed possible. I couldn't turn my thoughts away from America. I imagined living there and talking like my American teachers. My secret excited me but also confused me. What made me think anybody would send me to America to study? I struggled to get the idea out of my mind, but could not.

No matter how much happier I was at Marian College compared to Mhonda, and no matter how much I liked the American nuns, my childhood fears lingered beneath the surface like a smoldering fire that I just couldn't extinguish.

One nun, Sister Martin Corde, seemed to see straight into my heart. She was the only American nun who was Black. Sister was short and moved like she had no bones. Swaying gently from side to side, she looked like a big, cheerful cotton ball floating down the path. When she laughed, which was nearly all the time, her cheeks bunched around her eyes. Her teeth were wide and white, and her gums were violet.

She seldom walked by me without asking how I was and what I was thinking about. Every so often I'd tell her that I felt lonely. When I finished my homework in the evening, I usually went to bed early instead of waiting for the bell, and I'd talk to Fat Mary until I fell asleep. Sister Martin Corde often came to my bedside to keep me company.

"How's my special girl?" she'd ask. I'd mumble something about being fine and wanting to sleep. "Are you all right?" she'd ask.

"Yes."

"Then why do you go to bed when you should be reading or studying like everybody else?"

"I've finished my homework and don't want to go to the library. I just want to sleep."

"You know, I worry about you. Can you to tell me what's on your mind and why you seem so sad?" I was surprised by her observation, because I thought I kept my sadness well hidden inside, under the care of Fat Mary.

"What makes you think I'm sad?"

"I just know. What's bothering you?"

"My life."

"What about your life?"

"Everything."

"Like what?

"Like I'm poor. People who don't have families are poor. No matter what the girls say about my pretty Sunday clothes, they feel sorry for me, like they know my parents didn't want me and gave me away. I get jealous when I see their relatives come to visit them. In Kifungilo there were other orphans like me, but here I'm the only one."

"I understand, but maybe your parents had a good reason to send you to the orphanage. And not all the girls here are rich or have family. You should start counting your blessings instead."

"The one blessing is that the German nuns took care of me and gave me a home when my own parents didn't. Although I'm grateful to them, I sometimes wish I'd died. I'm tired of feeling alone in the world."

Sister paused a few moments and then said, "Another blessing is that you're a sweet, sensitive, and intelligent person. You think and feel very deeply. Your classmates tell me that you have a good sense of humor and they like you. If you stop hating yourself, you'll have room in your heart to love yourself like you deserve."

"I don't hate myself." I told her that the one thing that kept me sane over the years was the decision I made as a child to love myself unconditionally.

"That's wonderful. Now act like you believe it. I also know that God loves you, and the Sisters of Kifungilo love you, and I love you. Whenever you feel depressed or discouraged, you can talk to me."

I did feel free to tell her things about my life that I couldn't tell anyone else because with her, it was like talking to my beloved Blessed Martin at the orphanage. Maybe she would be a saint like him one day. Sister Martin Corde was the kindest and gentlest nun I'd ever met. She often brought me food when I was sick and stayed to listen to me and tell me stories about America. She wrote me letters and notes which she put in Sister Dolores Marie's mail window so it looked like I received letters too, and she gave me books to read and took time to discuss them with me. She watched over me and was my guardian angel at Marian College. Yet in all our talks, I never mentioned my secret desire to go to America.

48

Reel Life

Sister Martin Corde encouraged me to participate in clubs and extra-curricular activities so I could discover my "hidden talents." I stayed away from most clubs because I preferred spending my free time daydreaming or laughing with Henrietta, Sunny, and Smiley but I did join the drama and glee clubs. The drama club entered nationwide competitions in Dar and usually placed first, second, or received honorable mention for its plays.

The glee club loved singing "The Yellow Rose of Texas," "Home on the Range," "Git Along, Little Dogies" and many other songs about a country and a culture that was completely foreign to us. The Drama Club performed *The Ugly Duckling* and *The Knave of Hearts*, and the Glee and Drama Clubs together performed Gilbert and Sullivan's *H.M.S. Pinafore* and *The Mikado*.

The Mikado was special for me because with a few piano lessons from Sister Mary Ward, the glee club teacher, and a lot of practice, I played the "Overture Duet" with her for the performance. The piano was a magical instrument and much more fun than the organ that I tried to pump at Kifungilo. It seemed to me that people who played any musical instrument, especially European ones, were very special and I was surprised that an ordinary person like me could play the piano. Making music was definitely for me, but unfortunately my music teacher presumed that I had an emotional problem. She said my mood changed like the weather. Even though I showed talent, she thought I'd be hard to work with and didn't give me any more lessons after the performance. I taught myself how to read the notes for "Starlight Waltz" and "Long, Long Ago" from an elementary piano book she provided. I memorized them and added them to the repertoire of waltzes that Sunny, Smiley, and I performed whenever it was our Tanga Region's turn to provide music for Sunday evening tribal dancing in the recreation hall.

I also saw movies for the first time at Marian College. Students who lived in Tanga, Mwanza, or the capital city of Dar-es-Salaam had been to the cinema and watched Asian movies in Hindi or American Westerns, but I never believed them when they told me that people moved and talked, rivers flowed through valleys, horses ran, and trains and cars sped over the flat surface of a screen that was nothing but a big white wall.

Once introduced to movies, I discovered a resource that fed my curiosity and fueled discussions, and I eventually mastered the art of movie viewing in Africa. Westerns with John Wayne, Indians, and buffalo fascinated us; we imitated the yodeling songs of Roy Rogers, and the theme song from "Bridge over the River Kwai" became one of our favorite marching songs.

Scenes involving meals amazed us. In one movie, we saw an enormous dining hall with elaborately decorated tables covered with plates, bowls, glasses, spoons, forks, knives, pitchers, small buckets, and gold-edged tablecloths with matching serviettes, which Americans called napkins. Why did they need all those utensils to eat, and why did they eat so many different kinds of food in one meal? And they wiped their mouths continually during the meal instead of waiting until they finished. Also, the diners didn't use utensils correctly. They ate only with the fork, putting the knife down for long periods of time.

We watched sports movies about American football and noticed that the confused Americans called our football "soccer." Hockey movies inspired imitation, but we couldn't figure out how the players moved so smoothly on those sharp knives under their shoes. Our American teachers never explained to us that the game was played on ice. Having never seen a block of ice, much less a big rink made out of the stuff, we ended each hockey-imitating session with bruises and aching legs from trying to glide over the ground.

The best movies were the ones with what seemed to be dancing. We recognized the German waltz, but most of the time we couldn't figure out what the couples were doing. Why did they glue themselves to each other and stand in one spot? How can anyone dance when someone is holding onto their shoulders and waists? Most puzzling of all, why did they close their eyes when they danced? How did they know where they were going? Didn't they want to see others dance? I figured that this type of dancing must be the American tribal dance, just as the waltz was the German tribal dance. I definitely preferred the waltz because you could move around the whole hall, and you could even shake your hips and shoulders as you twirled when you got tired of dancing stiffly.

The music in the movies was also puzzling. We seldom saw a band with drums and guitars or musicians playing *wazungu* instruments during the entire movie, but there was always music. Was life in America accompanied by music? We also couldn't understand why all of the film stars looked alike except for the color of their hair. They were tall or short, but they decorated their faces the same way, and their figures were usually of the same proportions and very thin. They wouldn't bring a big dowry to their families.

I'm sure that most of the movies we saw had stories or a moral, but they were wasted on me. I couldn't add anything to a discussion of a movie except to ask questions about the physical surroundings: the cost of a gown or house, the appearance and disappearance of characters, and—the most annoying question of all to my classmates—could such things happen in real life? I wished that my questioning, analytical mind could relax so I too could laugh, scream, shout, or even run from my seat when a scene became frightening like my classmates did. By the end of my stay at Marian College, though, I had mastered the art of African movie viewing. I hit myself or whoever was sitting next to me during a fight scene, stood up and ran in place when someone was running, stirred a pot on my lap when someone was cooking, and answered most questions out loud, which often got us audience members into verbal fights if the answers conflicted. The most important thing to do at the movies was to let as many people as possible know while the movie was still playing that you'd figured out the story, and then make a big production of leaving the cinema hall long before it ended. Only slow learners stayed to the very end.

49

More Than Friendship

All in all, I felt very lucky to be at Marian College. Trying to understand and fit the American way into our lives made it interesting and stimulating. I sometimes felt that Americans were not *wazungu* at all, but simply foreigners with a mixture of whatever they liked and tolerated. I doubted that students in government schools run by British and British-trained teachers ever saw their unofficial side as we did with our informal American nuns. Our teachers at Marian College made us believe that anything was possible. They did and accepted many things that we had been taught were wrong. I think Sister Silvestris was correct in her assessment that Americans could never handle the job of converting pagans to Christianity because they might end up pagan themselves. The more rules they seemed to break, the more we loved them.

But Marian College, being an all-girls school, had its own special situations. We had a phenomenon called *kijembe,* which literally means "little hoe" but figuratively meant "my beloved friend." Having a *kijembe* was the closest thing to being in love with someone. A student without a *kijembe* was lonely and felt unwanted. We changed *vijembe* (plural form) when things didn't work out, but when your *kijembe* left you, it was like being thrown into hell. This special relationship was not sexual, but everything else shared by a couple in love was present just like we'd seen in the movies.

During my stay at Marian College, I had three *vijembe*. We exchanged love letters and gifts, acted coy and played hard to get, all the while trying to keep the relationship secret. Guessing who was whose *kijembe* was almost a full time job. Several students tried to have a *kijembe*-type relationship with the nuns which never worked.

Since everyone kept their *kijembe* a secret, rumors spread about some lay teachers having students as *vijembe*. It was considered a beautiful thing, and we were jealous of the students whose *kijembe* was a teacher.

I was not pursued to become someone's *kijembe* as much as my friend Henrietta was. She kept her *kijembe* secret and never showed me the letters she received, no matter how much I begged. Then, out of the clear blue one day, I found a lump of paper folded into a million folds and tucked into my composition book in my desk. I carefully undid the folds, but when I saw it was a love letter, I crumpled it in my hand and went to the toilet to read it. I couldn't believe my eyes. I finally had a *kijembe*! I read the letter over and over until it was etched in my heart and brain, never to be forgotten:

Oktoba of this year of 1960

My dear Water over all the Rivers.
Your name is Mary Ryne,
I am sitting here outside near your uniform. The sun it is shining on the blue color. I am watching it dry because I know that one day my tears they will dry too. I have been crying for you every night and every day, but you do not hear me and you do not see me.

You are a most beautiful creature from God to put on this place called earth. When I see you, my eyes become blind because your beauty is like the sunset there on the Uluguru Mountains. I will not wish to make you angry towards me, but I will wish you to take a pen and write to me a loving letter. Otherwise, I will die tomorrow morning, and you will never know why I went to heaven because of you.

Please my dearest person flower from the fields. You must answer this lovely letter and put it under my pillow. I live in St Mary's hall and my pillow has many joyful hearts on it.

Your truly loving you,
Me. Myself.

Who could be writing this wonderful letter to me? The only way to find out was to write her back, put the letter under her pillow, and catch the name on her cupboard. I had no idea how to write a love letter. I took my clues from the crumpled piece of paper in my hand and started composing my letter in my head right there in the toilet. I tucked the precious letter into my bra, taking it out to reread every time I got stuck. I memorized what I was going to say, went back to the classroom, and at age sixteen, sat down at my desk and hesitantly wrote my first love letter:

> *Dear You,*
>
> *You must be the nicest person on earth to love me. No one has ever written such a letter to me. I don't believe anyone who says that I am beautiful, but I will try to be beautiful for you.*
>
> *Do you want to be my kijembe? I will be very happy to be yours. I cannot praise you very much yet because I don't know who you are and I don't know if I will like you.*
>
> *I think if you continue to tell me such nice words, I will love you like the sunrise over my Usambara Mountains.*
>
> *I will count the minutes and seconds till I see you face to face.*

Your chosen girl,
Mary Ryne

I put the letter under the "joyfully hearted pillow" and saw that my *kijembe's* name was Zita. Her uniform was yellow, so I knew she was a freshman, a year below me. That explained why her English was not as good as mine. Her bed was as clean as the beds in Kifungilo, and there wasn't a single wrinkle on her white cotton sheet or bright red blanket. Anyone who made a bed with such care had to be good. The next day I received her reply under my plate in the dining room:

> *Dear Mary Ryne,*
> *Let us get behind the kitchen during Rosary and meet together.*

Your beloved one

We skipped Rosary and met in the shed behind the kitchen. Zita had bluish black skin and very short fine curly hair. She had no breasts at all, but her buttocks made up for the missing frontal lumps. The whites of her eyes were whiter than cotton in the fields and the blacks were blacker than the tar on the roads. Her lips were as full as African lips should be, and her nose was as tiny as an African nose shouldn't be. She showed her stained yet perfectly shaped teeth as we stood looking at each other with smiles we didn't know how to stop. All we did for what we thought was only five minutes, but actually lasted the entire half hour of the Rosary, was smile, shake hands, and say, "Thank you, thank you, ten times and then ten times more." We agreed to become each other's *kijembe* and to love each other until we died.

What that meant was that we wrote several letters to each other every day. Whenever we got together, we talked about how love felt, how much we missed each other, how jealous we were of each other, and how we would kill ourselves if the other ever found another *kijembe*. We told each other we were pursued by others but that we would always remain faithful and would never carry on in public like other students who constantly got into fights over a stolen or unfaithful *kijembe*.

One day when we were simply basking in each other's presence, we started talking about our homes and childhoods. I told Zita that I didn't have much to talk about because German nuns raised me in an orphanage. Zita was visibly upset with the summary of my first sixteen years of life and didn't believe that no one in my family would take me if my parents didn't want me.

"That cannot be. You're a nice person and someone was there to teach you how. I heard peoples from Germany they are bad. Did somebody be good to you?"

"Yes. Tell me about you—about your city of Tanga. I heard that Tanga was very beautiful and it was full of Arabs and Indians, but very few *wazungu*."

"I do not think Tanga is this beautiful place. Many people with sicknesses, dirt everywhere, and many people who are asking for money from the street. I heard Lushoto is this beautiful place, yes?"

"Yes. Tell me more about Tanga."

"Why you must know so much about it?"

"In Kifungilo there was a big girl named Rosa who took care of me. She was very beautiful and kind and she liked me very much. She got married and moved to Tanga. Maybe you know of her?"

"Rosa, the kind half-caste mama, and husband name of George?"

"Yes!" I was jumping up and down with delight. Someone knew Rosa.

"She has two girl childrens, yes?"

"Yes!" I couldn't contain my excitement. "Tell me how she is, where she lives, what she's doing. Tell me everything about her. Can you take me to her sometime? Will you take a letter to her when you go home for holidays next month? Will you—"

"Stop, my happy Mary Ryne!" Zita's face was long.

"What's the matter? Why did you stop me?" Zita put her arms around me and tried to say something. "Tell me what's wrong," I begged her.

"Mary Ryne, I have the bad, bad, very bad news."

"What bad news?"

"The nice mama Rosa is died."

"Dead? No! How do you know? When? How? " I started crying uncontrollably and my body shook as if I was trying to bring up Rosa out of my own soul to tell me that she wasn't dead. Zita just let me cry and cry. She said it was good to cry. It would make me "not feel the hurting in future days." When I calmed down, she told me that Rosa had died from kidney failure earlier that year. She said that she really died from a broken heart and from a hard life and that her husband George was a drunkard who beat her even when she was sick.

I wondered why in catechism class we learned that God was just. What justice was this? Why would Rosa, who never beat anyone, be beaten and mistreated? Was Zami beaten and tortured and mistreated by her husband like she deserved? And why did God take away the few people in this world who loved me? When would I stop hurting? Maybe I had to die first. Did God take Rosa to stop her suffering and that's what is meant by "God is just"? Yes. That's it. She's finally happy in heaven.

"It's okay," I told Zita. "She's not suffering anymore. Of all the girls in Kifungilo, she deserves the earliest call to rest, peace, and happiness. I'm glad she's dead."

"That's how it must be. Everyone in Tanga loves Rosa too much. She help my family not to be poorer, and I cry the same way when she die. Now it becomes that I love you because we love the same woman. But why did no person told you?"

"No one writes to me. Sometimes Sister Silvestris writes, but she didn't mention Rosa's death. Rosa left Kifungilo many years ago. Sister probably thought I had forgotten her."

"I will never forget you, Mary Ryne. I think you will cry very much like this when I die, yes?"

"Yes." What else could I say? How could she even begin to understand what Rosa meant to me? I cried like a child who lost her mother. I was grateful that little Monika had burst the dam of tears when I beat her, because if I couldn't cry over Rosa, I'd probably never ever cry again.

Zita and I promised each other that we would remain *vijembe* until we died and met in heaven. In spite of all our sincere intentions, as vacation time approached, Zita and I found ourselves drifting apart and becoming interested in other girls. I was the first one to be unfaithful. I didn't want to talk about Rosa, and I got a little bored with the same conversations and flowery words about my beauty, which I never believed, but had learned to accept the American way—superficially. I learned to say what I did not mean in order not to hurt Zita's feelings. When I finally told her the truth about our relationship, she screamed and pulled her hair. She calmed down only when I promised her that no other girl could ever mean more to me than she did because she was my first *kijembe*. I said many things just to soothe her. The day we said goodbye for the holidays, she told me that she too was tired of me and was ready for someone else.

It was only a few days before school was out for the year, but having no active *kijembe* made the days long and lonely, and even though I spent time with my friend Henrietta, I felt that something important was missing. In a way, my relationship with Zita prepared me for what happened on my return trip to Kifungilo.

50

Little Red Devil

 Right after Mass, about 7 o'clock in the morning, we all gathered excitedly anticipating the arrival of our bus. As I sat on my suitcase in front of the dorm, Henrietta came running toward me. She handed me an envelope that she said was on Sister Dolores Marie's mail window since the day before. I thought how wonderful it was to receive a letter on the last day of school, but to my disappointment I recognized Sister's handwriting.

Mary,

Mother Rufina wants you to ride to Lushoto with Father Michael, who works with the Education Ministry in Dar-es-Salaam and represents all the Catholic Schools in the Tanga Region. He will be stopping at Marian College on his way back from a meeting in Dar, so don't get on the bus. Come to the convent at noon. You'll make the long trip home by car, you lucky girl!

Have a great vacation and give my regards to the Precious Blood Sisters in Kifungilo.

Sister Dolores Marie

How lucky for me that Henrietta saw the note! Although I was going to travel with several Chagga students from Moshi to Mombo, I wasn't looking forward to the late night ride to Lushoto with only a handful of villagers.

I waved goodbye to the bus loaded with singing, happy faces and saw the concern of some students who thought I was being left behind. I told Henrietta that I was traveling by car with someone from the Education Ministry in just a few hours. She looked at me suspiciously. "Do you know this person?" she asked.

"No, but Mother Rufina says he'll drive me to Lushoto where I'll spend the night at the dentistry and then Sister Fabiana will take me to Kifungilo in the morning."

"Be careful. You shouldn't travel with someone you don't know. He could do anything to you."

That hadn't occurred to me, but if Mother Rufina had arranged things, that made it safe. "I'll be careful. See you in two months." I hugged her and she joined the students from the Tabora Region who had to walk to town for their bus.

At the appointed hour I went to the convent. The door opened as soon as I started to knock. A tall, thin, casually dressed man was speaking with some nuns inside and then turned to me.

"This must be the young lady I'm assigned to deliver to Lushoto." Father Michael spoke English with the same Irish accent as the Rosminian priests who still went to Kifungilo every year for their annual retreat. He looked at me with warm eyes, took my suitcase and headed for a small red car parked near the Sisters' huge aqua green Chevrolet. This European man didn't act like one. Since when did a *mzungu* man carry anything for an African women?

"My car is very small compared to that luxury American model, but I'm sure I can squeeze your big box in the boot," he laughed, tapping my tiny wooden suitcase. Although the car was small, it had four doors and two seats in front. I headed for the back seat but saw that it was littered with travel bags, folders, papers, books, and newspapers.

"That's your seat, my lady." He pointed to the front passenger seat. "Get in and we'll be off." I got in and sat up very straight with my legs together and my hands on my knees. "Those good Sisters didn't introduce us properly, did they?" he remarked.

"No."

"Well, I know who you are, of course. You've probably seen me in Kifungilo. My name is Father Michael, but you can call me Michael. Pleased to meet you, Mary!" He turned briefly toward me, made a mock bow, and smiled. I smiled too, but I didn't know how to take this play acting from a male *mzungu*.

"Now you can relax. Have you ever traveled this far by car?"
"No."
"Do you know any other English words besides 'no'?"
"Yes."
"You remind me of when I was trying to learn Swahili. *Ndiyo* and *hapana* was all I said for a long time. Do the American nuns speak Swahili to you?"
"No."
Father Michael was driving very fast and I was afraid. He seemed quite relaxed though, and sometimes hummed to himself. Occasionally he looked over at me and smiled.
"I think you're driving too fast. I'm afraid of an accident," I managed to say.
"Driving too fast, you say? I'm well below my personal speed limit. You're probably used to traveling in slow buses. Do you want to see how fast this little red devil can go?"
"No." He was right. This was only the second car I'd ridden, not counting the Kifungilo van, the first one being the Maryknoll Sisters' Chevrolet, and the nuns certainly didn't drive fast.
"I won't show you right now, but when you've learned to trust me, I will."
Despite my uneasiness at his driving, I liked the sound of his voice. And I liked to stare at him. He was clean-shaven and his unruly hair shone and smelled of Brylcreem or some other hair tonic. His hands held the steering wheel lightly, and the white of his trimmed, clean fingernails contrasted with the black of the steering wheel. He wore dark green corduroy slacks, a striped red and white shirt under a thin V-neck sweater. On his feet he wore black socks and bulky light brown sandals.
"I bet we can beat the Moshi bus even though we left three hours later. What do you say? Should we chase it?" he asked.
"No."
"Okay, I've a better idea. We'll find a nice spot in the shade of an acacia tree, rest a while, and have a Fanta or coffee." We drove a few kilometers more and pulled over by an acacia tree that had obviously been a favorite stopping place for many travelers before us. There were a few logs and flat rocks to sit on, egg shells, orange and banana

peels strewn here and there, and charred earth from a fire.

We sat on some grass under the tree and he handed me an opened Fanta bottle. "Cheers! Tell me about Marian College. Do you like the Americans? How would you compare them to the Kifungilo nuns? I must say, they scare me. Unfortunately, I have to visit them at least three times a year as part of my job."

"I like the Americans very much."

"Why do you like the Maryknolls?"

"I'm not afraid of them. They're not as strict as the Germans and they don't take everything, even religion, so seriously. When they make mistakes, they apologize even to us students. I can tell they're trying to teach us as much as possible. They smile a lot and always acknowledge our presence, even if they're talking with someone else. And they say nice things about us and about Africa."

"See, you can talk in paragraphs! What do you like the least about them?"

"I don't understand a lot of what they say. They use big words and American words that we've never heard, and they seldom explain what they mean. My biggest problem with the Americans is that I find it hard to know when they are sincere. Everything is always somehow okay. Even when you've done something wrong, they hardly finish their slight scolding before they say good things about you. I'm used to feeling miserable when I've done something bad, and not end up laughing with the person who just scolded me. They also don't care how they pronounce African names."

"You're fortunate to have dealt with other *wazungu* so you can learn about how different they are from one another. They're as different and the same as the tribes here in Africa. Tell me, what kind of horrible things would deserve a scolding from those easy-going nuns?"

"Many things."

"Sentences and paragraphs, remember?"

"Once my friend Smiley and I were in the auditorium listening to the words of songs on the gramophone for a singing competition. We were concentrating very hard trying to figure out the words to Elvis Presley's 'Jailhouse Rock.' All of a sudden the only no-nonsense Sister at Marian College knocked our heads together. We staggered up and found ourselves looking into her fuming crimson face. I saw darkness and stars. Furious, she whispered loudly, 'Where did you get that filthy record? What were you doing with your heads practically tied together?'

"Smiley explained we were listening to the words. Sister asked us why Marian girls would listen to an Elvis Presley song. When we told her we were preparing our song for the singing competition next week, she asked if we were really going to sing such a song in front of all the Sisters and students. I volunteered that we were going to dance too. Sister grabbed the 45-rpm record, hit it against the edge of the stage, and broke it in half. For our punishment, she forbade us to enter the competition. Then she stormed out of the room while we looked at each other wondering what we had done wrong."

"Naughty girls. Don't you know that Rock 'n' Roll is sinful? And Elvis is the personification of sin?" teased Father Michael. "In Ireland, young people are crazy about Elvis, but I didn't know he was famous in Tanganyika."

"We hadn't even heard of Elvis when Sunny brought the record from Dar. Mostly songs in English win the competition. Last year another friend and I won first prize for singing 'Devoted to You,' by the Everly Brothers. We didn't have the record, but we memorized as much of it as we could from a small transistor radio and made up the rest."

"Let me tell you something. You're *not* a bad girl," said Father Michael.

"Thank you." After being with the American nuns, I was accustomed to trying to figure out what people meant when they complimented me. Since he was being friendly, I decided to ask him, but before I could, he moved close to me, slowly and deliberately putting his arms around me. He lifted my head by the chin, and kissed me on the forehead and on each cheek.

"Thank you," I said, and abruptly stood up.

"Where are you going?" He tried to pull me down on the grass again and I resisted. "What's the matter?"

"I don't know what you want."

"Are you afraid of me?"

"I'm not usually afraid of priests."

"Then come back and sit by me."

"I've never sat so close to a priest. And I didn't think that priests were supposed to kiss a girl on the face." He didn't say anything for a long time as I stood hesitantly a few steps away.

"All I want to do is to hold you in my arms. There is nothing wrong with that. Mother Rufina trusted me to drive you all the way to Kifungilo and you won't even sit next to me?"

I was really confused. Mother Rufina, who preached that all men are evil, put me in his care for the whole day, so he must not be an evil man because he's a priest. I was taught to always obey a *mzungu,* especially nuns and priests. The nuns in Kifungilo treated priests with great reverence. I was afraid to disobey him, so I went back to sit next to him and said, "I'm sorry. I know you are a priest and you won't hurt me."

"You're right. I won't hurt you, but I must tell you that first and foremost I am a man and then a priest."

"I see it the other way around. You're a priest first, and then a man."

"I think I'm the best judge of that. But tell me, what are you afraid of?"

"I don't know. In one way I am happy that the Americans have given me enough confidence to be able to sit with a *mzungu* man in the car and carry on a conversation without feeling inferior, but my gut instinct tells me to be afraid even though you are a priest."

"One more time I will tell you that you mustn't be afraid of me. I will never hurt you in any way. I find you very attractive and beautiful. I want to hold you and be close to you. There's nothing wrong with that. Would you let me kiss you?"

"I have to think about that."

"Take your time."

How can I disobey him? Should I tell him that I'll ask Mother Rufina if it's all right to let him kiss me? What did he mean by beautiful? I wished he wouldn't lie. But this priest seems very gentle and considerate. He actually asked me for permission to kiss me. Father Michael didn't give me too much time to think. He pulled me towards him and kissed me again on each cheek saying, "I will never hurt you, never, ever!"

I made a point to pretend to relax as Father Michael held me tight and then I felt his lips sliding down my face and stopping on my mouth. They were very hot. I pulled away. I had a flashback to the kissing scenes I'd seen in the Indian movies in town, and I wondered if I was about to be kissed in that dirty way. He gently laid me on the ground and it looked like he might try to kiss me again. I tried to resist but I was also curious. I remembered that after the kissing scenes the couples got naked, and then we saw only the upper parts of their bodies, though they continued to gyrate and huff and puff and groan and scream.

"No, no, I don't want to do this."

"What's the matter? Did I do something wrong?"

"No."

"Then what's wrong?"

"I'm afraid."

"What are you afraid of?"

"I don't know." I pulled away from him, but he insisted on holding me.

"Don't be afraid. I won't hurt you. I'll never hurt you." We sat up and he put his arm around my shoulder. A million thoughts ran through my mind. Was this what Paulina told me about? That when a man kisses you, his penis gets hard and then he puts it into your vagina to deposit his seeds so that I would have children? Oh my God! I'm going to get pregnant today! I abruptly stood up and tried to walk toward the car, but he held me back and said, "We're not going anywhere until you tell me what's wrong."

"I'm afraid I'll become pregnant," I blurted out.

"I thought so. We'll go back to the car as soon as you've stopped shaking and as soon as you look into my eyes and smile."

I controlled my shaking as much as I could and gave him the required smile.

"Okay, let's go."

We got into the car but he didn't start the engine. Somehow the driver's seat fell back and he stretched out with his hands behind his head. He lay very still. I tried to sit still too, but my shaking resumed. He closed his eyes and gave several deep sighs.

"Stop shaking! I really will not hurt you or make you pregnant. Do you want to know how people become pregnant?"

"I think I know, though I've never seen the act done."

"The only way you could become pregnant is if I put this inside there." He pointed to his penis with one hand and touched me between the legs with the other. I stiffened up and continued trembling.

"I give you my word, I will never do that. First of all, I wouldn't do anything 'to' you. I'd do it 'with' you. I'm a man and you're a woman. I'm very attracted to you. It's that simple. There's nothing wrong with me wanting to express myself to you in that way. It's very normal."

"You forgot the part about being a priest."

"I didn't forget it. I left it out because God knows you can't let it go."

"You're right."

"Am I the first man to express this desire to you?"

"I think so." Juma had wanted to do the act to me on the bus, but he didn't ask me first.

"In the future lots of men will probably want to do it with you because you are very beautiful. We call it 'making love.' It's why people get married."

"You don't have to tell me I'm beautiful. I know the truth about that. But tell me if it's only married people who are allowed to 'make love' as you call it. And tell me that you won't make love to me because you're a priest."

"Right on both counts." He looked very serious.

"Then why were you trying to do the act to—I mean—with me?"

"There's a lot we can do without actually making love."

"I'm very afraid of becoming pregnant and not finishing school."

"Let me tell you one more time, I will never, ever get you pregnant. Please believe me. I know that coming from an orphanage you've been hurt in many different ways. I would never add to your struggles. Remember, my job at the Education Ministry is to see that you finish school and get a good education. Do you believe me?"

"I think so."

"You don't seem so sure. Repeat after me. I'm sure that Father, no, that Michael will never, ever knowingly hurt me. Say it!"

"Father Michael will never, ever knowingly hurt me."

"That's my girl. Shall we go now?"

"Yes."

The mood in the car had changed quite a bit from when we left Morogoro. Father Michael didn't ask me as many questions. He didn't drive as fast, and he smiled and put his hand on my lap anytime he didn't need it on the steering wheel. We stopped again but this time we didn't leave the car. "We have only an hour to go and there's one thing I have to do before I drop you off so I know you're not angry with me."

"I'm not angry," I said.

"Then will you let me kiss you?"

"Is that all you'll do? Just kiss me?"

"I promise."

"Okay." He pulled me over toward him and just looked at me. He lifted my head like he'd done before, so that I was looking straight into his blue bloodshot eyes, one slightly larger than the other. He gazed at my face for so long that I had time to notice his high cheekbones and a nose that was too big for the rest of his face. His mouth was small and the lips were cracked from the African sun. Knowing that kissing was all he was going to do, I relaxed a little and let him go ahead. He pulled a lever on my side of the car and my seat fell back, almost flat. He proceeded to kiss me all over the face, but then got on top of me. I stiffened and kept my eyes wide open. He slid one hand inside my blouse and moved it back and forth from one breast to the next. With the other hand he held his penis bulging inside his trousers. With his tongue pressing deep into my mouth and his hand in my blouse, he kissed me hard and long, and huffed and puffed for what seemed like an eternity, then suddenly calmed down and moved back to his seat. He rested his arms behind his head, stretched out on the reclined seat, and breathed loudly. His face was bright red. When his breathing got more regular, he abruptly sat up straight, turned to me and said, "Friends?"

All I could say was, "Friends."

We arrived in Lushoto after sunset. Father Michael looked totally different to me than he did that morning. I didn't know what to make of him. He said he wouldn't come in because he wanted to get to Korogwe before he was too tired to drive, so we shook hands in front of the dentistry and the little red devil drove away.

I couldn't get Father Michael out of my mind all night, and I mentally turned every loop of escarpment with him on the long journey from Morogoro to Lushoto trying to understand why he acted that way with me. He said he did nothing wrong. Was I just imagining things? Was I so brainwashed about priests that I believed he couldn't do anything wrong?

The following day, when Sister Fabiana came to take me to Kifungilo, he was still uppermost in my thoughts. Something in my chest got tight when I thought about him. It felt like pain—a very unique kind of pain, but pain all the same. I wished it would go away. It interfered with my breathing and traveled up and down my digestive tract. I tried very hard to concentrate on what Sister Fabiana was asking me about "those American Sisters" and Marian College, but as soon as I'd answer each question, the little red devil returned. She asked me how my ride with Father Michael had been. I told her it was much better than riding the bus. She said that Father Michael was a good priest and Mother Rufina trusted him.

I feared I was going to tell Sister that Father Michael had kissed me. I wondered if I should ask her if it was okay, and if I shouldn't worry about it, but I quickly came to my senses. I knew for a fact that if I told Sister anything, she would probably throw me out of the van into the ravine. I would be seen as a wicked girl who made false accusations about good Father Michael. Even if I could produce proof or if he were caught in the act, I would be accused of tempting him and seducing him and leading him astray from his divine calling as a man of God. I knew deep in my bones that no matter what a priest said or did to me, I could never, ever mention it to anyone. It would mean the end of my dreams, and if my dreams ended, so would my life. Without my dreams, what did I have to live for? If I mentioned what Father Michael did to me, it would be regarded as a fabrication or as my fault. No, I needed to forget about Father Michael's kisses and advances, and the sooner the better.

Yet during my two months of vacation I was haunted by every gentle word and act Father Michael had said and done. Could it be true, I wondered, that there was a man in this world who wouldn't hurt you or make you pregnant, even if he had the opportunity? Was this what made priests different from Mother Rufina's men? Could Mother Rufina have been wrong when she warned us that "all men are evil"?

This was so confusing. I kept telling myself one of those American "white lies"—that I only longed to listen to him speak gently to me and have him listen to me. But he was a priest. Could my studies be endangered? That surely would happen if the nuns found out. Would I ever see him again, or was this another predictable episode in my life so far—losing people who cared about me? Of course, he never said anything about how he felt toward me. How did I know that he wouldn't have acted the same with any girl he'd had in his car? Still the longing in his eyes and the gentleness in his touch, the sudden passion with which he'd kissed me, and the strength of his arms around me told me that he cared.

Being in Kifungilo, it was easier to find Fat Mary and have her come to my rescue. She came to me during Rosary one evening. Tears flavored by sad memories flowed down my cheeks when she appeared. I knew that I would never forget her, but I wondered if I would always feel afresh the pain she helped me endure in my childhood every time I saw her. This time I had an ocean of new feelings and concerns. Didn't time and growing up count for anything? Why did she look exactly the same as she did when we were both six years old? What did she think of me now? How could I tell her that something in me longed to be treated as an adult and no longer as a child? That I felt such powerful things inside? As always, she listened to my trials and tribulations and helped me. I was grateful she'd never left me. She rekindled my childhood resolve to take full responsibility for my life because I was alone in this world. I gave her all my new feelings for safekeeping.

My two-month vacation went quickly. I taught tribal dances to the little children to perform for the nuns at Christmas, I helped Sister Silvestris in the sewing room, and I went with her to take clothes and food to her *maskini* in the villages. About a week before I was to go back to school, Sister Silvestris and I went to Kiuzai to visit a very sick young woman. When we were about half a mile away from the village, we heard the screams and cries of mourning.

"Let's go back." Sister said, "She's dead. Let her family mourn her in peace, and we'll come back tomorrow for the funeral."

"Sister," I said, "did you know that Rosa died?"

"Yes, Mary. She was so weak from her asthma and her miserable life with her husband."

"A student from Tanga told me. I can't believe I'll never see her again."

"You'll never see her on earth again, but you'll see her in heaven. Her two children are coming to Kifungilo next year. If you were here, you could take care of them just like Rosa took care of you. She was one of the best girls we ever had. Having her children here means she will always be with us."

"In memory of her, I've decided my name should be Mary Rose Ryan. She will be a part of my name and me forever. And Father Michael told me that Ryan was a common Irish name. He said Irish people have been in Africa for years and have helped us a lot. So, I decided to take Ryan as my surname."

"You can change your name as often as you wish, but you will always remain Fat Mary to me. I named you Mary because it's a beautiful and holy name. Father Michael didn't like it when I called you Fat Mary, but I told him that as your orphanage mother, I had the privilege of giving you a pet name. He has been very helpful to us in his position at the Education Ministry. He helps us get qualified teachers and selects the students who will go on for higher education and finds schools for them. After your good results in the Standard Eight Exams, he picked you to go to the American school, and after several requests from him, Mother Rufina finally agreed."

So it was Father Michael who handpicked me for a highly sought-after place in the first secondary school for girls. I wondered if I would see him again to thank him. I was glad I had picked an Irish name as a last name.

From that day forward I had a great sense of peace about my name. Mary Rose Ryan. It sounded right. It sounded true.

51

The Awakening

 The way I remember it, the only highlight of my third year in secondary school came at the end of the year when Father Michael again appeared at Marian College to take me to Lushoto. I'm sure I participated in several after-school clubs, learned new tribal dances, entered singing competitions, and had new *vijembe,* but everything paled compared to that encounter with Father Michael. I was as confused about him as ever. During the course of the year, I'd succeeded in mostly getting him out of my mind, calling up his image only once in a while when I visited with Fat Mary. My childhood had prepared me well to accept every goodbye to someone who had been kind to me as final. In fact, when I received a letter from him telling me that he'd stop on his way from Dar to take me to Kifungilo, I thought that there'd been a mistake. No one ever came back for me.

For a whole week I waited for my trip on Saturday, wondering if I would feel comfortable with him. I enjoyed the attention he gave me and the fact that he talked to me as an equal, but I was uncomfortable with the kissing. At night, after the Sister on duty walked down the aisle in our dorm haphazardly sprinkling holy water over our mosquito nets, I prayed that the trip would go fast and he wouldn't kiss me again.

When Saturday arrived at last, I sat on my suitcase by the road near the convent waiting for him. I prayed to God and all the saints that I would act normal and not show that I was worried about what he might do. I prayed especially to Kateri Tekakwitha, the Native American woman being considered for sainthood who Sister Paul Catherine liked so much and had us read about and discuss in class.

I liked her because of her name. It sounded mysterious and pagan, and I felt that she and Blessed Martin understood me more than the other saints. When I saw the little red devil coming toward me, I stood up and managed to wave and give a very faint smile. The saints had answered my prayers. My fear of educated people, people in authority and *wazungu* left me. I saw Father Michael as a person who cared about me.

"How's my girl?" He shook my hand, put my suitcase in the boot (what Americans call the trunk), opened the door on my side, rushed back to get in on his side, and before I had time to straighten my dress, we were off. "I'm in a hurry today. You want to know why? I've been waiting a long time for an excuse to find myself at the Lushoto Dentistry for dinner. Those Germans can cook! But I don't have to tell you that?"

"No."

"Well, was your third year as wonderful as the other two?"

"Yes."

"What do you mean, just 'Yes'? Tell me everything about the whole year. Oh! I almost forget that you talk in monosyllables for the first hour. It's okay. You've changed a little. Is it your hair? Is it shorter? Curlier?"

He hadn't shaved, but his clothes were freshly laundered. He wore the same cologne as last year, but he had a different black leather watchband that wrapped tightly around his hairless arm like a little snake.

"Shall we time ourselves to see how long it will take us to get there?"

"Okay. But please, Father, don't drive fast."

"I'll drive only as fast as this unreliable Simca will allow me," he joked, referring to the little red devil.

"All right." We drove quietly—cutting, weaving, and speeding our way through the Uluguru Mountains.

Just before we entered the Pare mountain range, the little red devil huffed, puffed, choked, coughed a bit more, and refused to continue. I'd seen many abandoned cars and trucks along the roadside, and I wondered how long it would be before another car drove by and gave us a lift.

"Oh no! Not again!" Father Michael threw his head on the steering wheel and let his long arms hang on either side, exasperated. He got out of the car, took some tools from the boot, opened the hood, and started tinkering with the engine. I got out of the car too, but didn't know what to do or say.

"This has happened before. The engine is overheating. I tell you, Tanganyika lacks good mechanics and spare parts."

"What will happen if you can't fix it?"

"I'll fix it."

"But if you can't?"

"Then we'll have to flag a car down and hope for the best."

"Since we left, I've seen only one truck on the road."

"It might be tomorrow before another car passes. Don't worry, I've never been stuck for more than a day, and I'm sure I can fix it."

"A whole day? What if animals or robbers attack us?"

"I'll protect you." He stopped his fixing and looked up at me. "Remember, when you're with me you're safe."

I squatted on the ground beside his feet and prayed silently. This time I asked God to help him fix the car.

"There! She's fixed."

"*Yeba!* Hurrah!" I was relieved.

"Now to celebrate, I'll have a Coca-Cola and you'll have a Fanta." Since there were no trees or shade anywhere in sight, we sat in the car. He wiped his very dirty, oily hands on an old a rag that he'd apparently used for this purpose before, opened a Fanta, and gave it to me. As he handed me the drink, I saw a gentleness in his eyes that confused me. I wanted to look deep behind them and into his soul to discover what made me feel I could trust him. I realized I wasn't afraid of him, yet I felt uneasy.

He finished his Coke, reclined his seat, and stretched out with his hands behind his head like he'd done before. I was preparing to answer his many questions when he abruptly pulled me over on top of him, hugged me tight, and kissed me. I almost suffocated. I moved away from him and got out of the car.

"Please come back."

"No!"

"Okay. When you're ready."

I walked away from the car. What would happen if I didn't object and did whatever he said, I wondered? Maybe what he wanted was okay. He should know. He's a priest. He says he's concerned about me and wants me to get an education. Maybe he has some ideas about where I could continue school, and if I don't go along with him, I'll hurt my chances. I got back in the car, but before I could even start to ask a question, he had his arms around me again and was kissing me powerfully on the mouth. He hadn't kissed me like this before. I couldn't even move my tongue. I listened to him and tried to imagine what was going on in his body, but my own body was throbbing in a new way, and I could feel my own quick, thumping heartbeats.

He undid the buttons of my blouse with one hand, pulled my bra straps down, and kissed my breasts. He tried to touch me between the legs but I removed his hand. He unzipped his pants and rolled over so that I was underneath him. I felt his penis throbbing and pressing through my skirt to my groin. He didn't explain anything. He started groaning louder and louder and pushing and pressing harder and harder. His irregular breathing made me think he was gasping for air. His movements became faster and faster and I prayed to God that he wouldn't die.

Unexpectedly, he let out a prolonged loud scream that scared me. He kept shaking and pushing himself on my stomach before suddenly stopping. He weighed me down as he remained motionless on top of me before finally returning to his side of the car. What in the world happened, I asked myself. He continued shaking and shuddering while I questioned if he was the same gentle person that I didn't fear. At that moment, I was very afraid of him.

"I'm sorry. I couldn't help it." He repeated those two sentences over and over until his voice was steady and normal again. He turned to look at me. His hair was matted in clumps and the whites of his eyes were pink with tiny red veins. I felt the heat evaporating from his pores as he slowly inhaled and exhaled the hot air trapped in the tiny car.

"What happened?" I asked.

"Nothing bad. I hadn't planned for this to happen, that's all."

I saw some vile and slippery looking substance smeared on my skirt. It looked like he'd blown his nose there. "What's this?"

"That's, that's... uh, that's... uh, that's called semen."

"Who put it there?'

"I did."

"When?"

"Just now."

"Where did you get it from?"

"Look, I'm very disappointed in myself. I realized you'd never made love before, so I had planned to explain everything to you beforehand so you wouldn't be surprised. But I couldn't control myself. I'm sorry."

"But where did it come from?"

"From inside me, from my penis." I had a flashback to the planting-seeds-in-a-woman's-body conversation I had with Paulina in Mhonda.

"Is this stuff your seed?" I pointed to my skirt. I didn't want to touch it.

"Yes, in a manner of speaking. Here, I'll get it off." He took a dark brown handkerchief and wiped the white sticky stuff from my skirt. "Did you enjoy it even a little?"

"Enjoy?"

"I'm so sorry."

"Did you enjoy yourself?" I had to ask.

"Yes, but I'd have enjoyed it more if I wasn't controlling myself so much."

"Controlling yourself? Maybe I don't know the meaning of that word. You were like a charging elephant."

"Believe it or not, I wanted to make love to you the right way. I wanted to enter you, but only up to ejaculation."

"What's that?"

"That's when I release the semen."

"Did you put your seeds on my skirt because you didn't want to make me pregnant?"

"Yes."

"Is that the only way a girl can become pregnant?"

"Yes."

"Have you ever made a girl pregnant?"

"No."

"Would you like to some day?"

"Hmmm.... Probably."

"Does it happen every time you do the act?"

"Good Lord, no. Only at special times when the woman is fertile—ready to make a baby." He buttoned up. I was getting bolder and felt I could ask him anything.

"Did you commit a sin?"

"Yes."

"Would it be a bigger sin if you put your penis in me?"

"Yes."

"Will you have to tell it in confession? How do you confess to another priest? Will your penance be bigger because you've taken a vow not to do the act?

"Yes, and I will confess. You should too."

"Me? What did I do? Should I say a man was on top of me and put his seeds on my skirt?"

He laughed and kissed me on the cheek. His eyes were a mixture of gentleness and merriment. "You'd give old Father Van Leer a heart attack!" A fleeting cloud of seriousness crossed his face.

I wanted to talk some more about babies and seeds, but Father Michael said, "Now we're off to the nuns. Hold on to your seat, we're late." The car started just fine and shot forward as though it was as happy and satisfied as he was.

Many, many thoughts crowded my head. Finally, at age seventeen, I was beginning to learn about the act. Paulina had told me the truth, but how could I have imagined the urgency and force behind making love? And the power and ruthlessness that accompanied it?

We drove in silence until we arrived in Korogwe. The car acted up again and he fixed it. We started climbing toward the scenic Usambara Mountains, but instead decided to take a shortcut and drove down a little path that led to a singing stream. We both got out of the car and I surprised myself by putting my arms around him and hugging him. I was grateful that he had controlled himself for my sake. He kissed me and told me that whatever he did with me, he'd never, ever put his penis inside me.

"Is that what you meant when you said you'd never hurt me?"

"Exactly. Do you believe me?"

Did I believe him? Should I? He was a priest. He had helped me already. He treated me like an adult. He drove all this distance because he wanted to be with me. "I do."

We stretched out on the grass near the water. His movements weren't as urgent or demanding as before. They were smooth and deliberate and tender. I relaxed enough to enjoy the feelings he caused in me until I felt I was losing control. I let my body take charge. I felt like the blood in my veins was a river that had heated to the boiling point. He started kissing me again, but then abruptly stopped. He stood up and very officially announced, "I'll take good care of her and deliver her safely to Lushoto."

"I bet that's what Mother Rufina made you promise. I'll tell her that traveling with you is very educational."

"Let's leave that out. I can't believe that the nuns teach you nothing about sex. Are you supposed to find out by trial and error? No wonder so many half-castes also have bastard babies."

That hurt. "It's *wazungu* like you who make half-caste and bastard children."

"I'm sorry. I shouldn't have said that. It was insensitive of me."

"The nuns in Kifungilo told us about the big sin and what kind of girls do it before they're married. They've seen the poverty and suffering of children born that way, so they warn us about men— and I know now that it includes priests like you."

"Let's go. I think I should drive you straight to Kifungilo."

Neither of us spoke much as we zigzagged through my favorite mountain range. The Usambaras made me calm. I had a feeling of going to a place where I belonged. I knew that I belonged to no one, so I felt that I must belong to the land that raised me. I was grateful that these glorious mountains claimed me and welcomed me every time they saw me. I looked over at Father Michael and wondered if the feelings he caused in me would change me. He had come back for me and we were together again. What did this mean? Could I really trust him?

"What are you thinking about?" he asked me.

"Nothing. What were you thinking about?"

"I was thinking how I'll miss you when I go to bed tonight, and I know I'll be thinking about you much more than I should."

"Why shouldn't you be thinking about me? I'll be thinking of you."

"Good. I'll see you in February when I'm driving you back to Marian College."

52

The Telephone

"Fat Mary, you must be very happy that this is your last year of school," said Sister Silvestris one day toward the end of holidays when I was helping her sort supplies in the sewing room. "You'll be one of the first girls to reach Standard Twelve and take the Cambridge Exams. Everyone in Kifungilo is proud of you. Sister Theonesta always asks about you. She says not to forget that she was your first mother and first teacher."

"I think of her so often. She used to tell me that I was the prettiest little girl in Kifungilo when the other children called me ugly and stupid. She said that I would grow up to sing and dance for the glory of God."

"When you were a very tiny baby, she and I slept in that little room near the old sewing room. She took you into her bed at night. She loved you like a true mother. I wish she could see you dance and teach the little ones. *Mama yangu!* And hear you speak your American English, M*ama yangu!* And now you are ready to sit for the Cambridge Exams! All her dreams for you are coming true."

"Did she love me so much?"

"Sister Theonesta loved you more than she loved any other child in Kifungilo. But now tell me, when you complete Standard Twelve, will you come back to Kifungilo to help me?"

"If I don't pass the exams, I'll come back. But if I do, I'd like to continue with school. I want to be a teacher, or maybe go to a university in Europe or America."

"Kifungilo has no money to send you anywhere after Standard Twelve. But if you come back here to teach, you'll be the most educated girl we've ever had and a great example for our children. If you teach here, Mother Rufina will even pay your fees for teacher training college."

"As long as I pass my exams, am I assured of further education?"

"Yes, Mary, and you will pass your exams."

It seemed as though the nuns had discussed and even planned my future. I was thrilled that I could continue school, but the idea of working in Kifungilo was upsetting. When I left to go to Mhonda, I vowed that I'd do whatever was necessary to have a life away from the orphanage. I couldn't bear the thought of having struggled and persevered through so many hardships only to end up where I started. I imagined all kinds of scenarios for myself. The most desirable was to pass my exams and then study in Europe or America. If I failed them, then I'd become a middle school teacher. If I passed and didn't go abroad, then I'd go to teachers training and become a secondary school teacher. That meant I wouldn't teach in Kifungilo since it only went to middle school. If all else failed, maybe I'd ask Father Michael if he could find a way for me to continue my education.

With great anticipation I awaited the day of my departure for my final year at Marian College. Father Michael arrived at sunrise and we were on our way. Except for casual morning greetings, we didn't say another word until he parked his car in the forest barely a few yards from the long colonnade of eucalyptus trees that indicated we'd left Kifungilo behind. Father Michael took my face in his hands. He looked at me for a long time before moving his parted lips back and forth across my tense ones until I felt something inside me let go. He kissed me slowly and deeply, murmuring, "I missed you. I missed you so much."

I caressed his unruly hair and told him that I'd missed him too. He lowered the lever of his seat and pulled me on top of him. I kissed him the best I knew how. His passion ignited something in me. Resting in his arms felt so good. I asked him, "Do you love me?"

He didn't answer. He gave a big sigh, and right away I knew I shouldn't have asked that. He held his head in his hands and for a moment, I thought he was weeping. All he said was, "I'm sorry."

I wondered what was wrong. What was he sorry for? If he missed me and kissed me that way, what was the matter? Was he lying to me? Was he taking advantage of my ignorance? Although I was only eighteen years old, I knew there had to be something he was hiding from me because feelings don't lie. Was the fact that he was a priest getting in the way?

"Let's go," I said.

"Are you angry?"

"I'm confused."

"Please don't be angry with me. I'm confused too."

He started the car and we pulled on to the road. He drove faster than usual and we got to Korogwe in no time at all. As soon as we entered town, without any explanation he turned onto a long, narrow, winding, gravel road that ended in front of three large houses on a hill that stood out from the rows of African huts and shacks because they were *wazungu* houses.

"This is our Mission Post where I live when I'm not traveling. I want to get something from my office. Come in with me and we'll have tea." I followed him inside where I heard the clattering of cups and spoons and voices conversing and laughing.

"Frank, Ben," he said, "this is Mary, the girl I've told you about."

"How do you do?" they greeted me. I just nodded. I recognized the two priests. They had come to retreats at Kifungilo.

"I'll get you a cup of tea. Sit down." The man named Frank cleared a place for Father Michael and for me and called out to someone in the kitchen. I felt awkward and miserable. I'd never had tea with three *wazungu* men before. I felt a little better when an African woman brought in the tea.

"*Karibu binti*" (Welcome, Miss), she said to me, and poured tea for the men first and then for me.

"*Asante*," I said. When she went back to the kitchen, I instinctively stood up with my cup in my hand, ready to follow her.

"Where are you going?" Father Michael asked. "Have tea with us."

"I'd rather have it in the kitchen with her."

"Come on, don't be afraid of my friends."

I sat down and sipped my tea. I listened to their rapid talking but understood very little. I realized how slowly and clearly Father

Michael enunciated when he talked to me. My feelings of being left out and unable to participate only increased, and I began to feel that he wanted to show me off. I decided to go to the kitchen anyway. When I stood up to leave the room, the telephone rang.

"Since you're up, answer it for me, would you?" Frank said. I looked at him and tried to pretend he wasn't talking to me. I watched the contraption on the wall ring, but I had no idea what to do. I had never used or even seen a telephone before. I touched the little bell on the outside of the box. I tried to figure out how to stop the ringing. I stood motionless in front of the telephone, feeling stupid, backward and out of place.

"Go ahead, answer it," Frank said without looking at me. I just looked at the telephone as it kept ringing.

"I'll answer it." Father Michael came to my rescue. I ran to the kitchen and burst into tears after closing the door behind me.

"*Mwanang, usilie! Shida gani?*" (My child, don't cry. What's the problem?) The woman in the kitchen put her arms around me and consoled me.

"*Asante*" is all I could say to her after I'd stopped crying. I heard the conversation in the living room stop and everyone say goodbye. I said *asante* again to the African woman as I left and followed Father Michael to the car.

"What's the matter with you?" he asked as soon as we got to the main road. "You sat there the entire time and didn't say one word. I've been telling my friends how bright and delightful you are, but instead of impressing them like I thought you would, you ran and hid in the kitchen!"

"What's the matter with *you*? You talked to your friends the entire time like I wasn't there. You hardly even looked at me. What was I doing there?"

"That's no reason to act so primitive."

"I am primitive! Don't you know that? I've never even seen a telephone in my life, and Father Frank wanted me to answer it. Where has he been living anyway? Doesn't he know there are hardly any phones in the whole country?"

"So that's what upset you!"

"I felt so stupid. I have no business riding in a car with a *mzu-*

ngu. The only place you treat me nicely is in your car—and in the bush. I don't want to ride with you again." Besides the humiliation of feeling out of place and on display, seeing the other priests made me wonder: Wasn't he ashamed of bringing me to them? Did he tell his priest friends about what we did? Was it normal for priests to bring girls to the mission? Maybe these priests had young girls too. I thought he cared for me and that I was special. Was I just fooling myself?

"I'm sorry. I keep assuming that you're familiar with European ways because Europeans raised you. You certainly don't act like an African girl!"

"What's that supposed to mean?"

"You're not submissive, and you're not afraid to express yourself and speak your mind in front of a white man like me and—"

"It's because you fooled me into believing that you were differ-ent. I should have known better. Once a *mzungu* always a *mzungu*!"

"And what's that supposed to mean?"

"It means that you will always feel and act superior to an African."

"That's very unfair. Do you really feel that's how I am?"

"Yes. You and all the *wazungu* in Africa."

Father Michael stopped the car abruptly, reversed it, and by the time the dust subsided, we had settled into a shallow ditch on the other side of the road. I looked out the window wishing I wasn't there. Father Michael got out of the car and walked along a footpath until he disappeared into the bushes.

"Are you coming?" he called. I didn't answer. He waited for a while and then, as if in exasperation, he walked briskly toward the car. He opened the door and dragged me out. He held both of my hands behind my back and tried to kiss me. I resisted, but he squeezed me so tight and kissed me so hard that I succumbed.

"If I hurt you, I'm sorry. I promised I'd never hurt you. Don't be angry." He sat me on the ground next to him. "Please forgive me. Can I have a makeup kiss?"

Suddenly something inside me broke loose. Pain and passion blended within me in a bewildering way. A force I could only give in to poured through me. I attacked him with all my strength, groaning as I kissed every part of his fully clothed body. When I came to his penis, I ripped open the zipper, grabbed the heated organ, and realized that after years of speculation, I finally held a man's hard penis in my hand. Fully clothed, I sat on it and felt his arms tighten around me. We thumped and thrashed on the ground, rolling every which way until he screamed and shuddered and eventually loosened his grip. I slowly rolled off him and lay quietly a few feet away. I gazed into the bright blue sky above and wondered who taught me to behave like that. I looked at Father Michael. His eyes were shut but he was smiling.

"Will you ride with me again?"

"Only if you forget how I just acted."

He kissed my forehead. "I like it when you're on fire." He kissed my nose. "You're as free and natural as the wind." He kissed my hand. "Sometimes I wish I could surrender myself to you as you just did." He let go of my hand and looked the other way.

"Why can't you?"

He just held me tight and whispered in my ear, "We'd better be on our way, otherwise we'll arrive at midnight."

We stopped again just as we approached the Uluguru Mountains, in time to watch the sun set over Marian College. "Today I saw the angry and hurt Mary, but what I'll remember is your wild, hungry, powerful, natural, free spirit."

"You'll come to take me back to Kifungilo at the end of the year?"

"I think I can arrange that! Let me leave you with this thought: As long as you pass your exams, I can help you get into any school in the country."

53

Miss Murray

 My senior year in high school was one of the most eventful years in my life. It was the year of the Cambridge Exams, the only exams that really mattered so far. I was determined to do well, even though I had a hard time studying for a couple of classes with teachers I didn't like.

I was happy to reunite with Sister Martin Corde and my friend Henrietta and *Mwalimu* Fliakos. Another student from Kifungilo who had gone to Kongei for middle school was already at Marian College as a freshman when I arrived that year. Imelda was the little girl with mumps in the orphanage's infirmary whose bacon I stole from the bandage around her head. She became my little sister. I had the privilege of showing and teaching Imelda everything she needed to know about Marian College. I was very proud to explain menstruation to her, but was amazed that she already knew everything. I, on the other hand, could fill a book with all the questions I asked when I was her age and the many discussions with Paulina about it. Was I the only one who had to have it spelled out in detail, or was my deficiency about the whole "period" subject due to never learning about the reproductive system when we were studying the human body?

There was also a new lay teacher from America, Miss Catherine Murray. She was a friend of Miss Polga, the other lay American teacher, who was teaching English at Marian College with a program called Teachers for East Africa. As was our custom, we danced and sang and composed poems to welcome new teachers and guests. Sister Dolores Marie introduced her and said that Miss Murray would help prepare a small number of students for the Cambridge Oral English Exam and they would be chosen by their English teachers.

Miss Murray was short and plump and always carried a large black purse that she wouldn't let us carry for her. She probably didn't know that, out of respect, students customarily carried everything for their teachers. Her somewhat large face was framed by thin, dry, wavy, caramel-colored hair, and she had large, blue-green protruding eyes that seemed to wander aimlessly behind a thick pair of butterfly-shaped glasses.

After Miss Murray was introduced, she said a few words, but mostly she smiled and nodded her head a lot. I watched her very closely during the program. She seemed genuinely interested and amused by our entertainment. There was a certain vulnerability to Miss Murray. She let us know right away that she wasn't ashamed of making a fool of herself by trying some tribal dances with us and executing them just terribly in front of the amused students and teachers.

"Well, what do you think of Miss Murray?" I asked Henrietta as we discussed the new teachers.

"She's odd, don't you think? She smiles a lot and looks everywhere at the same time."

"She doesn't look everywhere at the same time. It just seems that way because her eyes are too big for her face and those glasses magnify any eye movements she makes. Her eyes move much faster than she walks or talks."

"I think she walks quite fast for a fat person."

"Just because you're as thin as a pencil, don't make fun of fat people."

"Mary, don't be so sensitive. Whenever I say anything about fat people, you become defensive."

"In my mind, I'm still fat, and I know what it feels like to be made fun of for being fat."

"Miss Murray is as round as a ball!"

"When we get to know her, her appearance won't matter. I have a feeling she's nice."

"I do too. She smiles too much to be mean inside."

When our conversation ended, I found myself wondering if Miss Murray was ever hurt because she was fat.

The next morning I learned that I was chosen to be one of the four students she would prepare for the Oral English Exam. Little did I know that this strange-looking American teacher with bulging eyes and thick glasses would change my life. She took an interest in me from the first day of class after she had us tell a little about ourselves. I always dreaded such self-introductions, which seemed standard procedure for Americans. The other students talked about their tribes, families, homes, villages, and their plans for the future. My introduction was: "My name is Mary Rose Ryan. I have no parents and I have no family. German Sisters at an orphanage called Kifungilo in the Usambara Mountains brought me up. In the future I would like to go to a university abroad or become a teacher in my country." Miss Murray just looked at me in silence and said a long "Goooooood." She didn't go on asking me all sorts of questions about what happened to my family, or whether I spoke any other tribal language besides my own like she asked the others.

Once the detested introductions were over, we started learning correct pronunciation, phrasing, and frequently used English idioms, all meant to increase our spontaneity when speaking. When Miss Murray gave us a new word or expression, her entire face, especially her eyes, got involved in over-enunciating. We had so much fun imitating her after class that the other students were jealous of us for having such an entertaining teacher. She also helped us practice reading the letters of praise we wrote to the Sisters and for visitors to our school.

We had two very important visitors that year. The first one was Cardinal Laurean Rugambwa, the first African cardinal of the Roman Catholic Church, and the second was none other than President Julius Nyerere, the first president of our newly independent country. On December 9, 1961, our country, still called Tanganyika, became independent. I was grateful we had followed the progress of TANU—Tanganyika African National Union, the political party formed in 1954 to gain independence from Britain—in *Mwalimu* Haule's Current Affairs class in Mhonda.

The Americans—Sisters and lay teachers alike—were excited about these visitors. We cleaned and scrubbed the entire school, planted flowers and trees, painted buildings, and built a stone-lined path with several archways decorated with leaves and flowers to lead from the car to Rosary Hall, as our auditorium was now called. We prepared tribal dances with colorful costumes, and the glee club taught us our new national anthem, *"Mungu Ibariki Tanganyika"* ("God Bless Tanganyika").

On the day of the President's visit, we dressed in clean uniforms and polished shoes, wore ribbons and flowers in our hair, and followed his Land Rover down the decorated path, singing and dancing, cheering, and tossing marigold bouquets over the car. He was smiling broadly as he descended, preceded by a host of government officials and security men. The Sisters and teachers lined up in front of the hall and shook his hand. It was obvious that the Americans were very impressed with the occasion.

We entered the hall and accompanied President Nyerere to his flower-decorated chair next to the headmistress Sister Dolores Marie and Sister Margaret Rose, the Mother Superior. We entertained with singing and dancing. After much applause, the President stood up to speak. I was expecting the strong voice of urgency that I'd often heard on the radio when he was campaigning for independence from the British. Instead, he was soft-spoken, very warm and sincere when he told us he was happy and proud to be invited to Marian College, the first secondary school for girls in Tanganyika. He said that only a hundred women had graduated from secondary school in the whole country. Our country needed educated women who would stand side by side with our new male leaders and who would raise educated children to lead our country.

After he spoke, we raised our right fists and cheered *"Uhuru!"* (Freedom).

He responded with *"Uhuru na Kazi!"* (Freedom and Work).

"Uhuru!!" we yelled.

"Uhuru na Maendeleo!" (Freedom and Development), he answered.

"Uhuru!"

He raised both fists saying, *"Uhuru na Kujitegemea!"* (Freedom and Self-reliance).

The visit was a thrill for me and for Miss Murray too. She had us describe the visit for her over and over during several classes, and she beamed every time we mentioned that the President held her hand the longest and he continued to hold her hand while he greeted everyone else. "You noticed! You noticed!" she'd shout with delight, forgetting that she was the teacher.

I loved Miss Murray. She was down to earth (to use a phrase she'd taught us) and really listened to what we had to say. Sometimes I'd catch her staring at me. I wondered why she paid so much attention to me even when not in class. I'd smile at her, and she'd smile back and blink her heavy eyelids.

Once she invited all four of us Oral English students to her house for tea. When we got there, she decided that she'd found something much more special for us to enjoy than tea.

"I have a great treat for us all," she said. "Wait until you taste it. You'll love it! I'm so excited I can't stand it. Let's have it instead of tea, shall we?"

"Yes, Miss Murray," we said in unison. I wondered what sort of food could make her so emotional.

"Guess what I found in town today—ice cream! Imagine ice cream in Africa! What more could anyone want?" She went to the kitchen and came out with a paper carton of something that she held with both hands as if it were gold. She carefully put it down on the coffee table in front of us. We stared at the carton. What on earth is this ice cream, I wondered. She dished out a stiff white substance into five bowls. She had a dreamy, faraway look on her face as she filled the bowls, and sounds of utmost delight came from her throat.

"Now let's feast!" She handed us each a bowl, but we all quickly put our bowls back on the table. She was oblivious to us as she raised the ice cream bowl close to her mouth, closed her eyes, and made sucking and smacking noises every time the spoon left her mouth. Finally, she cleaned the bowl, her spoon clanking loudly as she went after every last smidgeon of ice cream. I was expecting her to raise it to her mouth and lick it like we used to do in Kifungilo. She put her bowl back on the table with her eyes still closed. When she opened them, the smile that had never left her face while she ate turned into an expression of surprise and disbelief when she saw our untouched bowls.

"You must eat it before it melts," she said. We didn't know what to do. I took the bowl in my hands and began to stir the ice cream. The other girls did the same.

"What are you doing? That's sacrilege! Don't destroy the ice cream like that. Eat it before it's too late." The others looked at me as though I were their spokesperson.

"We can't eat it," I said.

"Pray tell me why?"

"Miss Murray, this food is too cold."

"Oh my God! It's supposed to be cold. I spent the entire morning trying to figure out how to keep it frozen long enough for you. We don't have a freezer, you know."

"What's a freezer?"

"All right. I should have explained everything first, but how was I supposed to know that you'd never seen ice cream before? Ice cream is the best, most comforting food on earth! All, and I mean all Americans love it. Here in Africa, they'd kill for it!"

Why, I wondered, would someone kill for something so cold and awful?

In spite of the ice cream debacle, Miss Murray continued to pay extra attention to me. In private, she asked me many questions about the orphanage and my life with the German nuns. She wanted to know who was in charge of me at the convent. She had done her homework and told me that she heard that Kifungilo was a very beautiful place and said she'd like to visit it someday. I told her that when I was little, we used to have many European visitors who came on Sundays just to see the place.

"Mother Rufina has invited Miss Polga and me to come for Christmas, and we're so excited! You'll be there, won't you?"

"Where else would I be? Anyway, I'd never miss Kifungilo at Christmas time. It's the best time for the children."

"Children all over the world love Christmas. Tell me, do you get many presents like we do in America?'

"Oh yes! We get a gingerbread man, some candy, nuts, holy

cards, and a new dress from the boxes that people in Germany send to the Missions, and sometimes we get a pair of shoes from those boxes as well." Miss Murray's face didn't smile like it usually did. Her eyes fluttered for a short time and she looked at me with an expression of either pity or lack of comprehension.

She invited me several times for dinner to "get to know each other." Why was it so important that she get to know me? I didn't feel such a need to know her. She encouraged me with my studies and wanted to know what I planned to do if I passed my Cambridge Exams.

"I have no definite plans. I just want to continue with school. I want to be a teacher."

"Is that all?"

"You won't laugh at me if I tell you what I really want?"

She put her arms around me for the first time and said, "I love you, Mary. I'd never ever laugh at you. I admire you." She was the first adult in my life who had ever said "I love you." I wondered if she meant "I like you" and what exactly was the difference between the two.

"I would like to continue my studies in a university in Europe or in America. I know it would take a miracle for that to happen."

"Do you believe in miracles?"

"Sometimes. Sister Martin Corde has really helped me believe in them because whenever I'm depressed about my life and cry to her about it, she tells me that she's always praying for a miracle to happen to me. I don't know what miracle she's praying for, but I'd like to find a way to continue my education. The nuns at Kifungilo can't pay for me."

"Maybe we can talk about it with Mother Rufina when I'm there this Christmas."

"Do you think you could convince her to continue to pay for my education?"

"I'll try."

Because we sat for our exams the end of the year and wouldn't receive the results until school was out, our American teachers decided to have what they called a "Graduation Ceremony" before we

Miss Murray 275

left. We had to wear long white robes and the most awful hats I'd ever seen—a square piece of cardboard covered with fabric with a silly thing hanging on one side called a "tassel." The Sisters and teachers took graduation very seriously. We had to rehearse for it like we rehearsed plays and performances. We stood on stage in the auditorium holding burning candles while the headmistress and students read speeches. Then the juniors came on the stage one by one, carrying unlit candles. The graduates lit the juniors' candles as they recited our school motto: *"As one candle lights another, nor grows less, so nobleness enkindles nobleness."* We were then given a rolled up paper tied with a ribbon to represent the certificates we'd get when the results of the Cambridge Exams came out in two months.

The best thing about graduation was the pin our headmistress gave each of us. The gold, black, and red enamel emblem of our beloved Marian College had an eternal flame burning in one corner. A giraffe, the national symbol of Tanganyika peered out from the opposite corner, and Mount Kilimanjaro, the highest mountain in Africa, and the Uluguru Mountains of Morogoro were positioned diagonally across from each other. I treasured it.

54

End of the Road

With most of the students gone and the rest of us in varying states of fear and anxiety, Marian College was like a mortuary during exam week. Failing would bring shame and disappointment to anyone who was even remotely involved with our education. For most of us, a secondary school education was the highest level we could hope to attain, and having attained it, we would be respected and valued. I knew I would be doomed to live in Kifungilo for the rest of my life if I failed. Would the nuns find a husband for me or would I have to run away in order to escape? I had now been exposed to and even tasted some of the fruits that life had to offer, so I knew I couldn't bear life in Kifungilo. I had reached the end of what I could do for myself and failing the exams now would be a death sentence.

We studied hard for the exams. Everything we had learned in seven subjects over the four-year period of high school would be tested. Teachers had to pry us off our desks and convince us to take breaks or go to bed. We moved about like robots ready to spit out correct answers on command. On the first day of the exams, Mass was said for us in the morning and we were treated like frail royalty. But once I was actually in the room with the exam in hand, I was no longer afraid of failing. I finished well before most students, but remained in class until others started leaving.

The week went quickly and before long we were weeping and saying goodbye to classmates and teachers. Because I had no idea what I was going to do with my life after I left Marian College, I felt once again that my goodbyes were forever. It was hard to say goodbye to Sister Martin Corde and to Henrietta. They were the two people I knew I'd do everything in my power to see again. I was relieved that Miss Murray was coming to Kifungilo for Christmas because I had become used to her smiles and frequent hugs. It was especially hard to say goodbye to Marian College. I had grown so much there. It introduced me to Americans and gave me the desire to travel to their great land. Going to America was a dream that most students had, but it was my special dream. Although the Sisters found scholarships to American universities for a few students from the last three graduating classes, for most of us it would remain only a dream. I left for Kifungilo with a heavy heart.

Sister Silvestris was very happy to see me and I her. Right away she acted as though I was back for good and gave me responsibilities. One of the things she had me do was help with showing the Kifungilo grounds to the *wazungu* who still came to visit or spend a quiet Sunday afternoon. "Your English is so much better than mine and you can also tell them about life here from the children's point of view." I didn't like the job very much because some visitors were rude and talked about the orphanage and the Sisters as though I wasn't there.

My third Sunday on the job, I took around an Italian priest, his parents, two brothers, their wives and a niece. They were very nice to me, especially the priest. They were full of life, and after they established that my name was really "Maria Rosa," they wanted to learn some Swahili words and even asked me to show them some tribal dances.

The priest had three big cameras and since none of his relatives volunteered to help him, I did. I carried just one and it was heavy. I had to laugh at him because he made such funny faces and contorted his entire body when he took pictures. He spent a long time arranging and re-arranging his seven-member family, and eventually they started arguing and refusing to cooperate. They spoke in Italian most of the time, and I couldn't tell if they were angry or enjoying themselves. They all talked at once and broke into singing and then they'd be shouting, and in the middle of it all, they'd sit down on the path to eat sandwiches and drink coffee. They were actually quite easy guests because they didn't ask me any of the questions I found hard to answer. They entertained themselves and me thoroughly.

When we arrived back in front of the convent, I said goodbye and started walking up the hill when the priest, whose name was Father Antonio, came to shake my hand. "You must excuse my family. They're always like this."

"Did they just arrive from Italy?"

"They've been here for a month already and they'll be going back in a week." Still talking and laughing at the top of their lungs, they piled into an old Land Rover and motioned for the priest to hurry up. "I'll be returning to Kifungilo to continue my work as soon as I see them off in Dar. Will you be here in ten days?"

"I'll be here forever."

"Then you can be my assistant and help me carry these cameras around when I come to take pictures for the book."

"A book?"

"I'm taking pictures for a friend's book about Christian missions in Tanganyika." His relatives blew the horn. He hurriedly shook my hand and said, "*Arrivederci, Maria. Bella Maria Rosa.*"

He returned in ten days in the same Land Rover, now filled with all sorts of photographic equipment and paraphernalia. We walked around Kifungilo again while he photographed the Sisters, children, church, and buildings. Often he'd ask me to pose among the flowers or next to my favorite calla lilies by the river, or he'd have me pretend to be picking and smelling roses while he took pictures with each camera. The moment he finished a series of pictures, he'd break into singing in Italian at the top of his voice, and I'd start laughing.

"Are you laughing at me?" he asked.

"Well …yes."

"And what's so funny?"

"The way you sing. Why do you sing with such a deep and unnatural voice?"

"Haven't you ever heard of opera?"

"Opera? Who's that?"

"That's what I'm singing. We Italians love opera, and very few people can sing this way." He continued singing and waving his arms and swinging his body and making strange expressions with his face while I laughed myself into tears. I'd never heard or seen such strange or funny singing. From then on, whenever he asked me to pose for a picture and I felt silly doing what he suggested, he knew how to make me laugh.

When we returned to the guesthouse, I walked into the living room and put his camera on the table only to feel very strong arms hug me from behind. "*Grazie, grazie.* We'll continue tomorrow, all right?"

"All right," I said, thinking that Italians overdid hugging just as they did their singing.

The next day we walked with two other girls to Gare Mission a few miles away. The trip, which usually takes only forty-five minutes, took three hours. Father Antonio sang his opera and hummed to himself while he took pictures of the countryside and of us, and we laughed uncontrollably. I walked close to him since I was carrying his cameras and I had to be very alert and hand him the camera he requested each time. It was hard work. When the other girls were a distance from us, he asked me to come to the guesthouse after dinner to keep him company. I was delighted, since I had nothing better to do and it would distract me from worrying about my exams.

He was waiting just inside the guesthouse door. I walked in and he quickly closed the door. Without saying a word, he kissed me passionately on the mouth.

"What are you doing?" I pushed him away. He stopped to look at me for a second and then reached for me again. "I'm leaving."

"Please stay with me."

"I'll stay if you promise not to kiss me."

"I promise."

I wondered if all priests did this when they found themselves alone with a woman, and if they thought it was okay. He asked me to sit on the sofa and he sat across from me. When I had the courage to look at him, it was as if I saw him for the first time. He sat at one end of the sofa holding his head in his hands, his long graceful fingers digging into his curly black hair. I noticed that he was shaking, so I asked him if he was all right.

"No, Maria Rosa, I'm not all right."

"I'll leave."

"No, no. Please don't leave. I...I...I asked you to come because I wanted to talk to you about a project I have planned, but as soon as I heard your footsteps I knew I would have to kiss you." He moved his hands from his head, moved closer to me, and held them around my face. "From the first time I saw you, I felt something inside. I've been unable to think of anything but you for the last two weeks."

Oh no! Here we go again. What is it with me and priests that they want to kiss me?

Father Antonio stood up and walked to the window. He stood there with his back to me and said nothing. I then noticed that he was quite tall, or was it his floor-length white cassock that made him look taller than life? His habit made him look more priestly than Father Michael, whom I'd only seen in lay clothes. He sat in a chair by a table and spoke as if he were discussing something with the floor. He said that he'd been in Africa on special assignments for six months and had been looking for someone to model for his photographs of the Virgin Mary.

"The Virgin Mary? What are you talking about?"

"You have the perfect face. It's serene. It's honest. It's beautiful."

"The Virgin Mary?" I repeated. "Do you mean that all those holy cards the Sisters give us are pictures of simple, poor people like me? That's a sacrilege!"

"Most of them are taken from statues, but mine will be special because I'll be able to feel the flesh and blood of my live model through the pictures." He was talking normally again. "Come, let me look at you." I felt nervous and strange. He took my hand and led me into one of the other guest rooms, which he had converted into a photo studio with huge lights and several lamps that had black and white umbrella-like cloths on them. He turned on the lights and the room became extremely bright.

Seeing my discomfort, he said, "There's nothing to be afraid of, Maria Rosa. You have the Virgin's name, and that makes you very special." He told me to stand on a low wooden stool. Then he draped a long white shawl over my head. He tucked my hair under the shawl, lifted my chin up to him, and looked down on my face. He rubbed some rouge from a round vial on my cheeks and put lipstick on my lips. The longer he took preparing me, the tenser I got. "There! *Bella!*" He went behind a camera that was mounted on a homemade wooden tripod. "I'll count to three, then you must smile, but don't show your teeth." He showed me how to tilt my head a little to one side and explained that what he wanted was called a "Mona Lisa" smile. I felt awkward and nervous. What was this priest up to? Why me? I had no intention of representing the Virgin Mary or any other Mona Lisa person in a picture. "Okay, ready? *Uno! Due! Tre!*" He took several pictures.

"*Meraviglioso!* Wonderful!" He changed my robes and veils and hair style often and gave me different sized black dolls to carry in my arms and on my lap. He folded my hands in prayer, had me raise them, and put shiny rosaries around them. Two hours later he turned off the bright lights and I felt normal again.

"It's very dark outside. I'd better go."

"Here, take this flashlight." On my way to the door he pulled me to him, looked at me for a while and then pressed my face against his chest. "*Grazie, bella Maria Rosa.*" I felt his heart beating. He held me tight and kissed me on the forehead. "*Grazie. Buona notte.*"

"*Buona notte,*" I mimicked him and left.

Father Antonio was in Kifungilo for a week. During the day, three of the big girls and I accompanied him on his photo safaris, sometimes on foot and sometimes by car. He asked me to come and visit him in the evenings, and since he hadn't kissed or touched me in five days, I was much more relaxed and I looked forward to my time with him. One evening he asked me if I'd always lived in Kifungilo. I told him that except for being away at school, Kifungilo was my home. I started fidgeting because I didn't feel like answering all the questions I knew were on his mind.

"I'm sorry for you."

"Don't be sorry for me. I've spent my entire childhood feeling sad about my life and situation. You don't need to be sorry for me." I changed the subject. "Where do you live in Tanganyika?"

"I'm stationed in the bush in the southern part of the country. I'd be the happiest priest in Africa if I were surrounded by the beauty of Kifungilo."

"What's more important to you, being a photographer or being a priest?"

"A priest, of course. But I love my photography almost as much. I'd never have met you if I worked only as a priest."

He walked to where I was sitting, kissed me, and pressed me against him with what seemed like super-human strength. I had all I could do not to collapse when he released me.

"I like you very much, Maria Rosa."

"You're the second priest who has acted like that to me. Aren't you breaking the rules of your vocation by liking a woman so much?"

"I believe that God has sent you to me for a reason. I can't stop thinking about you."

"Do all priests break the rules?"

"Do you love that other priest?"

"I don't think so."

"It's all right to tell me. I need to know."

"Why?"

"Because I love you. I know we just met, but look into my eyes. I've never felt this way about someone before. Never, never! I can't stop thinking of you, *bella* Maria Rosa. I'm a priest, but I need the woman you are."

He kissed me on the lips very gently. "I can give you everything you want, Maria Rosa. I want you. I want you to be a part of my life forever."

I looked up to see his face but instead my eyes fixated on a large wooden crucifix on the wall. It felt unreal that Fat Mary was sitting on a sofa in the guesthouse of the Sisters of the Precious Blood in Kifungilo with a *mzungu* priest professing his love for her. I abruptly got up from the sofa and moved away from Father Antonio.

"What's the matter? Tell me. What do you want, *bella*?"

"The only thing I want is to go to a university if I pass my exams."

"I can do that for you," he murmured as he pulled me back to him kissing my hand. I'm returning to Italy in six months and I will start looking for a school for you before I leave. I'm from Torino and I know people who can help us. What do you want to study?"

"Everything."

"We could have a good life together. You would go to school during the day and come home to me at night. I'm thirty-eight years old. I can find a good job with my photography skills. I'll take very good care of you."

"You're serious, aren't you?"

"Very serious. Because I am a priest, the Sisters will trust me and will agree that I would be like your father, and they will allow you to come to Italy for university. I'll tell them that you would stay with my family and I would care for you like a father."

"Wouldn't that be lying?"

"Not really. I don't have to tell them more than that for now. Will you think about it?"

I saw my opportunity to leave Africa, so I said, "Thank you, Father. I'll let you know soon." He held my head against his chest and stroked my hair.

"Thank you for coming to me," he said. "I will never be the same."

55

The Miracle

The morning Father Antonio left, we stood in front of the convent as he kissed me on both cheeks and gave me a box beautifully wrapped with blue paper. There was a letter attached to it. As soon as his Land Rover disappeared into the cypress trees, I opened the box to find chocolates individually wrapped in multicolored foil paper. I picked a heart-shaped chocolate, kissed it, and put it back in the box. I opened the envelope and saw that the letter was twenty-one pages long. I started to read it and before long, found myself fighting tears of happiness. He said that he didn't want to waste the few hours we were alone telling me things he could explain in a letter. He told me all about his parents and his two brothers and their families, how old they were, what they did, and which ones I would like the best. He wrote about his feelings since he met me, all the plans he had for me and for us, and his confusion about being a priest that he planned to resolve. He said he wanted to take me to Italy in June and find a good school, and that God would take care the rest. I believed every word he said.

I thought about the possibilities he was offering me. I imagined life in Italy and wondered how long it would take me to learn Italian. Then suddenly, while I was still thinking of life with Father Antonio, Father Michael entered my mind. I saw his serious and sometimes sad face that looked as though he was trying to hide something. I thought about his kisses and our love sessions along the road and in the car, and my heart started beating very fast. Thinking of the two men in my life made me feel confused but also happy. I didn't know what would happen with Father Michael, but I knew for sure that

Father Antonio loved me enough to take me to Italy for university. I was looking forward to Miss Murray's visit at Christmas because I wanted to tell her about my good fortune and ask for her advice.

In the morning, my head throbbed. By nightfall, what I'd thought was just a bad headache turned out to be full-fledged malaria. Sister Silvestris was quite concerned because I hadn't been sick at Kifungilo since I almost died of typhoid when I was seven.

"I don't like it when you're sick. You bring so much joy to us when you come back. I've been waiting for you to finish school so you can come to Kifungilo for good. When you're better we'll talk like *zamani*—the old days. Now sleep, my child. Of course you're a big girl now, but no matter how big you are, you'll always be my child, my Fat Mary."

A whole week passed before my fever went down. While I was recuperating, I tortured myself over what to do about Father Antonio. Everything, except my heart, told me to go with him. The way he kissed me and the way he planned and talked about our life together convinced me that he was sincere about loving me. I wondered if his love was enough to make up for the misgivings I had about leaving Father Michael behind. He was the first man who showed any interest in me—first as a student and then as someone he wanted to kiss and make love to. Would I be wasting a golden opportunity if I stayed in Kifungilo and waited for Father Michael to make up his mind about me? The fact that he was a priest didn't deter me from believing that if he loved me, he could do something about it like Father Antonio said he would. Would I, in time, feel the same way about Father Antonio as he felt about me? What was love anyway? Was it the painful and confusing feeling that these two men left in my heart? As agonizing as these thoughts were, at least they spared me from worrying over the results of my Cambridge Exams.

Miss Murray and Miss Polga arrived the day before Christmas and I was so happy to see them. Miss Murray gave me a big hug. "I missed you."

"I missed you too," I said, though God knows I had no time to think of anything besides Father Michael and Father Antonio.

"I'm very anxious to see how you celebrate Christmas in this most beautiful place on earth! You never told me how beautiful Kifungilo is. It's certainly worth the suicidal Mombo-Lushoto road. Miss Polga is brave. I wanted to turn around, but she inched her way up the steep pot-holed path that you call a road. No one in America would believe that road. I'm already afraid of the trip back."

They settled into the guesthouse and I had dinner with them. I hadn't seen *wazungu* devour food like that. They kept saying, "Isn't this magnificent? Oh my God! Just taste this! Have you ever in your whole life eaten such wonderful food?"

"I'm staying here forever!" Miss Murray announced.

I returned to the children's quarters and wrapped up the tablecloth I'd made and embroidered for Miss Murray for Christmas and the box of chocolates I got from Father Antonio for Miss Polga. On Christmas Eve, some of the big girls and I went to fetch our American guests to come to the recreation hall for the festivities. As usual, the little children performed a Christmas play and sang songs for the appreciative old Sisters. We then went to our gift piles on the tables along the walls. I showed off my gifts—a pink taffeta dress with huge sleeves, a pair of still usable black high heels, a small red purse with a broken zipper, a new rosary, a cup of nuts, and a gingerbread man. I was so busy showing my gifts that I didn't notice that Miss Polga had left the room and Miss Murray was weeping.

"What's the matter?"

"I'm sorry. I'm sorry," Miss Murray repeated and walked out too. I followed her out asking, "Did something happen?"

"I'm so sorry, Mary. It's awful to act like this. This is your Christmas and we should be happy to be with you, but it's so sad."

"What's so sad?"

"I'm sorry. Maybe I can explain later." Miss Polga was already halfway down to the guest quarters and Miss Murray followed her, leaving me confused and worried.

"We'll see you at midnight Mass," she sobbed. "I'm sorry." As she disappeared I heard her blow her nose as only she could, and the echo of that sound disturbed me throughout the night. I couldn't bring myself to talk to either of my guests after Mass. These Americans were so strange.

In the morning they acted as though nothing had happened. I decided not to bring it up. We opened our gifts and I was thrilled to see that Miss Murray had a brand new dress from America for me. She also gave me a beautiful three-strand gold and pink pearl bracelet that she said was a gift from her father. Miss Polga gave me a soft leather prayer book, which I knew I would treasure. They were very pleased with my gifts for them and I was happy. It was the first time in my life that I had given a Christmas gift to anyone. The happiness on their faces made me realize that the true joy of a gift was more in the giving rather than the receiving. I felt the same way when I gave Paulina the necklace set. I have always remembered that.

I ate all my meals with them and we toured the grounds. At times they were speechless and overwhelmed with the beauty and serenity of this German hideaway in the middle of Africa. Two days before they were supposed to leave, Miss Murray told me that she wanted to walk with me. We went down by the beautiful pond where Abbot Franz Pfanner, the founder of the Missionary Sisters of the Precious Blood, was immortalized in a statue inside a glass display case overlooking the pond that teamed with fish of every color and size.

She seemed anxious and nervous, and her eyes looked bigger and more apprehensive than usual. I thought she wanted to explain why she and Miss Polga showed such bad manners when they cried and left our Christmas Eve celebrations in the midst of the children's happiness. I had decided to tell her about Father Antonio and ask her opinion. She walked very slowly and breathed loudly and deeply as though something was weighing on her. We sat on the bench in front of the statue and she took my hand in hers.

"Mary, I have something very important to talk to you about. I have been thinking about it ever since that first class when you introduced yourself. It would mean very much to me if you would say yes, and to tell the truth, I don't know what I'd do if you said no." She took a deep breath and sighed heavily.

"Mary," she continued, "I would like to take you to America with me when I return in June. I want to be your mother and you to be my child."

What? Was I dreaming? Should I ask her to repeat "very slowly and clearly" what she just said like she asked us to do in class? How could she be my mother? She was only four years older than I was. She must be joking.

"I've already discussed it with Sister Clotilda, who is in charge while Mother Rufina is in Germany. She not only gave her permission, she promised to help me in every way."

"Did you say Sister Clotilda promised to help you?"

"Yes, and she is the one who invited us to come to Kifungilo for Christmas. Why are you so surprised?"

"She hates me. She almost beat me to death when I was a child." Miss Murray didn't like to discuss unpleasant things, so she just kept talking.

"I first wrote to Mother Rufina about my plans, not knowing that she was in Germany. The letter must have been forwarded to her and she instructed Sister Clotilda to do everything she could to help you get to America." She continued telling me all the plans she'd been working on. She'd get me a passport and apply for a college scholarship, hoping that I'd pass my exams. She'd take care of everything. All I had to do was say yes.

I would like to take you to America. I couldn't believe my ears! My delayed reaction worried Miss Murray.

"Please say yes. Say you'll come with me. I love you very much and I can't see going back home without you."

"Oh, Miss Murray!" I started crying when I finally realized that I wasn't dreaming. I couldn't stop crying. I buried my head in my skirt and sobbed until all my tears were gone, and I was left heaving with a joy that bordered on pain.

"Please say yes, Mary."

"This is the happiest day of my life!" I poured my heart out. "Oh, Miss Murray, you're the kindest person on earth! Are you sure you're not an angel from heaven? I promise I'll do anything you want me to do. I'll work very hard so you will never regret it. I always dreamed of going to America. I can't believe it! Sister Martin Corde was right. Miracles do happen! I will live my whole life, but I will never forget this moment, this day. You have saved me. It doesn't matter what I become when I grow up as long as I do it in America. Yes! There's nothing in the world I'd rather do than go to America with you. Yes!"

She hugged me and wept along with me. "Thank you, Mary. You've made me very happy!"

"When do we leave?"

"First, you'll be coming back to Marian College with Miss Polga and me to await the results of your exam. If you've passed, you'll help Sister Antonita and Miss Fliakos with the Domestic Science classes and Sister Paul Catherine in the library. If all goes well and I can get your traveling documents together, we'll leave for America in early June."

"What if I fail?"

"You can't fail! I'm hoping you'll get a First Class Pass because it will be easier to find a scholarship for you. But no matter what happens I'm taking you to America, because from this day forward, you're my daughter and you'll go wherever I go."

"Thank you, Miss Murray."

"And from this day on, call me Cathy."

"I'll try, Cathy."

Before I told the other girls my good news that evening, I went to the recreation room and knelt down in front of the same Nativity scene where I'd prayed to Baby Jesus to find my mother when I was a child. I looked at him lying there in his bed of hay and wondered why this scene never left me. Over the years, whenever I prayed, I prayed to Baby Jesus. He was the miracle baby who never grew up. I believed that he really listened to me and often answered me. As I knelt there I realized that Sister Silvestris was right all along. She told us every Christmas that whatever we asked of Baby Jesus he'd grant us.

"Baby Jesus," I prayed, "you really took a long time to grant my childhood wish of finding my mother. Were you waiting until you found a mother for me who truly wants and loves me?"

"Yes," Baby Jesus answered with a contented smile. "I wanted to find a true mother for you, and I wanted to give you the good news when you came back to me at Christmas time."

I thanked him with all my heart and asked him to forgive the occasional disappointments I had in him. I asked him to teach me how to be a good daughter. I asked him to find mothers for the other orphans in Kifungilo. I reached into the Nativity set where he was lying on a bed of hay and soft moss, picked up his statue, and kissed it long and hard on the mouth. I realized that no matter how advanced and complicated my instruction in Catholicism had become, my true religion would always remain my personal relationship with Baby Jesus, and I would take that with me to America.

From that moment on, I worked on getting used to the idea that I was no longer an orphan and getting used to regarding Miss Murray—Cathy—as my mother. My lifelong search and intense longing for my birth mother was over. I replaced her with Cathy.

56

First Job

It was strange to be at Marian College as a teacher's aide rather than as a student. I stayed at the teachers' house near the school and taught sewing to first year students. Since Christmas, I thought of nothing else but Cathy and America. Father Michael never entered my mind and neither did Father Antonio until one day I received a letter from Father Michael telling me that he was coming to Marian College in a week and would pick me up in the afternoon to have lunch in town. Since I was no longer a student, I didn't need permission to leave the school grounds, so I planned to see him and tell him of my good fortune. As soon as I saw him, I knew something was up. I hadn't seen him so happy before. This time instead of shaking my hand like we always did when we were in public, he kissed me on the forehead and opened the car door.

"How's my American girl?" he asked.

"How did you know?"

"I find out everything that's important to me."

"But really, how did you find out?"

"Don't forget that I work for the Education Ministry and the bishop, and he has to approve whatever goes on in Kifungilo or any other mission in our district."

"But who told you?"

"I once mentioned to you that I was at a meeting in Tanga when the possibility of you going to Marian College was discussed. You and a handful of girls from the region were being considered to attend the school. Because I knew about the fate of Kifungilo girls with no education, I voted for you. When I was in Kifungilo one day, you were pointed out to me. That's when my interest in you began and I vowed to see that you went as far as possible in school."

"How do you know I'm going to America?"

"I've been helping your new mother get a passport for you. I'm thrilled for you. You deserve everything good that will come from this."

"So you're not sad that I'll be leaving Africa for good?"

"I could be selfish, but your education is more important than the feelings of an old man. It always has been. Didn't you know that?"

"You won't be sorry to see me go?"

"Sorry? Let's see." He pulled to the side of the road and stopped the car. "Sorry, you say?" He turned to me and then abruptly looked away. "Let's drive a little further."

"Maybe you should just take me back."

"Will you be sorry to leave me?" he asked me instead.

"I asked you first. I think I'm mistaken about you."

"Please, Mary, I don't want to argue with you, especially not today." He drove off the road along a bumpy abandoned path and parked under a mango tree. I got out of the car and walked away.

"You never talk about your feelings or intentions like Father An —." I caught myself! "Why don't you just come out and tell me that you're amusing yourself, and as soon as I leave you'll find another innocent girl." He ran after me, grabbed my arms, and held them behind my back, but I kept my face away from him.

"You know that's not true. Look at me!"

"So you can lie to my face?"

"So I can kiss you!" I pulled away from him and sat on the grass.

"You don't understand. I'm tired of being used. I want to get back to school."

"Not until you kiss me and say you're sorry for acting like a spoiled girl!"

My hurt was turning to anger. "Take me back to school! I never want to see you again."

"All right. Get in the car!"

I did, and I slammed the door. I wondered what it was that I wanted from him. Was I upset because he hadn't offered to send me to Ireland for university? Or was it because now that I was going to America, my feelings were hurt that he wasn't going to miss me? We drove in silence and I pouted all the way to school.

Once there, I got into bed even though it was only four o'clock in the afternoon. I felt as though my heart was swelling and would eventually burst out of my chest. How could he say that he cared for me? What was it about Father Michael that made me feel he was insincere? Was it because I could read Father Antonio's feelings like a book? So many thoughts about priests and vows of chastity and innocent young girls filled my head. I pushed all thoughts of the two priests out of my mind and made myself think of Cathy and America until I fell asleep.

The very next day I received my sixth long letter from Father Antonio. I had written to him and given him my address at Marian College, but told him nothing about Cathy. When I arrived at school after Christmas vacation, there was a letter from him waiting for me in Sister Dolores Marie's office. Thank God I was no longer a student, so she hadn't read it. Cathy brought it to me and asked so many questions that I gave Father Antonio the address of a friend from Kifungilo who lived in town, and I went to her house to retrieve the letters. I had gone to visit her several times while I was in school and took gifts from Sister Silvestris to her each time I returned to Morogoro after my holidays. Kifungilo girls trusted each other like family.

When I couldn't postpone it any further, I wrote to Father Antonio telling him about my decision to go to America with Cathy instead of going to Italy with him. He said in his reply that he would respond in person the following Sunday. He asked me to meet him at the Savoy Hotel at 2 p.m. As I walked into town, I recalled most of what he said in his long letters in the last months, and I felt as though I'd known him all my life. Sadness settled in my chest and my steps became heavier as I approached the hotel even as my body remembered his strong embrace and loving words. I knew he loved me, and I had to admit that the love of a man, evil or not (forgive me, Mother Rufina), felt powerful indeed. It crossed my mind that Father Antonio would break his cameras and rip his heart out if he knew another man had kissed me, while Father Michael showed no emotions.

When I arrived in the little lobby, I almost didn't recognize him. He was dressed in street clothes instead of his usual cassock, and he'd shaved his beard. He looked much younger and quite handsome. He took both my hands into his and kissed them. "Bella Maria Rosa, I love you." I was a little embarrassed because there were other people around, but he proceeded to kiss me on the lips right then and there. We sat at a small round table by the window at the bar, and he had a beer and I had a Fanta.

"I'm so happy you came. I was afraid you wouldn't. Then I'd have to come to the school and get you, and I'd probably make a fool of myself." Seeing him in street attire relaxed me. We finished our drinks, and then he took my hand and led me down a narrow corridor to the back of the hotel. He took a metal key from his khaki slacks and unlocked his room.

"Welcome to my bed, Bella Maria Rosa."

"Shouldn't you welcome me into your room first?"

"How could I forget?" He had a bouquet of wildflowers and my favorite chocolates by the nightstand, and spread out on the bed was a very pretty short transparent nightgown with red ribbons and black lace along the hem.

"Let's talk about America," I said nervously as soon as we sat on the bed.

"I've been thinking of nothing else but your letter for the past week, so unless you've changed your mind about going to America with that woman, there's nothing to talk about."

"It's the best for me, Father."

"And for me? Do you care that you've destroyed my life?"

"I haven't destroyed your life. I've always wanted to go to America. It's a dream come true."

"And why didn't you tell me you wanted to go to America? Didn't you think I could take you there?"

"I never told anyone."

"I don't want to talk today. This is probably the last time I can have you for myself. I go to Italy next week because my mother is very sick and I probably won't return to Africa."

"*Pole sana,*" I said. "I'm very sorry."

"It's the will of God." He sat at the foot of the bed with his head buried in his hands.

"Is something wrong?"

"Everything is wrong. I had so many plans for us. Did you read my letters? I wanted to...I want...I wanted... He started to cry. I was shocked. I hadn't seen a man cry before, much less a priest. I started to cry too.

"No, you mustn't cry. I don't want to see your beautiful eyes wet."

"I like you without the beard," I said, wiping my tears. "You look much younger and very handsome." I sat down beside him.

He sighed deeply as he opened the box of chocolates and put a milk chocolate hazelnut in my mouth and sucked it along with me. He then undressed me and put the lace nightgown on me. I stretched out and waited for him to undress, but he didn't. Instead he kissed every inch of me softly and quietly first, but then loudly and passionately. I knew it was the last time we would be together, so I made a point to relax and let my body and emotions react naturally to his touch. As he got closer to my private places, his kissing turned into singing and then to laughing. I enjoyed the warmth of his lips on my skin, and I heard myself making groaning sounds that I thought only men made. I felt wonderful and relaxed. I had the presence of mind to ask him not to penetrate me and make me pregnant even if I lost control. He said he loved me too much to put himself first. I believed him and surrendered. He continued kissing me as he whispered words I couldn't quite hear. Before I knew it, I felt a crescendo of waves building and spreading the most indescribably pleasurable sensation spreading to my thighs, toes, up my spine, and to my head. My body jerked and tossed and rocked. I was breathless and helpless. Father Antonio held me tight until the involuntary movements of my body subsided. When all was calm, I sat up in the tiny room and tried to figure out what had just happened. Father was still fully dressed.

"Is this the first time you've felt the release of love?"

"Is that what happened?"

"I'm the happiest man alive. You'll always remember your first time and you'll always remember me, Bella Maria Rosa."

"Even if I tried, I don't think I could ever forget the feeling you gave me just now. I wish I could have it again and again."

"Come with me and I will give it to as often as you wish."

I lay in bed and watched him undress. He was a bigger man than Father Michael and his chest and most of his body were covered with dark hair, while Father Michael's body was smooth. Then I saw his erect penis. He was a very big man. I wondered how he could carry it, and how he could get it to shrink into his underwear. He came at me from the back, his organ between my legs. He tried to pull down the lacy negligee and undress me, but I pulled it back up. I stayed still for him until he finished, sobbing, "*Ti amo, Maria, ti amo.*"

I tried to pull away from him but his grip was firm and powerful. Finally he rolled away from me, shaking and muttering something to himself in Italian. In the calm moments between his shuddering, he had a beautiful smile on his face. Huge drops of perspiration rolled from his forehead to his neck and settled onto his hairy chest. He opened his eyes and brushed my hair from my face. "This is the best goodbye present you could give me. The way I feel right now is how I always want to remember you. Come with me to Italy. Please, please, Bella Maria Rosa."

We lay motionless on the bed, and then he called for the hotel attendant to bring hot water for a bath. As soon as the water was in the tiny tin tub, he removed my lacy nightgown, tucked it in a brown envelope that was near the little table, carried me to the tub, lifted me in, and then he got in. We bathed together in the small space and dried each other. Before I put my dress on, he removed a heavy chain that he was wearing on his neck and put it around mine. He kissed the chain.

"Thank you very much," I said, touching the gold chain.

"It belonged to my father and I haven't removed it from my neck since the day he put it there."

He took my hand and led me out of the room, and we walked down the hall and back into the little café where we spent two hours talking. I kept repeating that nothing would keep me from going to America with Cathy, while he kept telling me about his plans for us when he got to Italy. We were together, but we were each having a one-sided conversation.

It was very late when he dropped me off at school. Before he left me, he gave me a long passionate kiss on the mouth and said, "There's one more thing I need to tell you before we part. You can travel the world over, you can meet a thousand men, but you will never, ever find anyone who loves you more than I do. It's simply impossible."

Something told me that he really believed it and that he was probably right.

"I will give you my mother's address in Italy so you will always know where to find me. I will wait forever for you." His eyes were full of tears again.

"Thank you for so many things, Father. Mostly, I thank you for loving me. Thank you for respecting my wishes not to make real love to me or rape me. I know it must have been hard."

"Hard? It was a miracle. It's one small measure of my love for you. I've never been able to control myself like this before."

"Have you made love to many girls before?"

"Not many."

"Was that before you were a priest?"

"Yes and no."

"Will you remain a priest?"

"You're the only girl I'd leave the priesthood for. I have no regrets and I'm not ashamed of my love for you. God brought you to me, and you will remain in my heart until the day I die."

"I'll always remember that there is a man in this world who doesn't need a reason to love me," I said touching the gold chain around my neck.

"*Ti amo, ti adoro, Bella Maria Rosa.*"

It was midnight before I got back to school. I lay in bed feeling drained but happy. I touched the chain around my neck. I decided to hide it from Cathy. I shuddered at the thought of her reaction if I told her where it came from.

The next morning I woke up with Father Michael on my mind. What was wrong with him? Why couldn't he leave me alone? Why did I know Father Antonio so much better after a short time together, while I knew almost nothing about Father Michael after several years? These two men were as different as night and day. One was a gentle, intense, and secretive intellectual who seemed to carry the weight of his thoughts on his shoulders, but was mostly interested in satisfying himself, while the other was a fool for love who wore his heart on his sleeve and poured out his feelings in lyrical outbursts. How was it that Father Antonio could love me so unequivocally after knowing me only three months? Maybe I was merely in the right place at the right time for Father Michael. Weren't both men toying with a young and inexperienced virgin? And were both lonely, depressed, isolated priests in deepest Africa who shouldn't have become priests in the first place?

Where did that leave me? Was I so deprived of love that I easily gave in to the first men who showed interest in me? How could I have put my strict Catholic upbringing aside to spend romantic time with priests! I was petrified and traumatized by Juma on the bus, but trusted these men when they said they wouldn't get me pregnant. Perhaps my fear of disobeying the revered priests influenced my acceptance of their advances. They were men of the cloth. Did my indoctrination prevent me from disobeying them even though I questioned their actions?

Or was it that I really enjoyed the attention, adoration, and intimacy that, up to now, I didn't believe existed for me? Maybe I accepted it as part of my continuing education—the part that would never be taught in a classroom. Not having had the love of a mother or family as I was growing up, did I know that what Father Antonio felt for me was love? Why did I believe him when he said he adored me? He told me I was beautiful. How could I ignore what I knew was true from childhood—that I was fat and ugly? And what happened to Mother Rufina's maxim that all men are evil? Did she mean all men except priests?

I lay in bed roiling with all the emotions I'd experienced in the last few months. The questions didn't stop. Would Father Antonio's love bring me happiness? If Father Michael didn't love me, what kind of feelings did he have for me? What kind of love was Cathy's? How did she know she had motherly love for me when she had never given birth? Was the love of a birth mother the same as the love of an adopted mother?

My turmoil was interrupted by Cathy's footsteps.

57

An American Passport

"Oh rise and shine and give God your glory, glory...." Cathy, who couldn't carry a tune, was singing at the top of her lungs. She didn't even knock on the door. She rushed in and handed me the *Tanganyika Standard.* "Read this!" she commanded, but then read it herself. "First Class Pass! First Class Pass! Mary, First Class! How magnificently wonderful this is!" She hugged me and kissed me on both cheeks.

"This calls for a celebration," she said. "Tonight we're going to have a party at our house, so invite your friends, wear your pretty Christmas dress, and we'll be merry!" She twirled out the door still singing and talking, "Can't wait to tell everyone. Oh my God! First Class Pass!"

Her rushing footsteps faded and I was left with the paper in my hands not quite registering what had happened. I sat on the bed and read the short section Cathy had circled with a red pen. It said that Marian College Secondary School had the most notable performances of the private schools taking the exams with three First Class Passes awarded to Mary Rose Ryan and two other classmates. It suddenly hit me. My twelve years of struggling for an education had culminated with a First Class Pass when it really mattered!

How absolutely magnificently wonderful was that, I thought, quoting Cathy. The first thing I did was to kneel by my bed and thank Baby Jesus. I knew he had guided my life from childhood to this day.

Many emotions grabbed me as I prayed. I prayed for Cathy, for Father Michael, and for Father Antonio. I searched for Fat Mary and asked her to guard the special feelings the two men had introduced me to, and to give them back to me if I needed them in America. For the first time since I was five years old, I realized that Fat Mary was unequivocally happy. She was shaking with laughter as she hugged my skirt. "Isn't life just absolutely magnificently wonderful?" I said to her. I took her in my arms and kissed her. I reminded her to take with her to America all my childhood secrets of pain and joy. Although I didn't know what exactly to make of my feelings for Father Michael or Father Antonio, at that moment I was sure that I loved Fat Mary more than anyone in the whole world. With Fat Mary inside me, I was ready to face my unknown future.

All day long everyone I met on campus congratulated me. A few days later I received a telegram from Father Michael that read: HEARTIEST CONGRATULATIONS MARY, PROSPERA PROCEDAS, and that same evening I found a bouquet of wildflowers in front of the teachers' house with a note that said *Congratulazioni, Bella Maria Rosa! Ti amero per sempre!*

I was overwhelmed by emotions I couldn't begin to understand. I fell asleep holding the telegram and the note, feeling that I had already lost both of them. I knew I had to let them go, and the sooner the better. I tried to give my feelings to Fat Mary, but for the first time she refused to take them and kept giving them back to me all night long.

From the next day until we left for America four months later, it seemed there was one celebration after another. Some were for passing the exams and others were farewell parties. Cathy was very busy with her drama classes and seemed preoccupied with something or other all the time, but was the life of our evening parties. I kept busy in the library, and I loved sewing with Sister Antonita, visiting with *Mwalimu* Fliakos, and talking with Sister Martin Corde about America. She hugged me often and told me how very, very proud she was of me and of the woman she knew I would become. Since Christmas, so many positive things had happened to me that I almost believed that life would forever be absolutely, positively, magnificently wonderful!

One morning in late April, Cathy came running to me singing and humming as she usually did when she had good news. "Here it is! Your passport! I have your passport in my hand, Mary. And that's not all. I got a letter from the College of Saint Catherine, the best college on earth—I went there—saying that you have been awarded a four-year scholarship, renewable at the end of each year. Can you even think of anything more exciting?"

"Well, I have something exciting too. My Cambridge Secondary School Certificate arrived in the mail, and one of the subjects that I was awarded a distinction in was Swahili. Imagine, a First Class Pass with a distinction in Swahili!" Henrietta would have been proud.

I was thrilled to hold a passport, any passport, in my hand—let alone this one, which I noticed was an American passport. I wondered how Cathy managed to make me an American citizen, but I was afraid to ask. By now I had witnessed miracles and I believed that with Cathy, anything and everything was possible.

I held the gray-green document in my hand and ran my fingers over the gold emblem and the words on its surface. It said my nationality was American and gave my birth date. I was nineteen years old—exactly my age based on what Elizabeth guessed when she said I was five years old. Flipping through its empty pages, I felt an almost sacred reverence for it. My childhood dreams were dancing between its pages. I saw my dream of getting an education, finding a mother, leaving the orphanage, and going to America wrapped up as an enormous present inside the passport. To this day my passport represents the miracle of hopes and dreams.

I had so many questions to ask Cathy about my passport. But she took it from me saying, "I will guard this with my life!"

I was overwhelmed with the idea of having a passport, and I wanted to hug and thank Cathy, but instead I asked her why she had come to Africa as a volunteer teacher. She explained that her good friend from college, Miss Polga, wrote to her about her work at Marian College and mentioned that the school could use an additional English teacher. One dark, cold February afternoon she was on her way home from teaching high school in Minneapolis. She was so bundled up that she could barely move, let alone drive her car through the snowy, icy streets. I had no idea what she was talking about but listened with fascination. She said the temperature was below zero, her car wouldn't start, and she was so frustrated that she began to cry.

"What does below zero mean?" I interrupted. She sighed a huge sigh, and said it was so cold that her tears froze on her blue cashmere scarf that she wore over her nose and mouth.

"That was it!" she said, "I screamed: I'm sick and tired of winter! I'm going to Africa! I'm going to hot, sunny Africa! And here I am."

And here I was preparing to travel to America with her. Fat Mary assured me that these things happen for a reason. It was in the divine plan. It was our destiny.

At the end of May, I went to say goodbye to Kifungilo. I met Father Michael in Korogwe and he drove me there. Because we knew that my time in Africa was drawing to an end, we spoke little, stopped often, and enjoyed some of our best times together. He spent the night at the guesthouse, while I spent the evening telling the other big girls everything I knew about my new mother and my life in America. They said they were jealous of me, but they knew if anyone deserved a family, I did. I'll never forget what Julitta said. "Mary, when anything good happens to any orphan from Kifungilo, it happens to all of us. We can tell everybody that we have a Kifungilo girl living in America!" We cheered and hugged each other, and savored a rare feeling of pride in ourselves.

It was hard to say goodbye to Sister Silvestris because, when I entered her room next to the big girls' dormitory, her piercing blue eyes that I so feared as a child were gazing at me through a veil of tears. She handed me a bag full of gifts that she said she'd saved for a long time. We shook hands and then we hugged. "Don't change, my Fat Mary. You're a good girl. You must write often, and if God is willing, we will meet again."

I knew I would never see her again, not only because of my history, but because I had no intention of returning to Africa. I asked her to say goodbye to Sister Theonesta and to Zahabu, our old woodcutter. I went to say goodbye to Blessed Martin and I asked him to take care of Sister Silvestris.

Father Michael drove me back to Marian College. We knew that this was our last trip. We stopped at our favorite spots and reminisced about our many trips over this road, and how we knew every curve, hill, river, or tree that had been kind enough to shelter us and witness our relationship. We talked about the little red devil's knack for acting up whenever we were rushed for time, and recalled the day that a rock from the mountainside shattered the windshield and we wondered how we were not hurt. I thanked him for driving me back and forth to school in the miserable heat, on terrible roads, for hundreds of miles to make the trip safer and more pleasant for me. He told me he'd try his best to come to the airport in Dar to see me off.

58

Betrayal of Trust

That evening when I was in bed, I was overwhelmed by a deep, deep sadness. It centered on Father Michael and Father Antonio. I tried putting myself in their places and wondered how they really felt about my leaving Africa. Father Antonio had professed his everlasting love, but as much as I intellectually believed him, my heart didn't feel it.

Father Michael couldn't even tell me he'd miss me when I came right out and asked him. After several minutes of trying to remember if Father Michael had ever expressed anything close to love for me, I couldn't come up with a single emotion that I was sure he had for me. Was he angry and hurt that I wouldn't be there for him anymore? Was he hoping to see me again? Would he even think about me? Why, after all this time, was the only reason he ever gave me for wanting to kiss me or make love was that he was a man and was attracted to me because I was a woman? Was it all that basic and simple? I was starting to see that our time together was mostly for his gratification, and what I might have wanted never crossed his mind.

Father Antonio showed genuine concern for me, but was it real? Would he really give up the priesthood to be with me? Did he tell me whatever he thought I wanted to hear so he could have his way with me, knowing full well he was leaving for Italy and would never see me again? The more I thought about them both, the sadder I got.

I had asked Fat Mary so many questions about them in the past, but it seemed she wanted to give me the answers at a time when knowing the truth wouldn't crush me because now I had Cathy.

As I tried to understand both priests' motives and my reaction to them, I slowly started seeing things differently and clearly for the first time. The cloud of confusion I had throughout our time together was thinning and dissipating in front of my eyes. A lot of my confusion was based on trying to understand if what they felt for me was the same as what I felt for them. If they were using me only for themselves, did they feel responsible for toying with the young and tender feelings of love and trust I felt for them?

It was becoming obvious to me what had happened. I was an insecure, love-starved, lonely and needy young girl, and I interpreted every act of kindness by them—verbal or physical—to be as genuine as my need. I was also coming of age and curious about feelings I hadn't realized I was capable of having. I could now see that for them I was the right girl in the right place at the right time, and they maneuvered their way into my sexuality knowing full well that what they could give me was limited. Did either of them ever see my soul?

I felt an aching sensation in my heart that made me weep for the innocent and impressionable adolescent who justified their actions because she wanted to believe in their love for her. I stayed with the pain in my chest until I understood that there was nothing wrong with my feelings for the priests—those feelings were pure and honest and natural.

In my life so far I had lived with abandonment, hatred, humiliation, isolation, loneliness, physical, mental, and psychological abuse. It didn't seem possible that, at this point in my search for a better life, I would have to add sexual exploitation by priests—priests whom Mother Rufina, the Sisters of Kifungilo, and I trusted and respected.

I could hear Fat Mary trying to say something inside me. I wiped my tears on my pillow, and hugged her. *All of that is in the past now. Tomorrow you will be packing for your new life in America with a lady who loves you with all her heart. Isn't that just absolutely, magnificently wonderful?*

"Yes it is, Fat Mary. Yes it is!"

I fell asleep with the satisfaction of finally seeing the nature of the priests' relationship with me and gratitude for understanding my response to them. I had no regrets.

59

Kwaheri Africa! Goodbye Africa!

 Cathy was not very organized, so I took over and packed everything for both of us. She gave me a small, smooth, leather-like suitcase made of pressed cardboard and painted brown, but instead of the traditional locks I'd seen on suitcases, it had a huge metal zipper. She told me that her father sent the money to buy it, and I admired it more than any other farewell gift I'd received so far. I packed several souvenirs from Marian College and the gifts that Sister Silvestris had given me: a ten-inch black wood-and-silver crucifix with a note attached that said "Always remember to be a good Catholic," a box of note cards with pictures of the saints and a note saying "Write to me many times," a pale blue pillow case with an embroidered red rose in the center and another note that said "You cannot take 'the best pillow on earth' to America, but you can take the pillow case." I was touched that she remembered the exact words I said to her when I begged her to let me take my pillow to Mhonda. I packed the beautiful Job's tears rosary that Sister Martin Corde made for me.

I put the telegram of congratulations for passing the Cambridge Exams—the only item from Father Michael—in my suitcase. He had played a role in my coming of age and paved the way for my education when it really counted.

I had already put aside, ready to pack, the lacey nightgown, gold chain, and all my letters from Father Antonio, who continued to write from Italy. I thought the letters would be a source of comfort and joy if I ever felt unloved and lonely in America, as they had been in Africa. He had sent me several envelopes full of the photos that he had taken, including some beautiful ones of me posing as the Virgin Mary. Although I enjoyed looking at them all, the ones of me as the Virgin Mary made me uncomfortable. I decided to take only a few photos of me alone and none of us together and to burn the ones of me as the Virgin Mary because they were a lie. I had written to Father Antonio asking him to destroy them but he wrote back, "Never would I do such a thing!" I prayed that Mother Rufina or Sister Silvestris would never receive holy cards from Europe, only to recognize that the Virgin Mary was none other than their Fat Mary! I packed a few of my favorite letters from him and remembered the feeling of being loved when I read them the first time. Those feelings were as real as the letters in my hand. I wrapped the heavy gold chain from Father Antonio and the nightgown with white tissue paper, wrote a note, and put them in a large brown envelope to give to the Kifungilo girl who lived in town.

You should leave the pain of both priests in Africa, advised Fat Mary, verbalizing my thoughts. *If you don't, you won't be able to lift your suitcase. Take with you only what was good about them.* I raised both fists to salute Fat Mary. Once again she had put everything in perspective and lightened my heart.

On June 13, 1963, the morning before our departure, the Sisters had a coffee party at the convent and we received more gifts. We said our final goodbyes at that time and went to wrap up things at Cathy's house. I was very calm while Cathy was a bunch of nerves. She cried on and off and sighed as she tossed things in her suitcase. In the morning, we left Morogoro for Dar and found Father Michael waiting for us at the airport. At the check-in counter, I was a little reluctant to hand my suitcase over to the clerk. Cathy hadn't explained checking bags to me, and I was confused when I saw them disappear behind the wall. I ended up doing whatever she did, got my boarding pass, and then went to say goodbye to Father Michael.

He came toward me and took my head in his hands and kissed me on the mouth, right there in front of Cathy. It was the first time he'd kissed me in public. I hugged him back.

"Look after yourself, young lady, and write, write, write."

"Thank you for supporting my quest for an education and for everything you did to make this trip happen. I will always remember that." I watched him disappear down the hall.

Cathy took my hand and we went to board the plane.

60

Africa's Gift

 Cathy and I pushed our weary but excited bodies down the narrow aisle of the East African Airways DC-3 plane and slumped into our seats. The airline squeezed as many seats as possible into this small plane, and we sat like stick figures with our carry-on luggage and purses on our laps, trying hard not to exhale down the backs of the passengers in front of us. Cathy was buried under her huge purse and I was grateful that I couldn't see her face. I swallowed once, twice, three times, but the pain refused to leave my chest. I looked out the window, letting my warm, heavy tears flow as they pleased. Wasn't this my lifelong desire? Then why was I so sad? Was I grieving for people I left behind and for the country of my birth?

Slowly I started noticing my surroundings and truly realized I wasn't dreaming. This enormous metal box, suspended between heaven and earth, was lifting me away from Africa. Our word for plane is *ndege*, which literally means "bird." The only airplanes I had seen before were the occasional noisy dots in the sky that Sister Theonesta let us out of class to search for. I could still see my classmates running every which way following the first child who spotted the plane and joining in the refrain, "*Ndege, ndege, ndege ya wazungu!*" "A plane, a plane, a European airplane!" we'd chant, waving at the dot long after it was swallowed by the horizon. Sister patiently awaited our return to the classroom where she'd laugh and ask, "Are you sure you were following the same plane?" after we reported our diverse interpretations of its color, size, speed, and sound. Babu, who had followed it up the mountain and said he almost touched it, claimed that a plane could be as big as our classroom. From that day on, Babu earned the nickname *Mwongo,* the liar.

Apparently he hadn't lied. Our plane was larger than I'd imagined. I pondered the metal mass with its funny barrel shape. Could this bird really fly across the ocean? I worried about my small suitcase containing the accumulated wealth of my nineteen years in Africa ending up in the ocean to intrigue sharks and other sea creatures. The puzzled expression of the smartly dressed clerk in the blue and gold East African Airways uniform at the check-in counter as I reluctantly let go of my suitcase now made sense. I could see there was no room for a suitcase inside the aircraft cabin.

I sank deeper into the seat as my new reality hit me. My lifelong prayers had been answered, hadn't they? I kept asking myself this as though I had to give myself permission to bask in my good fortune. I had a mother and I was leaving Africa. And didn't this mother sitting beside me want me and love me and promise she'd never leave me? Could I be sure that, once we got to America, she would continue to love me the way she says she does? What if I don't fit in and I embarrass her? I realized that now I really had no choices. I was moving farther and farther away from the only country and life I knew to begin a new life in a promised land. Would its promises be for me too? I looked over at Cathy and prayed intensely for her. I prayed for her not to leave me until I could take care of myself and that I would always show her I was worthy of her love and sacrifices. I didn't want to think what might happen if things didn't work out for us. It scared me, because if I thought I had no one in Africa, I truly had no one in America.

I hoped that the terrible noise of the engines would drown out my doubts since I was sure Cathy and everyone else in the plane, including the pilot, could hear my heart speak. I tried very hard to empty my mind of all emotions except joy, and after a while I succeeded. As my ears grew accustomed to the clamor of the engines, I pretended that I was flying the plane. My body felt lighter and lighter. I imagined the plane was a majestic, tawny eagle in flight, and that I was riding alive and carefree on its back, urging it to fly faster and faster to its destination. I became the eagle itself, soaring toward the country of my dreams, determined to let nothing stop me. It was an unforgettable sensation. Every so often I was overcome by the miracle of flying higher and higher beyond the clouds into a heaven that awaited me in America.

Was America the heaven in the beatitude, "Blessed are the poor in spirit, for theirs is the kingdom of heaven?" Would God follow me to America? Or would he be angry with me for abandoning the land of my birth? I looked out the window and down at Tanganyika. She demanded that in my final hours in Africa, I take stock of her. The rugged coastline, the silver sands of the miles and miles of beaches, and the sapphire blue Indian Ocean shimmered and undulated under the sun as they performed a farewell dance for me.

The rugged topography of Tanganyika, with its neighbors Kenya and Uganda to the north, Congo (now Democratic Republic of the Congo) to the West, and Nyasaland (now Malawi) to the South, reminded me how little of my vast country I'd seen. I imagined Victoria, Tanganyika, and Nyasa Lakes to be like giant octopuses, with their meandering tentacles gathering water from scattered mountain ranges to form rivers and streams for the one hundred and twenty tribes of Tanganyika. The land spoke to me. The Ngorongoro Crater, the Serengeti Plain with its treasure of wild animals, and the haunting Usambara Mountains that sheltered me in my childhood, whispered that I would come back as did the fruits, flowers, and foliage. Yellow mangos, papaws and bananas, purple jacarandas and orange flame trees, and the dark, thick forests with their abundance of unique plant species in myriad shades of green formed an exotic bouquet for me.

I saw the proud Maasai in their *manyattas* scattered around Mount Kilimanjaro. At home in their compounds, they were involved in circumcision celebrations, drinking fresh calf blood in defiance of Christianity and modernization, yet attracted to Western merchandise and showing off their wristwatches and transistor radios. I envisioned them halting their festivities to look up at me and wave goodbye. From among them emerged a tall, dignified woman who tucked the gathered population under her skirt of cowhide as she slowly ascended toward the plane. She had a determined look on her powerful face—as though she planned to set the plane on her head and carry me back to African ground.

As my vision continued, she moved closer, and I saw that she had become a Sambaa woman from Lushoto. In celebration of her recently acquired status of independence from Britain, she was dressed in the brilliant *kitenge* cloth that proclaimed the blue, green, black, and gold colors of her flag. Her outfit consisted of a short overskirt attached at the waist to an ankle-length one, a fitted bodice with huge puffed sleeves, and a headpiece of the same cloth. This was her new national dress. In her arms she carried a traditional, woven *kikapu* filled with fruit. Her feet, wrapped in crudely made black rubber thongs, took giant steps as she seemed to pursue the plane and me across the African continent.

In the course of the flight, it was as if her breathing became labored and her tired feet dragged until they couldn't support her weary body any longer. I watched as she slowly retreated. With great effort, she lifted the basket of fruit above her head and offered it to me. She spoke loud, elaborate words, but only "Africa! Africa! Africa!" echoed in the widening space between us. Her form gradually disintegrated.

A deep sadness choked me and when I swallowed, the big lump in my throat told me that I must have been crying since we left Dar-es-Salaam. Soon we would be in Nairobi, Kenya, where we would board our international flight.

I left Tanganyika with this image of a caring, protective, strong, determined, generous, struggling yet very elegant African Woman etched in my mind. I can't tell you the exact shade of black she was because her color changed with the moving sun and the cloud shadows that lingered over her face. I did not know it then, but she would become the source of strength and inspiration and my rock of stability in America.

As is the African custom, she came to *kusindikiza*—to accompany me a little way on my journey out of the country and to give me her final gift. My farewell gift from Mama Africa was priceless and a gift only she could give. Her gift to me was the knowledge and absolute certainty that my long search for belonging was over. No matter where on earth I found myself, and no matter what lay ahead of me, in my heart I knew I would always remain Africa's child.

GLOSSARY

Pronunciation

    In Swahili the accent of a word almost always falls on the next-to-last syllable: **Tan-zan-I-a**. There are only five vowels and they are always pronounced the same. All vowels are pronounced and two vowels together are each pronounced: **Haule = Ha-u-le**.

adhabu – punishment
asante – thank you
asante sana – thank you very much

baba – father
bibi – grandmother
binti – Miss, unmarried girl
bladiful – bloody fool
Bondei – name of tribe living in the Usambara Mountains around the coastal city of Tanga

Chagga – name of tribe living in the foothills of Mount Kilimanjaro
chotara – person of mixed race, often used as a derogative term
chura – frog

dawa – medicine
debe – large metal container for various uses
dereva – driver
Dettol – an antiseptic
dudu/wadudu – any insect or creepy crawly bug (singular/plural)
duka – store
Dummkopf – stupid person

Fanta – orange-flavored carbonated drink
Fipa – name of tribe in Southwestern Tanzania
Funga mdomo – Shut up!
furaha – joy

Gare – Mission station near Kifungilo

hafukasti – half-caste
Handeni – village in the Tanga region
hapana – no

hasira – anger
Hehe – tribe living in South Central Tanzania

Iringa – major city in the highlands of Southern Tanzania

jambo – hello
Jina langu – My name is...

kalaba – Color bar
kaniki – shinny, black, very cheap cotton worn by poor people
kanzu – white loose-fitting robe Muslims wear
karai – large tin basin
karibu – welcome, near
kitenge – heavier, more expensive cotton fabric (often Java print) used for
    women's and men's shirts
khanga – colorful cotton cloth worn by East African women
Kifungilo – name of the little village where the orphanage school is located
Kihehe – a tribal language from the Iringa region
Kijembe/vijembe (pl) – a person of the same sex with whom one shares a
    platonic love and friendship
kikapu – basket
kilokote – gutter child
Kiluguru – language of the Luguru tribe
Kimya – quiet, silence, Hush! (name of Christmas song)
Kiondo – the postman for Kifungilo
Kisambaa – language of the Sambaa tribe
Kiuzai – name of a village near the orphanage
Kongei – African Middle School run by Precious Blood Sisters
Korogwe – town on the railway and bus routes
kunguni – bed bugs
kuru – crow
kusindikiza – to accompany a parting person as a gesture of friendship
    and respect
kusonya – a sucking sound used in East Africa and the Caribbean ("ste-
    ups") to show annoyance or anger
kwaheri – goodbye
kwisha – done, finished

Lady Twining – wife of the British Governor to Tanganyika, Sir Edward
    Twining
lala salama – sleep safely, sleep well
Laurean Rugambwa – First African Cardinal of the Roman Catholic
    Church

Luguru – name of tribe living in the Uluguru Mountain range in central Tanzania

Lushoto – name of the small town closest to Kifungilo

Maasai – a Nilotic ethnic group of semi-nomadic people, located in Kenya and northern Tanzania.

Magamba – little village in the Usambara Mountains where the British Governor's lodge was located

magazine – storage room

makarai – tin basins

Mkuzi – village five miles away from Kifungilo

Mama yangu! – My goodness! (lit. Oh my mother!)

mandazi – a pastry made of fried white flour dough dipped in sugar

manyatta – Maasai compounds

mapenzi – love

maskini – the poor

Mastiff – stiff person, nickname of Sister Agathana

matajiri – rich people

matata – trouble, problems

mchawi – witch (*wachawi* – plural form)

mdogo – small one

merikani – cheap, shinny, white cotton fabric from America

Mhonda – Middle school near Morogoro run by Precious Blood Sisters

Milele na milele – forever and ever

mnenguo – name of one of the Luguru tribal dances

Mombo – town near Lushoto

Mono Snow – skin bleaching cream

Morogoro – large town at the foot of the Uluguru Mountain range

Mother Ancilla – founder and builder of the orphanage

Mother Majellis – Mother Superior at Mhonda Middle School

Mother Rufina – Mother Superior of the convent in Kifungilo

mtu wa mandazi – gingerbread man

Mungu Ibariki Tanganyika – God Bless Tanganyika (title of National Anthem)

Mungu wangu wee – Oh my God!

mwali – young girl just reaching puberty

Mwalimu – teacher; used as a form of address

mwamba – rock, "brainy" (slang)

Mweta – farmhand at the orphanage

mwongo – liar

mzungu – white person (plural form: wazungu)

ndala – flip flops
Ndanda – Mission and hospital in southeastern Tanzania run by Benedictine priests and nuns
ndege – bird
ndiyo – yes
Ngoma – drum, tribal dance celebrations
Ntendezeze – Mother Rufina's nickname (*zeze* – name of stringed instrument)
Nyamwezi – large tribe living in the southeastern part of Tanzania
nyumba ile – lit. "that house" where clothes were kept in cublicles
nyumba mpya – new house

panga – machete
Pemba – small island off the coast of Tanzania
pipi – candy
pole sana – so sorry
pombe – homemade beer

Rangwe – Benedictine Order Mission Station in the Usambara Mountains
Rosminian – Catholic Order of priests founded by Italian Antonio Rosmini.

sadaka – sacrifice
Sambaa / Wasambaa – tribe living in the Usambara Mountains
sambusa – samosa, fried or baked pastry with a savory filling originally from India
sanduku – suitcase
schwarze Kinder – black children
schwarze Teufel – black devils
schwarzer Ziguener – black gypsy
shenzi – pagan (often use as a derogatory term)
Shikamoo – a greeting of respect to an elder
simama – stand, stop
Simca – French make of car
Simsim – cooking oil from sesame seeds
sindimba – a Nyamwezi tribal dance
Sister Agathana – nun in charge of sewing
Sister Antonita – Maryknoll Sister who taught Art and Domestic Science at Marian Collage
Sister Clotilda – teacher at Kifungilo
Sister Fabiana – driver of Kifungilo van, in charge of farm animals, orchards and vegetable gardens.
Sister Florestina – Headmistress of Mhonda Middle School

Sister Ignatis – Headmistress of Kongei Middle School
Sister Martin Corde – African-American Maryknoll Sister
Sister Nerea – dentist in Kifungilo and Lushoto
Sister Silvestris – nun in charge of all the orphans
Sister Theonesta – nun, who cared for Mary as an infant and taught grade
   school (Standards I to IV)
steups – a sucking sound used in East Africa and the Caribbean to show
   annoyance or anger
sukari guru – unrefined brown-sugar
suruwali – shorts
Swanglish – slang (mixture of English and Swahili)

Tabora – name of major town in central Tanzania
Tanga – large city on the East Coast of Tanzania, also a region
Tanganyika – original name of the former German then British Colony on
   the East Coast of Africa which gained its independence in 1961.
Tanzania – mainland Tanganyika united with the Island of Zanzibar to
   form The United Republic of Tanzania in 1964.
Toka! – Get out! (broken Swahili)
Tosamaganga – Italian run Catholic Mission and School in the southwest-
   ern district of Tanzania
Tumsifu Yesu Kristu – "Praise be to Jesus Christ" (used as a greeting for
   religious)
Turiani – little town near Mhonda Middle School

uchafu – filth
ugali – a stiff porridge used for lunch or dinner made of corn flour, water,
   and salt
Uhuru! – rallying call for independence (freedom)
uji – soft porridge used for breakfast, made of water, corn flour and salt
Uluguru – land of the Luguru tribe
umeme – lightning
upepo – wind
Usambara Mountains – range of mountains surrounding Kifungilo
uvundo – odor, smelly

vikatasi – menstrual period cloths
vushti – sausage (from the German 'wurst')

wachawi – witches
wadudu – insects or bugs (plural)
wafariseo – hypocrites
Wasambaa / Sambaa – tribe living in the Usambara Mountains

washenzi – heathens, pagans (plural form)
wazungu – white people (plural)
wazungu weusi – Africans who act like Europeans

yeba! – hurrah!

Zahabu – name of the woodcutter at the orphanage (lit. gold)
zamani – long ago, old times
zawadi – gift, present
zeruzeru – albino

ACKNOWLEDGMENTS

Without Cathy Murray Mamer, there would have been no hope, no love, no America, no college, no mother, no children and no book in my life! You believed so much in me and in my potential, that at age twenty-three, you moved mountains to get me, a 19-year-old African orphan to America, and provided me with my first real home. In America you and your dad were my everything! How can one say thank you to someone like you? You are my guiding light, and your love keeps me soaring. Your unconditional love gave me what I needed to become me. I will write a lot about you in my next book, because I hardly knew you when I entrusted my life and future into your hands. Our finding each other is proof of Divine Intervention.

My children Kata and Karl: This book contains many answers to your questions about my parents and family that I could not answer when you were growing up, because I simply didn't know. I thank you for being the catalysts that encouraged me to face the truth about my humble beginnings in Africa and now the cycle of ignorance that I grew up with will not be perpetuated to other generations. I thank you for your patience and acceptance of my evasive responses to your questions and observations. I thank you for cheering me on when I shared bits and pieces of my story even though you couldn't understand me at the time. I thank you for your constant love and protection of me. I thank you most of all for making me a Mother. Motherhood was an unknown mystery, an abstract concept when I was growing up. Because of you, I no longer have to wonder what it felt like having a mother who loved you, or about being that mother who loved her children. You gave me both gifts. *Nawapendeni sana!*

Jacqueline Mosio, my chief editor, my first friend in America, the person who could look at me and see my Soul. You loved me at first sight as we sat in our Bible Study class at the College of Saint Catherine seemingly oceans apart culturally, linguistically, ethnically and financially yet drawn together. You stood by me through many years of insecurity and doubt about my story, my writing and myself. Your brilliant understanding, deciphering and explanation of my poorly articulated thoughts and emotions, your sensitive and sensible questions about my country and myself forced me to resurrect and re-live parts of my past, and gave me the courage to write my story. You validated my uniqueness and encouraged me not to try too hard to become too American too soon. Jackie I have no words to thank you for the role you played in my life from that first day of college to today, to becoming my maid of honor, the godmother to my two children, now my editor. Thank you for letting me expose my vulnerability to show me its reflection in your soul. You are truly my Soul Sister. I thank you for your hard work on polishing my manuscript, and for your insistence that I tell my story the way I want to tell it.

Twenty-five years ago when I decided to write my story, I didn't know where to begin. I knew my personal story of life at the orphanage but knew next to nothing about its history. It was Sister Eileen who obtained the original handwritten diaries of Saint Mary's Convent, in Kifungilo (written in German) and helped me make copies. It took three years to have them translated. Without those diaries, my knowledge of the founding of the orphanage would have been very limited.

Thank you, Sister Eileen, for always welcoming me and my family to the Dentistry in Lushoto every time we made a trip back to Tanzania. It was your stories during those visits that clarified the incidents of my childhood, which I remembered only in bits and pieces. You told the good and not so good incidents of life at the orphanage in such a way that we held our sides with laughter even as our eyes filled with tears! I am mostly grateful to you for being the voice for the children and for protecting us from abuse and neglect while we were together at the orphanage.

Betty, thank you for sharing your little sister Imelda with me. Thank you for always opening your heart and home whenever I came to visit Kifungilo from America. Being in your beautiful home in Lushoto reinforced the closeness of sisterhood that all Kifungilo girls shared. Thank you for the many nights we sat in your living room listening to old vinyl recordings by your husband and his group, "Frank na Dada Zake." Singing along to his songs cemented the fact that life in Kifungilo was often rich and good.

Imelda, you know my story inside out because it is your story too. We were together at the orphanage. Even though you were two years younger, we latched on to each other so very long ago until your sister Betty was always surprised to see one without the other. Thank you for reading the manuscript and for your excellent suggestions and clarifications. Thank you for being the sister I never had. Thank you for loving and accepting me so unconditionally. A huge thanks to Dallas Browne, your husband and my brother, for reading the manuscript. Thank you both for your faith in me and for your encouragement. Thank you for being family to me.

Thank you to my Central High School teacher colleague and world traveler Maureen Mashek for always encouraging me to tell my story. Thank you for reading my very first manuscript, chapter by chapter, and for your invaluable input. Your love and encouragement along with your pride in me carried me through difficult bouts of insecurity about this book.

To all my friends, thank you for your friendship, love and belief in me. Thank you for your patience as you gently nudged me along, and not so gently told me "Hurry up or we'll be dead before your book comes out!"

A big thank you to Kjell Bergh, the father of my children. You were one of my earliest and most enthusiastic supporters. Your encouragement and enthusiasm convinced me that I had a story to tell. You made several trips to Tanzania with our children and me and you charmed my African family and friends to the point where they all agreed that our marriage was made in heaven.

I owe a debt of gratitude to Arlene Mathews for taking my first manuscript and giving it shape and form. You asked questions that made me remember that I was writing mainly for a Western audience and thus had to clearly describe cultural aspects of my story that I had taken for granted.

A very big thank you to my readers who gave their time to go through the early manuscript and make comments, corrections and suggestion: Carletta Smith, Salma Faraji, Natasha Vaubel. Margaret Wong and Walter Graff, Diane and Jim Gayes, Anna Fitzsimmons, Rachel Soffer, Dr. Joyce Jackson, Helene Turnbull, Abdu Faraji, Catie Balek, Miggs Reiman, Grace Rogers, Barbara Owens, Reverend Nancy Norman, Kristen Bomas, Carole Nelson Douglas, Patricia Bohen Crowley, Meryl Price, Beth Anderson and Rebecca Sorenson.

Thank you to Barbara Cronie Editor, Editing Par Excellence, for her professionalism, enthusiasm, and support of **Africa's Child**. Thanks also to David Unowsky of SubText Books and Richard W. McCormick, Professor of German, University of Minnesota.

I first met Rachel Soffer when she was a student in my African Studies class at Central High School. We formed a deep connection and since then she has become an *Aerobics With Soul®* instructor and has helped me with many legal matters as an attorney.

I am eternally grateful to Marian Wright Edelman for reading the manuscript and agreeing to write the Foreword, I could have searched the world over, but wouldn't have found a better person to present **Africa's Child** to the Reader. **Africa's Child** embodies everything you have dedicated your life to advocate for and protect. It is proof that your work on behalf of children all over the world is needed and attainable. I bless the day I met you and am proud to consider you a dear friend.

My deepest gratitude to the Order of the Missionaries of the Precious Blood Sisters and in particular, Mother Ubalda and Mother Ancilla who founded the Kifungilo orphanage; Sister Silvestris, my orphanage mother, and Sister Theonesta who showered me with love when it mattered most. Your tutelage, dedication, and commitment laid the foundation for the person I became.

Thank you to the many Kifungilo Benefactors, known and unknown to me, who provided critical support for the nuns and children in times of need.

To the Wasambaa of the Lushoto area: You surrounded my childhood with your warm presence and let me partake in your songs and rituals. From you I first learned the meaning of belonging to a tribe. *Asanteni sana.*

About the Author

Maria Nhambu, an educator, dancer, writer, mother, entrepreneur and philanthropist, was raised in an orphanage for mixed-race children high in the Usambara Mountains of Tanzania. A 23-year-old American woman adopted her and brought her to America at age 19 for college.

Nhambu is the creator of *Aerobics With Soul® The African Workout,* based on the dances she learned growing up in Tanzania. She prefers to be known simply as "Nhambu" which means "one who connects" or "bridge person." She is the mother of two and a grandmother, and lives in Delray Beach, Florida. *Africa's Child* is the first in a three-part memoir of her life.

www.MariaNhambu.com

More to Come...

My life story continues. Arriving in the United States with Cathy Murray, I faced proving I was worthy of being adopted, taken to America, and receiving a four-year college scholarship. I also had to wend my way through an unfamiliar culture that included shocking doses of American-style racial discrimination. I had to learn to be a Black American. I graduated from college, thus fulfilling my dream of becoming a teacher, and taught high school in the inner city. I married, had two children and was becoming established in the American way of life.

Then the Spirit of Africa came back to claim me. A visit to Africa, and especially to Tanzania, was a revelation to me. It woke up the drum beat and dancing that I always carried in my body and soul. I began teaching Swahili and African Studies and performed African dance at schools. Urged to do more by that energetic African Spirit, I created *Aerobics With Soul®*, a fitness workout based on African dance. Look for the next installments of my memoir: *America's Daughter* and *Drum Beats, Heart Beats.*

CPSIA information can be obtained
at www.ICGtesting.com
Printed in the USA
FFOW03n1854140716
25797FF

9 780997 256109